RAPID INFORMATION
SYSTEMS DEVELOPMENT:
a non-specialist's guide to
analysis and design in an
imperfect world 2/e

R

INFORMATION SYSTEMS SERIES

Consulting Editors

D. E. AVISON
BA, MSc, PhD, FBCS
Professor of Information Systems,
School of Management,
Southampton University, UK

G. FITZGERALD
BA, MSc, MBCS
Cable & Wireless Professor of
Business Information Systems,
Department of Computer Science,
Birbeck College, University of London, UK

Editorial Board

This series of student and postgraduate texts covers a wide variety of topics relating to information systems. It is designed to fulfil the needs of the growing number of courses on, and interest in, computing and information systems which do not focus on the purely technological aspects, but seek to relate information systems to their business and organizational contexts.

INFORMATION SYSTEMS SERIES

RAPID INFORMATION SYSTEMS DEVELOPMENT:
a non-specialist's guide to analysis and design in an imperfect world 2/e

SIMON BELL
Systems Department
Open University

TREVOR WOOD-HARPER
Information Research Centre
University of Salford

THE McGRAW-HILL COMPANIES

London · New York · St Louis · San Francisco · Auckland
Bogotá · Caracas · Lisbon · Madrid · Mexico · Milan
Montreal · New Delhi · Panama · Paris · San Juan
São Paulo · Singapore · Sydney · Tokyo · Toronto

Published by
McGraw-Hill Publishing Company
Shoppenhangers Road, Maidenhead, Berkshire, SL6 2QL England
Telephone 01628 502500
Fax: 01628 770224

The LOC data for this book has been applied for and may be obtained from the
Library of Congress, Washington, D.C.

A catalogue record for this book is available from the British Library.

Further information on this and other McGraw-Hill titles is to be found at
http://www.mcgraw-hill.co.uk

ISBN 0 07 709427 1

3 4 5 CUP 2 1 0

Typeset by Mackreth Media Services, Hemel Hempstead
Printed in Great Britain at The University Press, Cambridge

In memory of my Father, Ted Bell

CONTENTS

SERIES FOREWORD

The information systems series is a series of student and postgraduate texts covering a wide variety of topics relating to information systems. The focus of the series is the use of computers and the flow of information in business and large organizations. The series is designed to fill the needs of the growing number of courses on information systems and computing which do not focus on purely technical aspects but which rather seek to relate information systems to their commercial and organizational context.

The term 'information systems' has been defined as the effective design, delivery, use and impact of information technology in organizations and society. Utilizing this broad definition it is clear that the subject is interdisciplinary. Thus the series seeks to integrate technological disciplines with management and other disciplines, for example psychology and sociology. These areas do not have a natural home and were until comparatively recently, rarely represented by single departments in universities and colleges. To put such books in a purely computer science or management series restricts potential readership and the benefits that such texts can provide. The series on information systems provides such a home.

The titles are mainly for student use, although certain topics will be covered at greater depth and be more research oriented for postgraduate study.

The series includes the following areas, although this is not an exhaustive list: information systems development methodologies, office information systems, management information systems, decision support systems, information modelling and databases, systems theory, human aspects and the human–computer interface, application systems, technology strategy, planning and control, expert systems, knowledge acquisition and its representation.

A mention of the books so far published in the series gives a 'flavour' of the richness of the information systems world. *Information and Data Modelling, second edition* (David Benyon) concerns itself with one very important aspect, the world of data, in some depth; *Information Systems Development: A Database Approach, second edition* (David Avison) provides a coherent methodology which has been widely used to develop adaptable computer systems using databases; *Multiview: An Exploration in*

Information Systems Development (David Avison and Trevor Wood-Harper) looks at an approach to information systems development which combines humand and technical considerations; *Relational Database Systems* and *Relational Database Design* (Paul Benyon-Davies) are two books which offer a comprehensive treatment of relational databases; *Business Management and Systems Analysis* (Eddie Moynihan) explores the areas of overlap between business and IT; *Decision Support Systems* (Paul Rhodes) places management decision making in perspective of decision theory; *Information Systems: An Emerging Discipline?* (John Mingers and Frank Stowell – Editors) debates the practical and philosophical dimensions of the field; *Why Information Systems Fail* (Chris Sauer) looks at the reasons for IS failure and the problems of developing IS in organizations; *Human–Computer Factors* (Andy Smith) emphasizes user-centred design, usability and the role of the users; *Transforming the Business: The IT Contribution* (Robert Moreton and Myrvin Chester) discusses the role that IS/IT can play in organizational change; and the second edition of *Information Systems Development: Methodologies, Techniques and Tools* (David Avison and Guy Fitzgerald) provides a comprehensive coverage of the different elements of information systems development. *The Information Systems Life Cycle: A First Course in Information Systems* (David Avison and Hanifa Shah) covers the basic material necessary in a first course in information systems. It can be used as a 'prequel' to Avison and Fitzgerald but can also be used 'standalone' where the teaching of IS does not go beyond a first course.

We welcome the second edition of Simon Bell and Trevor Wood-Harper's book on rapid information systems development to the series. Most books in the series are directed specifically to students althought they will have relevance to practitioners. This book is equally, if not particularly, relevant to practitioners as they grapple with situations requiring efficient and effective development of information systems. These developers may not be specialists but users (perhaps in developing countries) who are required to develop their own applications. Rapid applications development is often referred to as a 'quick and dirty' approach. Simon and Trevor's book provides support for 'quick and clean' development. The book is written in a friendly style and it abounds with examples and cases which all help readers in picturing how their real-world problems might be tackled.

David Avison and Guy Fitzgerald

FOREWORD

This book is intended as a practitioner's guide to those non-experts who are intending to plan and develop information systems, that is become involved with the process of systems analysis and systems design (SA&SD). The authors recognize that many other approaches are possible in this complex and evolving field and that greater depth of understanding than that which arises from the reading of one book will be required before exponents could be said to have achieved mastery of all the techniques included here. Nevertheless the authors believe that at the time of the first edition of this book in 1992 and at present there is a lack of understanding in the information system planning profession of the need for planning tools for non-IT specialists and that these tools do exist and can be understood and applied by non-specialists relatively quickly. This book should be seen as an introduction to the information systems development process and as a guide to one particular method. It is to be hoped that this may encourage more professionals working in this field to write training materials of value to non-specialists.

The authors welcome any constructive comments and observations arising from the application of principles contained in this text, especially from users working in situations of rapid change and minimal time for long drawn out development procedures. This book is written in recognition of the need to draw together 'clean' theory and what is often 'dirty' practice in one view.

The examples used in this book are amalgams brought together from field experience, theory, teaching and anecdote. They do not represent any one single context. Any resemblance to any real organization is coincidental.

PREFACE

It is not the authors' intention to produce a work of pure systems analysis and systems design theory. If this is what the reader is hoping to find then he or she will be disappointed. Nor is it our intention to provide readers with an idealized analysis and design procedure. This book is about doing systems analysis and systems design under conditions where the only alternative to rule-of-thumb methods is to not use any methods at all. This book is intended for those whom the information systems profession would refer to as amateurs but we prefer to label as non-specialists. It is aimed at assisting non-specialists in doing the preparatory work (called systems analysis and systems design) which should occur before an information systems is installed. We wish to assist those involved in doing this work because, to date, there has been precious little support for them in their travail unless they proposed undertaking a three-year university degree or expensive professional training courses, sometimes of dubious value.

This book does not contain pure examples of applied methodology. Almost all the examples discussed here are drawn from work undertaken in the challenging environment of developing countries where computer awareness and computer systems development remains in its infancy. Therefore the analysis and design tools discussed here have had to be adopted and adapted rapidly when there has been little time and in low support environments (low support in terms of poor climatic conditions, poor infrastructure and low awareness among stakeholders in the IT systems). Nevertheless, we believe that an adapt-and-adopt approach used in imperfect conditions is better than no approach to planning at all and it is with this in mind that the following is offered.

The main method set out in this book is a variant of Multiview (for more details see Avison, D.E. and Wood-Harper, A.T. 1995 reprint: *Multiview: An Exploration in Information Systems Development*. McGraw-Hill, London) but also contains a number of other analysis and design approaches which have deviated from their original state to meet the needs of variable situations. The approaches have been adapted in the light of participatory and thoughtful consideration with the stakeholders in information systems. If the adaptations made here are offensive to the authors of these approaches we offer our apologies but also invite their consideration of our central point:

> In learning how to provide an analysis and design tool for non-specialists one must learn what the non-specialist can usefully do and occasionally adapt the tool in the light of this learning.

Introduction to the book structure and contents

This book attempts to provide the user with an understandable set of rules of thumb for planning an information system without there being 'experts' available to fall back on. As a 'user's guide' this text does not go into great detail concerning the theoretic context of the planning tools we apply. A listing of publications for further study, many drawn from the McGraw-Hill Information Systems series, is included in the text.

The book is organized so as to reduce the amount of time which the reader has to spend on areas which may not be of immediate interest. Implicit in the approach we are adopting here is the understanding that in many situations where information systems are required **there is not always a lot of time to carry out in-depth planning. Because of this a** *rapid information system planning or development technique is required* to enable organizations to develop effective information systems.

With this in mind we will briefly outline the structure of the book.

Chapters. These are organized so as to cover the sequence of activities involved in planning any potential information system. As we are chiefly dealing with the **practical details** of planning unnecessary **theory** which may be of interest but is not central to this theme is located in **theory appendices** at the back of the book. Each appendix provides the reader with further insights into the subject and lists key texts which can be pursued for further reference.

Each chapter is opened with a listing of the **major keywords** to be dealt with in the body of the chapter.

Each chapter begins with a brief **summary** of contents and an indication of how long each stage of the method applied would take to carry out in practice.

The chapters that deal with the fivefold aspects of the method we are going to use are each closed with a **tutorial or sequence of exercises**. These are intended to be of value if the book is to be used directly as a stimulus to the planning process in an organization or set as an introductory text in analysis and design teaching.

Our final appendix sets out a model approach to answering the exercises in the tutorials.

The chapters contain an explanation of the working of our analysis and design methodology and contain examples of each stage.

Glossary. Much of the vocabulary used in information systems and information technology related areas consists of jargon. Some jargon is useful and some is unavoidable. In order to assist the non-specialist all major jargon and abbreviations used in the text are covered in the **glossary**. Words that appear in the glossary are identified on their first appearance in the text by appearing in bold print.

As a guide, we have provided a schedule of the progress of the planning process as we go through. This is not intended to be absolute but should provide the reader with a rough guide as to the amount of time to be devoted to each activity in the planning process.

Overall book structure

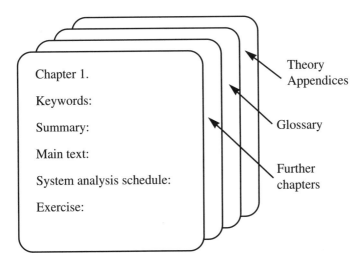

We shall not cease from exploration, and the end of all our exploring will be to arrive where we started and know the place for the first time.
                              (from T.S. Eliot's 'Little Gidding')

ACKNOWLEDGEMENTS

The authors wish to express their gratitude to L. Antill for inputs to earlier, collaborative work (1985) which provided inspiration for the present volume. Thanks also to Martin Sewell who provided much support in the application of this approach in Developing Countries and Ian Shephard for his comments and insights.

Words fail to express the gratitude which the authors owe their families for their support and patience.

Chapter 1

INFORMATION SYSTEMS AND ORGANIZATIONS

Keywords:

planning, change, risk, learning organization, methods

Summary:

Information as a commodity is briefly discussed. The need for information systems planning is introduced and described. Incidental virtues of information systems planning (e.g. learning about and with your organization, developing an understanding of the stakeholders, assumptions and mindsets of colleagues) are discussed. Common problems with information systems are reviewed.

1.1 Introduction

It may appear to be obvious but **information systems** (IS) are supposed to inform people. In the planning or development process we should never lose sight of this primary objective. By informing, the **system** assists people (generally referred to in the IT context as the 'users') to make intelligent decisions. Therefore, if information is:

- poorly gathered and sorted
- inadequately edited
- incorrectly analysed
- analysed for the wrong things
- badly presented

the information system will fail in its primary function. This in turn has a knock-on effect on decision making, the results of which feed through to the effectiveness of the organization as a whole. Therefore any information system needs to be carefully planned in terms of:

- The **data** to be gathered.
- The **information** products being derived from the data.
- The ultimate **knowledge** which is thought by the planner to be the final requirement of the system (a very difficult thing to define).

All too often an information system will be designed prior to anyone having asked the question which it is intended to answer. Thus, incorrect data is gathered, inappropriate information products are generated and insufficient knowledge is derived for effective decision making.

Organizations of all kinds, be they small private companies, non-governmental agencies or large government departments, are primarily users and producers of information. Information is a most versatile and pliable commodity. Literally anything that leads to any form of action could be seen as being information. A kick in the rear or a bank statement will lead to action, immediate or delayed, positive or negative, brief or sustained. It is worth briefly describing some of the major attributes of information systems:

- They deal with an endlessly changing commodity.
- They are required to facilitate decision making.
- They exist in all organizations.
- They are vital to an organization's function.
- They are increasingly available in a computer-based form.
- They are frequently badly planned.

An information system, particularly a **computer-based informa-tion system**, can appear to be efficient and yet be perceived by end users as being unhelpful or even hostile. There can be many reasons for this, some of which we look at in the section dealing with 'Problems with Systems' towards the end of this chapter. At this point we need to make clear that an information system is an inte-gral part of the social system that comprises another part of the organization. This relationship is illustrated in Figure 1.1.

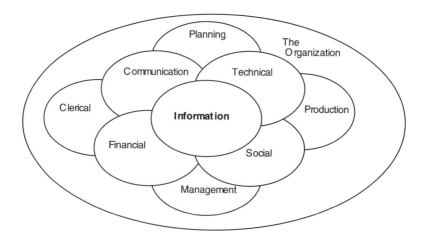

FIGURE 1.1   *Linked aspects*

The way in which an organization functions is very complex and information systems impinge upon most of the features of organizations. Therefore, as well as being established on technically sound principles, the planning process needs to be both diligent and sensitive to organizational needs and user thinking.

AUTHORS' ASIDE

There is a great deal written about organizations and their capacity to deal with change including the changes that IT brings with it (see Further Reading at the end of this chapter). This book focuses on analysis and design but we would particularly like to flag the work of Morgan (1997). In his book he indicates a range of metaphors which can be used to help us in describing organization (e.g. organization as machine, as brain, as prison). In Chapter 3 we make use of metaphors to describe the systems analyst. Metaphor is a useful devise to develop insights into a complex context. To think of an organization as being 'like' a brain is to raise questions such as:

'Is this organization behaving rationally?', 'Is this organization learning?'. These types of question are provoking and can be really helpful in the early stages of systems thinking when we are trying to identify problems. We will return to this approach in Chapter 5.

When we refer to 'organizational needs and user thinking' we mean such common issues as:

- Lack of experience of the planning or **systems analysis and systems design** process in the **recipient community**.
- Senior management reluctance to adopt suggested change.
- Junior staff reluctance to adopt new practices and procedures.
- Absence of local, reliable support for incoming systems.
- Sense of risk and uncertainty in a new endeavour.
- Staff too stretched to accommodate changes gladly.
- Distrust of change processes.

This book is designed to introduce a means for effective information systems planning for organizations while taking into account this range of issues.

While not wishing to give the impression that information systems in use today are generally unfriendly and inappropriate, it is our experience that there are a large number of such systems that fail because they do not take into account the views and worries of the end users. A glance through just about any edition of *Computer Weekly* would confirm this statement; the litany of disasters relating to IT are numerous (Lyytinen and Hirschheim, 1987; Bicknell, 1993; Collins, 1993, 1996a, b, 1997a, b; Davies, 1996; Drummond, 1996; Schneider, 1997). The headlines themselves are instructive:

- *Lack of systems back-up causes hospital chaos.*
- *Bank chief learns from computer failure.*
- *GP's network buckles under huge workload.*
- *How British Gas took the blame and still managed to survive.*
- *Why British Gas jumped out of the frying pan...*
- *The politics of risk: trials and tribulations of the Taurus project.*
- *Bug delays £25m court case system.*

Both private and public sectors are prone to massive IT project failure (£80 million in the case of the City of London computerization 'Taurus' project).

One of the problems that often arises with new computer-based information systems is that users feel that the new information system is being imposed upon them with little or no discussion. It is our contention that generally speaking, the end users of information systems do not have enough say in the analysis and design process.

AUTHORS' ASIDE

There are a number of approaches to information systems building which are intended to develop the users' input to the system, e.g. Rapid Applications Development (**RAD**) and **prototyping**. However, these approaches require that the user be given technical support in developing new information systems making use of software tools. In this book we wish to focus on empowering the user to think about and plan his or her information system and not on the approaches designed by technical facilitators.

Lack of input to processes leads to a lack of sense of ownership among the end users of the system supposedly being implemented to improve user efficiency. Further, the information systems analysis and design process is suffering from a dose of '**expert imposition**'. To explain what we mean by 'expert imposition' we have to look no further than the types of problem that have been confronting architects in recent years.

After years of quiescence the end user (in this case the home owner or office worker) is asking architects questions such as: 'Would *you* live in one of your buildings?'. The question being asked of information system planners is: 'Would *you* like to work with one of your information systems?'.

Simply stated one of the major problems implicit in information systems design appears to be that if information systems are planned at all they tend to be planned *by* and *for* computer experts not general users.

By this we mean that information systems suffer from a highly technocratic approach derived from experts of the computer profession. Those that use this approach tend to be large companies and/or government departments and agencies that have access to the necessary financial resources required to purchase the professional skills for systems analysis and systems design. This type of planning is characterized by the information system being designed in isolation from the end user in most stages. *Systems for smaller organizations usually develop on an evolutionary, piecemeal basis with little or no overall planning.* The problem can be broken down as follows:

- Between the computer profession and the general user there is still a considerable knowledge gap. This gap is partly incidental because of the newness of the computer profession and partly contrived by the computer profession due to a tendency to obscure simple or obvious ideas in confusing jargon.
- The knowledge gap is a convenient means for information system analysts and designers to keep away the uninitiated and the eventual user of the system under design.
- This tendency leads to professional conceit on the one hand and user mistrust on the other.
- Yet, returning to our initial problem, users do require working information systems and they often require them rapidly.

For the majority of organizations without access to professional skills, how are the information systems to be planned? What features of an organization need to be analysed? How is the final information system to be implemented?

If computer experts are not available, are too busy, too intimidating or cost too much, users will tend to fall back on their own means and muddle along. This situation can lead to considerable difficulty and cost but it is an increasingly apparent tendency. Unplanned or poorly planned systems are on the increase because:

- There are literally millions of **desktop microcomputer** sites globally that are not run by experts from the computer profession.
- Contrary to the opinion of some computer experts 10–15 years ago, microcomputers, far from being a 'blip' are becoming increasingly sophisticated and undertake an immense range of tasks.
- Powerful **hardware** and **software** require exceptional and new skills from users.

- User training has tended to be badly organized and under-subscribed.
- This has resulted in lack of method in planning information systems and to massively under-utilized technology (e.g. powerful microcomputers, intended for sophisticated accounting operations, being used for **word processing**).

The purpose of this book is to demonstrate an easy-to-use method for:

- Identifying what the information system planner (that is you) needs to know.

Following this we:

- Demonstrate ways to model the range of technical, economic, social, cultural, political, etc. issues which may be critical to the running of the information system.
- Produce a definition of the proposed new information system.
- Identify key technical and social combinations that will achieve the new system requirements at a given cost.
- Plan for the interface between users and technology.
- Outline the major technical processes and facilities that need to be in place for the system to work effectively.

Finally we:

- Set out software and hardware selection procedures and the implementation process.

We need to make clear several major features of this book:

1. You do not need to be a system engineer or even know much about computers to be able to make effective use of the book, this book is intended for non-specialists.
2. The book deals with information systems design. The end product probably will be automated but *may be semi-automated or even manual*.
3. Many people put in charge of new information systems have little previous experience. Therefore the book is aimed at managers who need a simple-to-use, non-technocratic analysis and design tool.
4. Existing workers in the profession sometimes doubt the value of current technical analysis and design tools and may have very limited time to come up with an end product. Therefore, we also intend the book for information systems analysts and designers who need a rapid-use tool.
5. Finally, many disciplines make use of information systems but do not always have specialist computer professionals on call to deal with planning. Hence we have made provision for the book

to be useful to both a wide range of professionals working in their own disciplines and lecturers and students interested in bringing some design skills into their specialist area (e.g. management, business, economics, planning, etc.).

For all the end users of the book we hope that they find in it a technically sound but rapidly applicable and socially sensitive planning tool.

THINK POINT

Before continuing, think about the following questions. In this chapter we have set out reasons why planning at the **stakeholder** (rather than IT expert) level is important.

- Are you aware of planning in your organization's adoption of IT?
- Does your organization involve a wide range of stakeholders in its IT planning?
- Can you think of five problems that might arise from the exclusion of stakeholders who are not IT specialists in the IT planning process?
- Can you think of reasons why including people is a problem?

1.2 Problems with information systems

A central theme for this book is the problem of devising a clear and user-sensitive approach to determining exactly what is the problem for which an information system is perceived as being the answer. How do we plan this system and offer a reasonable chance of successful use? With this in mind it is useful to look at some of the standard problems that we have encountered in previous systems planning exercises. The types of problem that are in some ways typical of information technology adoption include:

- patchy understanding of the computing involved by the potential users
- very wide range of requirements by the user
- awkward environmental factors involved in the placement of sophisticated systems
- high-cost training and staffing implications.

These points lead us to an observation concerning the impact of information systems in organizations where situations of risk and uncertainty prevail:

> Users appear generally to believe that little can be understood about an information system prior to installation. Further it is often believed that information technology will probably lead to negative rather than positive work experiences.

Taking this as our lead point, our approach is to reassure the user on these counts. But why are users apparently so wary of information systems? Some examples may help to explain.

Our first example in Figure 1.2 shows that the problem for the analyst is not the data to be prepared or the staff to be trained. It consists of senior management intransigence. If management is left out of the decision-making process and is not included in discussions or consulted then systems can fail.

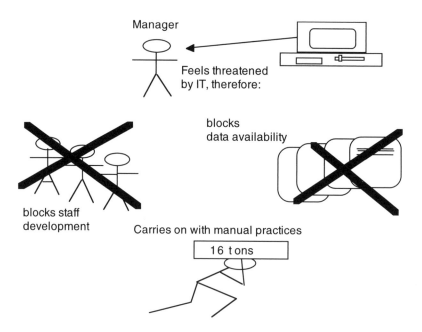

FIGURE 1.2   *Problems with IS 1: senior management intransigence*

This demonstrates that it is vital to get the support of major stakeholders in the system. In this case the failure results in continuation with existing manual practices that could be easily, technically improved upon.

The first learning point would seem to be – *always draw management into the analysis and design stage – do not make the technology appear threatening (or any more threatening than it is already!).*

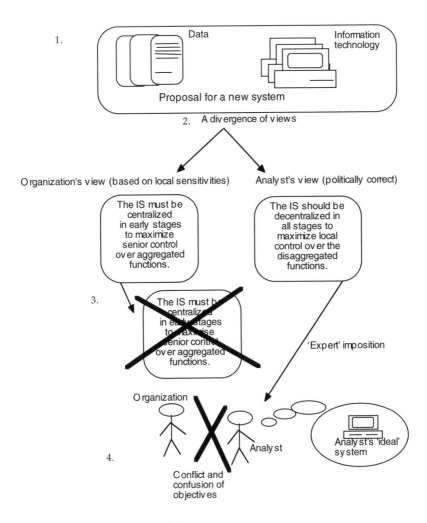

FIGURE 1.3   *Problems with IS 2: Poor analysis perspective*

Figure 1.3 demonstrates our second problem situation. Here the problem is the planner or system analyst.

In this example the planner devises and suggests a new system but this is quite different from that which the major stakeholder in the organization requires. Problems arise when an analyst's enthusiasm to create systems that are theoretically sound (in terms of the personal preferences of the analyst) rather than **contextually** appropriate (i.e. what senior management wants) predominates. The result is that the analyst is at odds with the preference of the end users or clients and ends up creating conflict and ultimate failure.

This situation can be resolved in two ways: either the client tells the analyst to think again, or as in this case, the analyst imposes the system. This example will generally be restricted to cases where either the planner has been given *carte blanche* to impose his or her will or if a larger, parent or funding body outside the organization that is being studied and which is possibly commissioning the study, backs the analyst's judgement.

The result is fairly predictable – a conflict of objectives between planner and client and ultimately systems failure. The learning point is: *irrespective of professionalism the planner/analyst must have the humility and common sense to see the client as central to a working system.*

Our third example is shown in Figure 1.4 and can be seen as a problem of over-ambition and the price of initial success.

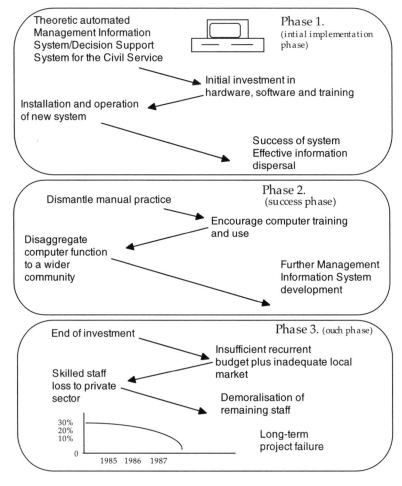

FIGURE 1.4   *Problems with IS 3: Over-ambition*

Information systems like any other systems have to provide their utility to the end user for some considerable time. If they do not provide this utility they can end up being more disruptive in their effect than continuing with outmoded and outdated manual practices. In Figure 1.4 the organization is left with a potentially catastrophic situation where the system ultimately fails but the confidence during the first few years has been so high as to lead to the dismantling of existing manual systems. The learning point is again quite stark: *short-term success can lead to long-term failure unless real long-term support is built into projects. This is a danger for all information system projects.*

Our fourth example demonstrates again the problems of short-term successes. The problem in this case is the over-adoption of a computer system. This type of problem can manifest itself in many ways. Examples include microcomputer systems running for over 20 hours a day, seven days a week and printers outputting day and night. In Figure 1.5 the computer-based information product

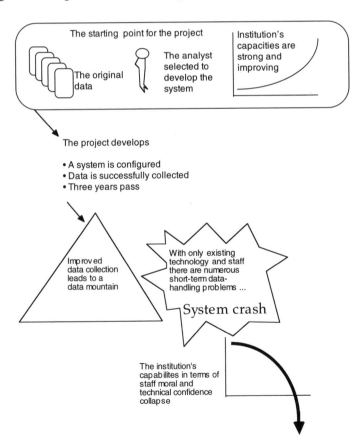

FIGURE 1.5   *Problems with IS 4: Task/machine development mismatch*

produces such a positive response from the organization that it encourages a massive increase in use.

The learning point from this is again predictable: *a system should be designed to meet the needs of today and tomorrow and the next day so far as we can predict it!*

Our fifth and final example depicts what might be thought of as the usual problems that a computer-based information system might have to deal with.

The key to almost all the problems depicted in Figure 1.6 is poor security. The requirements for security are directly related to the specific factors at work in the potential information systems context (that word context again!). Generally there is a trade-off between ease of access to information systems and security. The higher the security the more difficult the system is to use. Conversely the more open the system is the easier it is for computer **hackers** to gain access, for computer **viruses** to be imported into the system and for software to be **pirated**. All of these problems tend to be sympto-

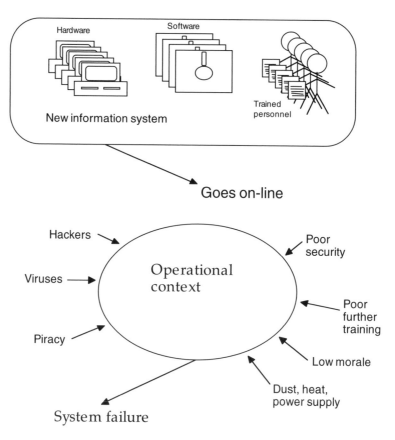

FIGURE 1.6   *Problems with IS 5: Technical management breakdown*

matic of a less than adequate approach to information systems design. Related issues include insufficient attention being devoted to training of computer staff and the resulting lack of confidence and morale of these staff members. Finally, we must recognize that information systems are often being installed in high-risk contexts. Risk varies with situation but can refer to:

- organizational and problems such as lack of training
- local infrastructure factors such as intermittent or fluctuating power supply
- climatic factors such as heat or humidity
- financial risks such as insufficient recurrent budget for computer support
- social risk such as antipathy to the incoming system, etc.

The learning point we draw from this is: *it is good practice always to ensure that an information system is going into a hostile environment. Modest systems planned for difficult situations can always be built upon later. Technically sound, ambitious systems may suffer teething problems which take years to recover from (if ever!).*

1.3 Conclusions

From the foregoing we would like to draw out some conclusions:

- All information systems exist to support efficient decision making.
- Efficient decision making is vital for personal and organizational well-being.
- Therefore information systems have to be properly planned for.
- Poorly planned or unplanned systems can (and do) lead to catastrophe.
- Many planned systems are too technocratic and also lead to problems for the end users.
- Therefore a key requirement is for an easy-to-use method for planning information systems.

The usual term used to describe information system planning is 'systems analysis and systems design' or SA&SD. This is rather a mouthful and can appear to be quite an off-putting expression to the non-specialist. However, in order for us to make sense of the planning process we need to understand analysis and design in outline at least – much of it is proceduralized common sense. Later on we will be using tools drawn from various types of analysis and design to plan for our own information systems but first it is useful to know what is analysis and design.

1.4   Exercise

Read through the following article and consider the following question, do the problems evident in the context relate closely to the problems for IS set out in section 1.2?

A National Health Service network used by four out of five GPs has buckled under high workloads, losing messages, delaying patient's test results and throwing surgeries into confusion.

Many of the 7,500 GPs on the network have invoked paper and clerical back-up procedures in an attempt to restore normality and to trace messages that have not reached their destinations.

The problems have delayed test reports, including breast screening and cervical smear results.

They have been caused by an unexpected surge in demand for the Healthlink service, from an average of 40,000 to 75,000 messages a day between January and October. The system allows GPs and health authorities to swap information on practice patients lists, treatments carried out and laboratory results.

Racal Managed Services, the network supplier, said there has been a strain on the central systems controlling the Healthlink X.400 (84) network. To cope with demand – 90,000 messages a day – Racal has boosted the system's processing power, disc capacity and disc cache.

Racal said it has accelerated the testing of a major upgrade to the X.400 (88) standard, expected to go live early next year.

The problems have led to GP surgeries spending thousands of hours over several weeks trying to resolve the difficulties.

Health authorities and doctors claimed this week that difficulties are continuing. Dr Grant Kelly, a GP, chairman of the General Medical Services Committee's IT sub-committee and head of the Joint Computing Group of the Royal College of General Practitioners, said test results were taking longer to arrive than by post. 'You have to see a gain from these systems and we haven't yet,' he said.

Linked to Healthlink:

7,500 GP practices
500 hospitals
17,500 NHS users
51 breast clinics
increasing by 200 users a month
sending 90,000 messages daily

The problems have particularly hit GPs who sent 'items of service' invoices to health authorities for registering and treating patients.

This has led health authorities to consider giving GPs emergency 'hardship' payments based on previous records to maintain surgeries' cash flow.

In a statement to *Computer Weekly* Racal said that with BT now operating in the same market 'the message throughput on Healthlink is very much against expectations. It was anticipated that the growth would be shared between the two service suppliers. However, the market has voted with its feet and continued to support Healthlink.

'GPs' network buckles under huge workload' by Tony Collins.
Computer Weekly, **28 November 1996.**

An answer is provided to this exercise in Appendix C.

References and further reading

(For reading on the nature of organizations and their capacity to deal with change see Argyris, 1960; Burrell and Morgan, 1979; Argyris, 1982; Checkland, 1984; Argyris, 1985; Gotsch, 1985; Barlow, 1991; Dykman and Robbins, 1991; Calhoun and DeLargy, 1992.)

Argyris, C. (1960). *Understanding Organizational Behaviour*. London: Tavistock Publications.
Argyris, C. (1982). *Reasoning, Learning and Action*. San Francisco: Jossey Bass.
Argyris, C. (1985). Making knowledge more relevant to practice: maps for action. In Lawler E. *et al. Doing Research that is Useful for Theory and Practice*. San Francisco: Jossey Bass.
Avison, D.E., Fitzgerald, G. and Wood-Harper, A.T. (1994). The 'Discipline' of information systems: The inter discplinary thing. *Systemist*, vol. 16, no. 1.
Barlow, J.F. (1991). Group decision making in computer project justification. *Journal of Systems Management*, June, 13–16.
Bicknell, D. (1993). Any takers for a stretcher case? *Computer Weekly*, **14**.
Burrell, G. and Morgan, G. (1979). *Sociological Paradigms and Organizational Analysis*. London: Heinemann.
Calhoun, C. and DeLargy, P. (1992). Computerization, aid-dependency and administrative capacity: a Sudanese case study. In S. Grant Lewis and J. Samoff. Boulder (eds), *Microcomputers in African Development*. Westview.
Checkland, P.B. (1984). Systems thinking in management: the development of soft systems methodology and its implications for social science. In H. Ulrich and G. J. Probst (eds), *Self Organization and Management of Social Systems*. Berlin: Springer-Verlag.
Collins, T. (1993). Lack of systems back-up causes hospital chaos. *Computer Weekly*, **2**.
Collins, T. (1996a). Bank chief learns from computer failure. *Computer Weekly*, **24**.
Collins, T. (1996b). GP's network buckles under huge workload. *Computer Weekly*, **1**.

Collins, T. (1997a). How British Gas took the blame and still managed to survive. *Computer Weekly*, **20**.

Collins, T. (1997b). Why British Gas jumped out of the frying pan... *Computer Weekly*, **26**.

Davies, T. (1996). GP link suffers network blockage. *Computer Weekly*, **4**.

Drummond, H. (1996). The politics of risk: trials and tribulations of the Taurus project. *Journal of Information Technology*, **11**, 347–357.

Dykman, C. and Robbins, R. (1991). Organizational success through effective systems analysis. *Journal of Systems Management*, **42**(7), 6–8.

Gotsch, C. (1985). Application of Microcomputers in Third World Organisations.

Lyytinen, K. and Hirschheim, R. (1987). Information systems failures: a survey and classification of the empirical literature. *Oxford Surveys in Information Systems*, **4**, 257–309.

Morgan, G. (1997). *Images of Organization: New Edition*. London: Sage.

Schneider, K. (1997). Bug delays £25m court case system. *Computer Weekly*, **1**.

Chapter 2

WHAT IS SYSTEMS ANALYSIS AND SYSTEMS DESIGN?

Keywords:

systems analysis, systems design, **learning organization**, exploration/research approach, **systemic**, **reductionist**, methodologies, tools.

Summary:

How do we plan an information system with systems analysis and systems design? The experts have produced a vast range of **methodologies** for the planner with a bewildering array of approaches. The incomprehensible language often used and the belief that analysis and design takes months rather than days often invokes the question from the non-specialist: 'how is any of it of use to us?'. In this chapter we look briefly at the range of methodologies and focus on some major, useful themes.

2.1   Introduction

Systems analysis and systems design (SA&SD) describes the means used to plan an information system. Usually SA&SD is set out within the context of an exploration into a problem of some sort. The exploration (or research approach) will contain a methodology of some form. Generally the methodology will tend to have the following range of elements:

Basics of a systems analysis and systems design methodology

1. Discover what the information problem/s is/are?
2. Discover what is the setting for the problem/s?
3. What resources and constraints are evident?
4. What are the major information components of the problem/s?
5. Structure the problem/s into a model.
6. Design model solutions to the problem/s
7. Test and cost the model.
8. Implement the model as appropriate.
9. Monitor and evaluate the results.

AUTHORS' ASIDE

At this point we would like to make a major aside. This ninefold list
of activities for analysis and design raises an issue which we consider to be of the highest significance, the opportunity for SA&SD to
provide organizations with a learning opportunity.

The virtues of the 'learning organization' as described by Peter
Senge (Senge *et al.*, 1994) relate to a number of practices carried
out within the organization. Senge sets these out as five disciplines
which are:

- Systems thinking
- Personal mastery
- Mental models
- Shared vision
- Team learning

The five are set out in more detail in Table 2.1. The overriding
virtue of the five disciplines is that together they constitute a short-cut
to organizational learning. By team learning, the organization shares
learning allowing the knowledge that arises from information and
data (as set out in Chapter 1) to be widely shared and known around
the organization. Systems thinking provides a tool for thinking about

TABLE 2.1   *What are the five disciplines?*

Discipline	Definition	Where applied?	Outcome?
Systems thinking	The main components here are links and loops – loops can be re-enforcing (small changes become big changes) or balancing (pushing stability, resistance and limits)	Contexts where cause and effect are unclear	Description and insight
Personal mastery	Numerous variations but one three-fold view is articulating a personal vision, seeing reality clearly and making commitment to the results you want	Contexts where individuals are in transition	Empowerment
Mental models	Based on reflection and inquiry but also the recognition that we all create unconscious mental models all the time	Any action learning situation	Clear self-analysis

TABLE 2.1 *(Continued)*

Discipline	Definition	Where applied?	Outcome?
Shared vision	Built around six core ideas: organization has a destiny, deep purpose is in the founder's aspirations, not all visions are equal, there is a need for a collective purpose, it is useful to have forums for people to speak from the heart, creative tension	Contexts of dramatic change	Organization-wide clarity of purpose
Team learning	Learning through conversation, dialogue and skilful discussion – the aim is to achieve 'collective mindfulness'	Contexts of team development	Group consensus

the organization as a whole. Mental models provide teams with the ability to step back from reality and question assumptions about what 'is'. Shared vision is a powerful tool to building a consensus within the organization and personal mastery is the outcome of a deep understanding of issues and tasks within organizational settings. Together they can lead organizations to move from relative self-ignorance to relative self-understanding of how the organization works and of how it is reacting and integrating with its environment.

In the example below we show how the general stages of SA&SD can be seen as relating to the five disciplines and how these in turn can be seen as leading to a rich learning experience.

EXAMPLE OF A SYSTEMS ANALYSIS AND SYSTEMS DESIGN METHODOLOGY IN ACTION

1. *Discover what the information problem/s is/are.* In this stage systems thinking and team learning are used to discover that there is an unacceptable lag between the preparation of departmental budgets and the presentation of these budgets to central financial committee for approval.
2. *Discover what is the setting for the problem/s.* Again systems thinking and team learning combine here with mental models to arrive at the shared vision that three major departments are the main offenders – Planning, Design and Maintenance but all

Continued

departments are occasionally late with their presentations. Rather than seeing this as a problem for ascribing blame, the issue is seen as an opportunity to develop new and improved practice.

3. *What resources and constraints are evident?*   Personal mastery is the lead of the five disciplines here. Central management has indicated a budget of several thousands pounds on a feasibility study into the problem and procurement of information technology and related staff. There is evidence that young, junior staff would be keen to see changes. One important learning point is that in the past there has been senior staff intransigence to change and to the perceived whittling down of responsibility and power implicit in a computer-based solution.

4. *What are the major information components of the problem/s?* Systems thinking and mental models are useful in drawing out the information components (such as departmental projections and agreed performance criteria).

5. *Structure the problem/s into a model.*   This requires the production of an overall plan encompassing an organizational chart of some kind giving key departments, stakeholders in the proposed system and identifying where the existing blockages and delays are with regard to setting projections and performance criteria. The development of a shared vision of the context is important at this stage.

6. *Design model solutions to the problem/s.*   Team learning, systems thinking and mental models are used at this point to identify issues in terms of blockages and delays. When these have been identified, model solutions can be designed that focus initially on the main centres of concern.

7. *Test and cost the model.*   Depending upon the resources available a thorough examination of any new model is required. The examination would normally take the form of a pilot study developing the shared vision and involving the team and wider organization with the suggested improved system with key information indicators being monitored for comparison with existing practices, e.g. how long did it take to get manager reports assessed on the new information system as opposed to the original system?

8. *Implement the model as appropriate.*   Implementation will build upon the shared vision and personal mastery developed so far and will normally follow successful pilot study and can take a wide variety of forms – e.g. parallel systems, a continued pilot approach or simple switch over (these and other implementation strategies are described in Chapter 10).

9. *Monitor and evaluate the results.*   All five disciplines are involved in the monthly and/or six monthly reporting upon criteria that measure the processes and impact of the project (this topic is covered in much greater depth in Chapter 9).

The purpose of the above example is to show how the SA&SD process is a rich opportunity for organizations to learn from an examination of information process and development within the organization. If treated in a learning-organization fashion then the explicit learning of the exercise (e.g. technologies and techniques to improve IS) can be linked to a range of implicit learning (e.g. senior manager intransigence to change) to lead to improved efficiencies in the organization as a whole. As well as the learning organization approach, a vast array of different methods are available for fulfilling this sequence of nine tasks. The approaches all have their own benefits and weaknesses. Generally they vary from each other along the lines of the different experiential and research backgrounds and training of the individuals who designed them. One way of understanding what is meant by 'research background' can be seen in terms of an axis (Figure 2.1) which shows a range of approaches to problem exploration or research. (Brief resumes of the eight approaches are in the Glossary.)

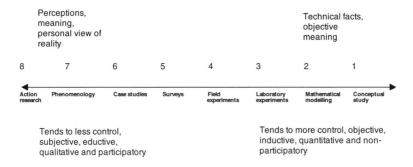

FIGURE 2.1   *Problem exploration approaches continuum (adapted from Wood-Harper, 1989)*

Do not panic about this. A few words of explanation may be required! The axis (called a continuum) is shown here with eight points on it. There may be many more points that we could add but the eight shown here should be sufficient for our example.

To the left are what we refer to as the *soft* or generally social sciences based approaches to exploring problems; to the right are some of the technocratic, *hard* science approaches. All eight of the approaches briefly shown here have salient features making one different from all the others. Each has its own assumptions or **worldview**. This is an important point.

The assumptions of the methods to the right of the continuum are derived from sciences akin to engineering and are focused on a controlled and controllable universe in which science knows or can know all that is needful to know. In contrast the assumptions of the approaches on the left are based upon the difficulty of saying one 'knows' anything with regard to the vagaries of human nature. They assume that there are very few fixed points upon which the analyst can depend and often assume that no thing can be absolutely known.

Before we go any further we need to make it clear that understanding and applying techniques of exploration is important for our main task – namely making working information systems. Setting up an information system requires the user to undertake research, to explore the context. To understand problems, deduce the strengths and weaknesses of the environment, plan a new system and test it prior to implementation requires some skills in exploration. The main point that needs to be understood is that most people are quite able to undertake research, indeed we explore difficult new contexts most days of our lives. All that is required is for the potential researcher to see research in the context of the problem.

For our purposes we use the world 'exploration' instead of research and in this text it refers to the adoption of an overall framework for the application of a methodology and the tools that comprise a methodology. The tools have then to be applied in a sequential and logical manner in order to arrive at an understanding of the problem, some suggestions for improvement, and means for producing the improved situation (see Figure 2.2).

How does the exploration, methodology, tools sequence work?

In one example, a management systems planner wants to know if a

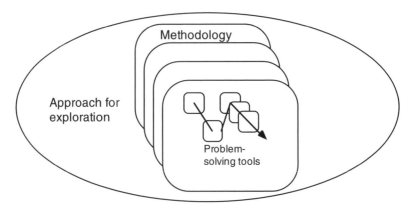

FIGURE 2.2   *Exploration, methodology and problem-solving tools*

series of measures aimed at supporting decision making at middle management level will be accepted by staff. Because she is working for a large, multinational company she cannot ask every single member of middle management if they agree with the proposed system. So, the first priority is to specify means to begin exploration. In this example a case study (point 6 on our axis in Figure 2.1) approach is used. Certain representative departments are checked. The methodology applied is called participative interaction which requires the problem-solving tool of questionnaires to be applied.

In another example an agronomist is employed to discover the most appropriate of six seed varieties for the production of maize. He applies the mathematical modelling research technique (point 2 on the axis), uses a sampling methodology and makes use of tools for measuring leaf growth and seed production among the six varieties.

As planners of information systems we need to be sure that we are fully aware of our approach to exploration, the methodology to be used and the range of tools which that methodology makes use of. Before we get to this point it is useful to first explain a little more of what the continuum means to us as planners. How do the eight approaches affect us?

The eightfold division is not definitive and could be added to. However, this range of backgrounds indicates two basic schools of thought or systems of analysis and design. These are known as the hard science school which is often argued to be **reductionist**, and the holistic or **systemic** (see Figure 2.3). Although we go into some greater detail concerning various methodologies in Appendix A, it is useful to get an overview of the two main traditions of thinking behind methodologies of all sorts here.

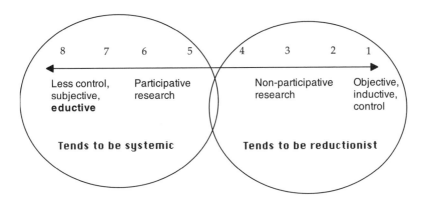

FIGURE 2.3   *Systemic and reductionist tendencies and the continuum*

2.1.1   The reductionists

Reductionism is the core behind most of the hard sciences and is centred on the philosophical teaching of positivism.

> All genuine human knowledge is contained within the boundaries of science. That is, the systematic study of phenomena and the explication of the laws embodied therein. Philosophy may still perform a useful function in explaining the scope and methods of science, pointing out the more general principles underlying specific scientific findings, and exploring the implications of science for human life. But it must abandon the claim to have any means of attaining knowledge not available to science.
>
> **(Flew, 1979)**

With a reductionist approach out go ideas about the reality and importance of 'unscientific' aspects of life (hunches, guesswork, instincts for rightness and even in certain circumstances illogical activity, i.e. activity that is not consistent with a narrow definition of efficiency). The universe is seen as fixed, knowable, measurable and, therefore, predictable. Of course, this is an ideal definition of positivism but we would argue that this is the underlying structure of thinking behind three of the analysis and design methods in common use today, i.e.:

1. Structured Systems Analysis (SSA)
2. Technical Specification (TS)
3. Data Analysis (DA)

2.1.2   The systemic

This is not yet a term to be found readily in dictionaries of philosophy but the approach arises from the systems thinking and therefore is embraced by the term holism:

> The contention that wholes, or some wholes, are greater than the sum of their parts ... A theory that claims that society may, or should, be studied in terms of social wholes...
>
> **(Flew, 1979)**

Systemisists are involved in the necessarily subjective world of real human activity. Central to systemisism is the belief that social and political forces will and must interfere with any technocratic information system – they are elements of the whole. Further, the information system planner will impose opinions and beliefs upon logical and objective new systems that are being planned – as will all other stakeholders in the context. The systemic view of reality is characterized by an inter and trans disciplinarian approach, i.e.

linking together various sciences and approaches and not compartmentalizing the world into exclusive boxes. Again we have three main approaches to SA&SD which we might use to illustrate its working in practice:

1. General Systems Theory (GST)
2. Soft Systems Methodology (SSM)
3. Socio-Technical Systems (STS)

(Refer to Appendix A for a discussion concerning approaches to analysis and design.)

THINK POINT

If you were asked to set out the single, major difference between systemisism and reductionism what would it be?

2.2   What is our research approach and methodology?

This is the most subjective question to ask. Implicit in the continuum shown in Figure 2.1 is the observation that all methodologies have their strengths and weaknesses. It is not a question of selecting the 'right' methodology, rather we believe that a better approach is to select the *appropriate combination of methodological tools for the particular situation* in which you are working.

Before going on to this, however, we should define the form of exploration or research approach of this book. Generally speaking we assume that you, the planner/analyst and designer are a member of the organization for which an information system is scheduled. In this case you will figure in your own analysis, you are part of the **problem context**.

In our situation – a situation which often prevails – irrespective of any reductionist, 'hard', objective planning tools that we might use later on, an overall systemic, 'action research' (point 8 on the axis in Figure 2.1) approach is essential. Figure 2.4 demonstrates the major components of an action research approach as set against the situation that can prevail if the approach is wrongly applied or not applied (anti-action research).

The action research approach (Figure 2.4(a)) shows several important and useful themes:

• The analyst and the client for whom the system is being designed

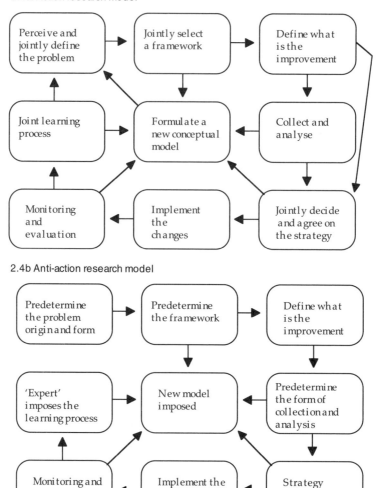

2.4a. Action research model

2.4b Anti-action research model

FIGURE 2.4   *(a) Action research model; (b) Anti-action research model (adapted from Warmington, 1980)*

work together as a team (an important point from a learning organization point of view).

- Strategy is jointly agreed on.
- Final policy is jointly undertaken.

While not wishing to imply that any other approach would be fatally flawed, the anti-action research model (Figure 2.4(b)) shows some of the range of problems that can arise if less emphasis is paid to the major stakeholders in the context.

The methodology that we will be using will be based upon this approach. By this means we intend to encourage planners to draw in interested parties to the work that they are involved in thereby reducing the possibilities of alienating stakeholders and/or missing vital organizational constraints that lie outside the narrow confines of the proposed information system. Further, the approach will allow us to see the way in which we as planners fit into the system that we are devising.

The second question is that relating to methodology. The methodology we use here goes by the rather grand title of a *multiperspective*, **eclectic** *methodology* evolved from field work based upon 'Multiview' (see also Warmington, 1980; Antill and Wood-Harper, 1985; Wood-Harper *et al.*, 1985; Avison and Fitzgerald, 1988; Wood-Harper, 1988, 1990; Avison and Wood-Harper, 1990, 1991). If you think that this sounds off-putting perhaps we should explain that the approach is difficult to define without the use of terms such as these but is much easier to understand and apply. What the title means is that the methodology makes use of a wide range of tools (it is eclectic) and attempts to perceive the problem that an information system confronts from a number of different directions (it is multiperspective). The methodology consists of five components or tools. Four of these relate to methodologies that we

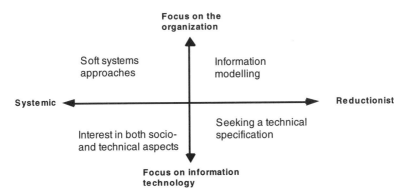

FIGURE 2.5   *Multiview and its constituent parts*

have already discussed. Figure 2.5 shows one way in which these four relate to each other and to wider issues already discussed in this chapter.

The diagram shows that two of the approaches are largely systemic and two broadly reductionist. Also two tend to be more concerned with the needs and demands of the organization while two have more focus on the technology. The fifth component of our methodology is that which deals with the interface between the user and the computer itself, the **human–computer interface** (HCI).

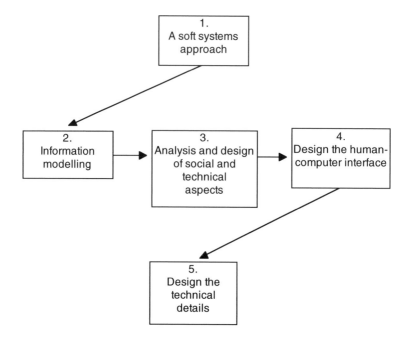

FIGURE 2.6   *A rapid planning methodology for information systems implementation*

We will go into greater depth concerning the specific details of the methodology in Chapter 4, but it is useful to see the overall layout now, and this is shown in Figure 2.6.

Before we discuss this methodology in depth we must define the role of the analyst, the person who is the central actor in the exploration (i.e. you).

2.3   Conclusion

In this chapter we have identified the approach to information systems planning that we are going to adopt and have demonstrated our reasons for selecting this approach in particular. Key points to remember are:

- Our approach will involve the active assistance of the recipient community – we look upon them as participants in the exploration.
- The approach is not intended to be confrontational to any other but adopts:
    - Key ideas from methods designed to improve the social significance of information systems and information technology;

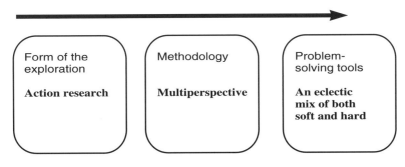

FIGURE 2.7   *Systems analysis and systems design approach of this book*

    – Key ideas from technically rigorous methods that produce well-designed, technologically sound systems.
- We can therefore state our approach to have the characteristics shown in Figure 2.7.

2.4   Exercise

Read the article below. Would you think a systemic or reductionist approach to this project would be most effective?

> Technical problems have stalled a £25m project to computerise all 250 county courts in England and Wales.
>
>   Roll out of the Caseman system has ground to a halt just five months into the contract, which EDS won with a bid believed to have been 50% lower than those from rivals such as Sema.
>
>   The system manages the progress of cases through the courts. But a key part of it, the printing of documents such as bailiff's reports, is still not working.
>
>   EDS has developed software to tackle some of the problems but says there is a bug in the Unix version of the Wordperfect word processor package.
>
>   .... The system was due to go live in the first batch of courts next Monday. EDS says it now has a fix for the bug and will ask for roll out to start in early March.
>
>   But the Court Service want two trouble-free days of printing at the proving courts before it starts the programme. Senior staff were due to meet EDS this week to review progress.
>
>   The delay has disrupted a massive training programme to familiarise 3,000 court staff with the system ...
>
>   **'Bug delays £25m court case system' by Karl Schneider.** *Computer Weekly,* **20 February 1997.**

    As with Chapter 1, an answer to this question is provided in Appendix C.

References and further reading

(The soft systems topic is well covered in Checkland, 1981;
Checkland, 1984; Checkland, 1985; Open University, 1987;
Checkland, 1988; Checkland and Scholes, 1990.)
(More general work on IS development from a more technological
focus is provided by Lucas, 1973; Lucas, 1976; Lucas, 1982; Lucas,
1985.)
(Kozar 1989 focuses on the human side of IS.)
(For informed discussion on the nature of action research see Heron,
1990; Reason, 1994; Heron, 1996; Reason and Heron, 1996.)
(For more discussion on the way in which we choose approaches to
exploring complex contexts see Galliers, 1985; Galliers, 1987;
Galliers, 1990; Galliers, 1992.)

Antill, L. and Wood-Harper, T. (1985). *Systems Analysis*. London:
Heinemann.
Avison, D.E. and Fitzgerald, G. (1988). *Information Systems
Development: Methodologies, Techniques and Tools*. Oxford:
Blackwell Scientific Publications.
Avison, D.E. and Wood-Harper, A.T. (1990). *Multiview: An
Exploration in Information Systems Development*. Oxford:
Blackwell Scientific Publications.
Avison, D.E. and Wood-Harper, A.T. (1991). Information systems
development research: an exploration of ideas in action. *Computer
Journal*, **34**(2).
Baskerville, R. and Wood-Harper, A.T. (1996). A critical perspective
on action research as a method for information systems research.
Journal of Information Technology, vol. 11, no. 2
Checkland, P.B. (1981). *Systems Thinking, Systems Practise*.
Chichester: Wiley.
Checkland, P.B. (1984). Systems thinking in management: the
development of soft systems methodology and its implications for
social science. In H. Ulrich and G. J. Probst (eds), *Self Organization
and Management of Social Systems*. Berlin: Springer-Verlag.
Checkland, P.B. (1985). From optimisation to learning: a develop-
ment of systems thinking for the 1990s. *Journal of the Operational
Research Society*, **36**(9), 757–767.
Checkland, P.B. (1988). Information systems and systems thinking:
time to unite? *International Journal of Information Management*,
8, 239–248.
Checkland, P.B. and Scholes, J. (1990). *Soft Systems Methodology in
Action*. Chichester: Wiley.
Flew, A. (1979). *A Dictionary of Philosophy*. London: Pan.
Galliers, R.D. (1985). In search of a paradigm for information
systems research. In E. Mumford (ed.), *Research Methods in
Information Systems*. Manchester: North Holland.

Galliers, R.D. (1987). An approach to information needs analysis. In R.D. Galliers (ed.), *Information Analysis: Selected Readings*. Wokingham: Addison Wesley.

Galliers, R.D. (1990). *Choosing Appropriate Information Systems Research Approaches: A Revised Taxonomy*. Amsterdam: North Holland.

Galliers, R.D. (1992). Choosing information systems research approaches. In R.D. Galliers (ed.), *Information Systems Research*. London: Blackwell Scientific Publications.

Heron, J. (1990). *Helping the Client*. London: Sage.

Heron, J. (1996). *Co-operative Inquiry: Research into the Human Condition*. London: Sage.

Kozar, K.A. (1989). *Humanized Information Systems Analysis and Design: People Building Systems for People*. New York: McGraw-Hill.

Lucas, H.C. (1973). *Computer Based Information Systems in Organizations*. Palo Alto: Science Research Associates.

Lucas, H.C. (1976). *The Implementation of Computer Based Models*. New York: National Association of Accountants.

Lucas, H.C. (1982). *Coping with Computers: A Manager's Guide to Controlling Information Processing*. New York: Free Press.

Lucas, H.C. (1985). *The Analysis, Design and Implementation of Information Systems*. New York: McGraw-Hill.

Open University (1987). T301 – Complexity Management and Change: A Systems Approach. Open University Systems Group. Milton Keynes: The Open University Press.

Reason, P. (1994). *Participation in Human Inquiry*. London: Sage.

Reason, P. and Heron, J. (1996). Co-operative inquiry. In R. Harre, J. Smith and L. Van Langenhove (eds), *Rethinking Methods in Psychology* (in press).

Senge, P., Ross, P., Smith, B., Roberts, R. and Kleiner, R. (1994). *The Fifth Discipline Fieldbook: Strategies and Tools for Building a Learning Organisation*. London: Nicholas Brealey.

Warmington, A. (1980). Action research: its methods and its implications. *Journal of Applied Systems Analysis*, **7**, 23–39.

Wood-Harper, A.T. (1988). Characteristics of Information Systems Definition Approaches. Norwich, School of Information Systems: University of East Anglia.

Wood-Harper, A.T. (1989). Role of methodologies in Information Systems Development. Norwich: School of Information Systems, University of East Anglia.

Wood-Harper, A.T. (1989). Comparison of Information Systems Approaches: An Action-Research, Multiview Perspective. PhD Thesis. Norwich: School of Information Systems, University of East Anglia.

Wood-Harper, A.T., Antill, L. and Avison, D.E. (1985). *Information Systems Definition: A Multiview Approach*. Oxford: Blackwell Scientific Publications.

Chapter 3

THE ROLE OF THE SYSTEMS PLANNER OR SYSTEMS ANALYST

Keywords:

the function of the analyst, past experience, methodology, area of use, self-analysis, reflective practice.

Summary:

The role of the analyst is to help the end user of the information system clarify his or her information processing requirements and choose the most suitable systems design to meet these requirements. The analyst must perform the detailed analysis and work with programmers and others to help to build and implement a working system. This role, or some parts of it, may be carried out from different positions within the organization, or from outside it. The analyst is part of the context. The analyst brings his or her own ideas, baggage, agendas and preferences. It is our contention that these personal issues are best addressed at the outset of analysis in order to clarify commitments and surface personal issues which, if left, might jeopardize the IS project. A little self-knowledge is a powerful thing. This chapter looks at how the analyst can arrive at a clear idea of his or her own background.

3.1 You the analyst – first thoughts

All analysis must start from the basis that *reality is complex* and *the analyst is part of this complexity*. Information systems, intimately linked to so many elements of the social, technical, political and cultural aspects of our lives are also very complex. What we often fail to fully recognize is that we, as analysts, are also part of the overall context within which our information system will work. As our action research approach recognizes we are within the research frame and we will influence what goes on. Our own personal preferences will have an impact upon our planning and we will, consciously or unconsciously, attempt to influence stakeholders towards our own pre-set ideas about what is 'right' (as we saw in problem 2 in Chapter 1). This cannot be avoided and therefore is best understood at the outset.

It is not the purpose of this book to set out the complex and often confusing aspects of behavioural psychology and self-analysis. In this chapter we wish to make clear that our perceptions change over time, that these changes can be monitored and that the understanding of our own personal bias will help us to understand the decisions that we make.

First of all, what is it that we as analysts and designers are trying to do?

Our first task is to attempt to understand local context, to make generalized models of the existing situation in order to go on to create an information system. By formulating generalizations about current practices in organizations we can develop models of reality which we can then test for adequacy in hypothetical situations (e.g. 'will this model pay-roll system cope with 23 new staff being re-employed following dismissal notices being sent out accidentally?'). If our model is proved by experience to be adequate then we can, with humility (that is recognizing that the system will always contain some faults and thus can always be improved upon), plan the working automated (or non-automated) system.

Understanding the complexity of reality is the nub of the analyst's dilemma with regards to making a reasonable model. Before going on to look at the tools the analyst employs we need to consider the role that the systems analyst plays in an organization. Let us start with a very general definition:

> The systems analyst works with the user within his or her socio-political and economic context to specify the information system requirements of an organization. The system is modelled according to terms of reference and the final outline plans are produced for hardware, software and necessary processing.

This conveys the intermediary, 'go-between', aspect as well as the architectural aspect of the job. The title Systems Analysis and System Design is often used to convey the creative aspect of the role. There is a sense in which the analyst is like an architect producing designs to the client's specification, or for their approval, which can then be turned into an actual construction by the implementing agency although this view minimizes the importance of the final system user in the analysis and design process. Our focus here is to set out:

- How different types of individual will conform to different types of analysis and design stereotypes.

Our stereotypes of analysts form a similar function in aiding our understanding to the organizational metaphors of Gareth Morgan's, set out in Chapter 1. The stereotype does not represent an actual person but provides a metaphor that we can use as a means to understand our own strengths and weaknesses. This is described in more detail shortly. Building upon this reflection we see:

- How the recent history of analysis and design indicates how these stereotypes arose.
- How a quick review of one's own intellectual background, methodologies and work environment helps in assessing how our current approach has arisen.

First, and generally speaking, we identify four types or categories of analyst. These four are not definitive and more could be added but, we believe, they represent a cross-section of the major tendencies among the professionals working in the area. The technocratic analyst (Figure 3.1) 'fixes' problems. He or she is best thought of as a technical expert like a doctor. The tendency of this approach is to take over the situation and impose one's 'expert advice'.

Self-image: 'I am a technical expert'

Seeks to: 'Fix' a problem with objectivity and rigour

FIGURE 3.1   *The technocratic analyst*

In our second example the radical analyst (Figure 3.2) seeks to overthrow existing wrongs and bring in new and improved systems. The metaphor of a warrior might appear to be a bit strong but the underlying tendency of wishing radically to alter what currently exists is a fundamental aspect of the resulting approach. Here the analyst will attempt to assert the radical reform of current practices.

Self-image: 'I am an agent of social change'

Seeks to: Change radically the existing status quo

FIGURE 3.2   *The radical analyst*

The third image (Figure 3.3) is the one which most would probably wish to be associated with. It is a benign metaphor and has close associations with the learning organization approach which we have already discussed in Chapter 2. In the case of the facilitator and teacher the analyst seeks meaning and attempts to assist clients by facilitating their own problem-solving efforts. The analyst attempts to draw the clients into the problem-solving process and encourages them to become involved in all stages. Analyst and stakeholders are drawn into a learning process.

Problem context

Self-image: 'I am a facilitator to assist with problem solving'

Seeks to: Find the meanining of problems

FIGURE 3.3   *The facilitator/teacher analyst*

In our fourth example (Figure 3.4) the analyst is an agent of change again but now in the sense of an emancipator – a catalyst assisting others to change their own lives. The difference between this analyst and the facilitator is that here change and confrontation are inevitable. Therefore, the approach is 'hands-on' and can be highly assertive.

Change!

Self-image: 'I am a catalyst of change'

Seeks to: Change states of mind and behaviour

FIGURE 3.4   *The emancipator analyst*

All four of our examples of analysts can be seen on two axes as shown in Figure 3.5.

The self-image of the analyst is very important. The four options we see here are derived from four very different perspectives, con-

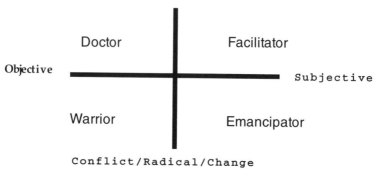

FIGURE 3.5   *Four metaphors of the analyst (adapted from Burrell and Morgan, 1979)*

sensus seeking at the top and radical at the bottom. Similarly the analyst can be seen as moving between the points of objective, 'scientific' behaviour (tending to the reductionist) and that of subjective preference and possibly more holistic.

THINK POINT

At this point it is useful to ask yourself some questions:

- In developing IS am I seeking change or meaning?
- Am I planning a technical fix to the problem in hand or am I assisting others to recognize existing problems and develop internal solutions?
- What is my self-perception – what kind of person am I?
- How will this affect the way in which I carry out my analysis and design?

What are the answers you come up with? What type of metaphor best describes you in your analysis and design context? Maybe skilfully thinking ahead and acting with caution – a snooker player? Maybe you see yourself as drawing out the stakeholders but at the same time keeping a degree of order in a discordant context – a facilitator with 'attitude'? Whatever the metaphor that comes to mind what does it tell you about the way you get on with others in the context? What about the metaphor that best sums up your main stakeholders? If you are a facilitator type but working in a 'thrusting' new agency, surrounded on all fronts by emancipator and warrior types does this inform the way in which you will go about your business?

The review of types of people we and our stakeholders are is a useful precursor to undertaking our exploration of the analysis and design context. Of course, any action arising from answering such questions is largely dependent upon ourselves and how we interpret what we discover. But it may well be that if one approach to analysis and design does not seem to be working, a different one can be tried that fits in better with the mood of the organization and the stakeholders within it. Of course, other types of metaphor might be employed in the understanding of the actors in the context. In our own practice we have employed a range of such tools from the formal to the highly informal. Morgan's approach to considering organizations as metaphors (Morgan, 1977) can provide valuable insights. The Myers Briggs personality index (there are a number of reasonably priced introductory booklets to this: Hirsh and Kummerow, 1990; Briggs *et al.*, 1994; Myers and Kirby, 1994) is a useful tool for getting stakeholders to see themselves in a powerful positive light. Astrological signs can be used as a means to open up stakeholder groups to views of themselves in a light-hearted fashion (an excellent book that produces astrological types quickly is Harvey and Harvey, 1994). We have even made use of the Winnie the Pooh characters for people to identify with (Bell, 1997)! Whatever the tool used, self-reflection is a powerful aid to understanding the analyst in the context.

The answer to the questions set out in the Think point above will largely depend upon where we see our own point of origin in the development of the present situation. To understand this it is useful briefly to look at the history of the analyst and designer in the wider history of the development of information technology.

3.2   The history of the analyst

Some (e.g. Awad, 1988) have attempted to break down the recent history of computer development into distinct periods or epochs. Here we take an adaptation of such a model and apply the salient features of the epoch as they concern the planner/analyst.

In the early days of **isolated computing** (25 plus years ago) the hardware system was all important. The main use of computing systems was cost reduction accounting. The salient features of the period were:

- **mainframe** orientated
- computer experts were extremely remote (in terms of physical location and general attitude) from users
- the analyst was invisible in the system and dealt with technical matters.

Then followed the second period of **consolidated computing** (roughly 25 years ago). This was a period that was dominated by programmers and poor documentation! The salient features were:

- mainframe and **minicomputer** orientated
- programmers – no user interface!
- analysts or, more properly, programmer–analysts, were still buried in the system. They were mainly involved with designing systems for computers, not systems for people.

When the power of technical systems began to be appreciated by a wider managerial audience faults arising from systems orientated to the wishes of programmers were recognized. This was the third period when **management controls and restraints** were imposed (20 years ago). The key to this process was the enforcement of standards in terms of programming, new systems development and system functions. The key features were:

- mainframe, minicomputer and microcomputer orientated systems (the 'micros' were disliked by some professionals and were considered to be not serious, a 'blip'!)
- computer expert worked directly under business management control
- the beginnings of crude user interfaces
- the analyst became a management aid. The beginning of the 'humanization' of many of these individuals began. Problems became organizational and less machine-based (not 'what can the machine do?' but 'what can the machine do for me?').

This approach still did not allow easy access to computer power. The development of microcomputers (the 'PC') has ushered in the (much celebrated) **role of the user** (15 years ago) – focusing on applications software (e.g. packages), distributed computing to remote officers (via the desktop PCs), far from the computer department. Key features included:

- the advent of microcomputer networks
- the expert operating as a *facilitator* of user needs
- the emplacement of strict control of the computer function by the organization
- the analyst becomes central to understanding the needs of the user.

Most recently, but still beginning some 10 years ago, following the trend above, we have seen the focus on the **user/machine interface**, making users and computers more equal to the struggle of communication. Key notes for this process have been the development of user-friendly approaches.

- networked information technology becomes the norm in all parts of the organization – most recently this can be seen in the form of the **internet** and the **intranet** and the rise of the **World Wide Web**

- invisible technology – 'I don't want to understand it, I just want to use it'
- invisible experts – 'Don't get in my way, just make the system easy to use'
- The era of 'We are all users now'.

The theme here is that information systems are generally becoming more available to the user and they are losing their technical/programming appearance. The analyst is now concerned with understanding users and making information systems dovetail into their needs. The movement from isolated computing to the user/machine interface (which has taken a mere 25 years) can be summed up by two statements which convey the focus of epoch 1 and epoch 5.

Epoch 1

The computer expert is the centre of the system. The computer expert is given the necessary support to indicate priorities and to control the process of providing automated procedures to alleviate problems. The user is peripheral to the needs of the data-processing department and acts as a problem object to the computer expert.

Epoch 5

The user is the centre of the system. The user is given the necessary support to indicate priorities and to begin the process of providing automated procedures to alleviate problems. The computer expert is peripheral and acts as counsel and support to the user.

Perhaps the most striking point that arises from the two statements is the movement between two metaphors – from the hard, technocratic view to one that focuses on facilitating the needs of the often despised user. In a sense the five periods can be seen as being not just representative of periods of history but also of states of mind. In this sense there are still plenty of epoch 1 people around!

3.3   You the analyst – second thoughts

Because background determines the approach for our exploration into information systems needs of organizations, and this in turn influences our selection of methodology which then goes on to determine the problem-solving tools applied, it is quite useful (although still largely not practised by analysts and designers) to review one's own background and assumptions with regard to the particular situation in which you are going to work. The analyst is as human as anyone else and if you intend to carry out your own analysis it is useful to have a system to recognize, before beginning the process of analysis, where your own ideas and concepts arise and possibly how likely they are to influence the task in hand.

3.3.1   Present reflection and self-analysis

One means for such self-analysis is shown in Figure 3.6. The figure demonstrates a fairly simple and easy-to-use tool for identifying the predispositions of the analyst with regard to the background, immediate problem context and methodology being used.

If you have never undertaken analysis and design before you should still be able to express a methodology preference from the information given in Chapter 2.

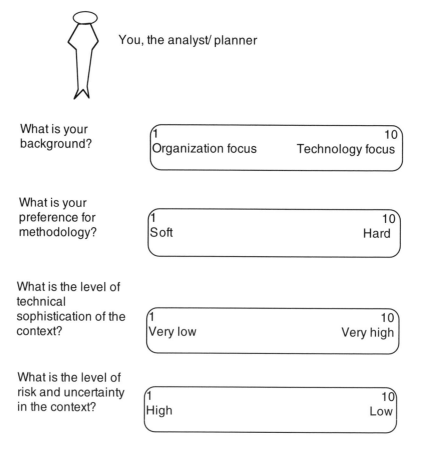

FIGURE 3.6   *Self-analysis – analyst 'know thyself'*

The first question is to identify background. On the scale provided here this ranges from organizational interest to technical interest, from largely soft to largely hard, from generally systemic to generally reductionist. The second question – with regard to methodology – similarly sets the task of identifying a preference to a soft or hard approach. The third question indicates the technological sophistication of the area being worked in (e.g. a computer-wise city bank or a naive farmers' co-operative), and the fourth question asks for an indication of risk and uncertainty for IT in that environment (e.g. is it well understood, financed and supported, low risk, or the reverse of these, high risk?). The result will be a mark between 1 and 10 for questions 1 and 2 and 3 and 4. For questions 1 and 2, marks tending to 1 indicate a soft background, marks tending to 10 indicate hard. For questions 3 and 4, marks tending to 1 indicate high risk, low sophistication, marks tending to 10 indicate low risk, high sophistication.

A useful rule of thumb for understanding this type of exercise is shown in Figure 3.7. The tool can be used as a rapid way of assessing the value and appropriateness of the analyst's approach in the given situation.

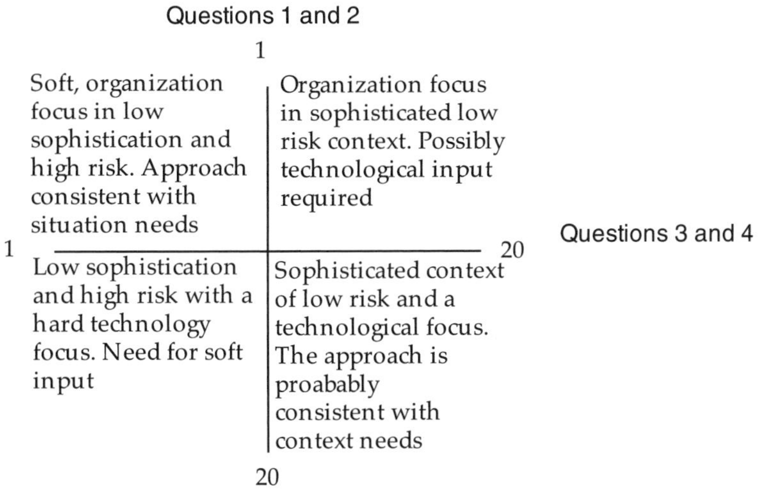

Questions 1 and 2

1	
Soft, organization focus in low sophistication and high risk. Approach consistent with situation needs	Organization focus in sophisticated low risk context. Possibly technological input required

1 ————————————————— 20   Questions 3 and 4

Low sophistication and high risk with a hard technology focus. Need for soft input	Sophisticated context of low risk and a technological focus. The approach is proabably consistent with context needs

20

FIGURE 3.7   *Assessing the four questions*

THINK POINT

Try the criteria on yourself and the organization you are working in. What are the omens for systems development?

3.3.2   Reflecting on the development of the analyst

This is another approach that can be used in conjunction with that set out in Figures 3.6 and 3.7 – it is developed more fully elsewhere (Bell, 1996). The method is intended for those who have undertaken systems analysis and systems design before and consists of reviewing personal development over several years. This can be undertaken focusing on three key areas (see Figure 3.8).

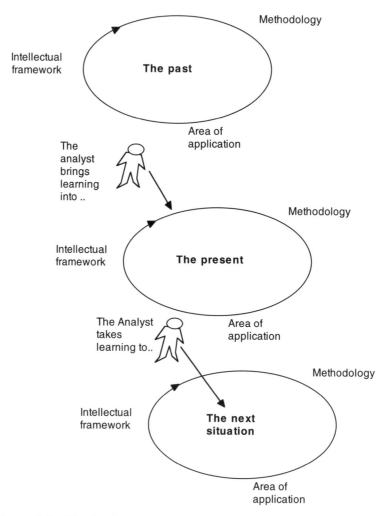

FIGURE 3.8   *The developing analyst*

- What is my intellectual framework? – the set of ideas and principles that underlie the way I work.

- What methodologies have I applied? If you have not undertaken systems analysis and systems design before what is your manner or style of working?
- What were the situations in which I worked?

In Figure 3.8 the analyst can be seen as developing and learning from past to present to the next context for intervention. In each case the intellectual background develops, the methodology may well change and the area of application of that methodology will also change. The process is dynamic with many opportunities for learning.

Look at your own intellectual framework as thoughtfully and impartially as possible. It will tell you a lot about how you will approach the subject of the analysis (warrior or doctor?) and may also indicate whether you will tend towards technical solutions or soft measures to make systems work. 'Man know thyself' is as relevant to the systems analyst as it is to the mystic. One example of such an analysis is shown in Table 3.1. The table shows five major

TABLE 3.1   *The chronological development of an analyst*

Frame	Intellectual framework	Methodology in use	Area of application/ problem context
Frame 1	Development studies literature	Technical specification type approaches (TS)	North East Africa
Frame 2	Hard systems, operations research literature	Increasing focus on mathematical and quantitative methods	West Africa
Frame 3	Critical of reductionism, 'muddling along', a time of drift	Amended TS	West Africa
Frame 4	Web modelling, soft systems approaches	Multiview	Asia
Frame 5	Soft systems and other qualitative approaches	Multiperspective methodologies	Several areas of Africa

shifts in the intellectual background, methodology and area of application of an analyst. It generally indicates a movement from hard to soft approaches. Table 3.1 shows five 'snapshots' in an individual's development. The example is academic but gives some general themes that are of interest The snapshot shows five frames over five years. Intellectually the analyst moves from his university concentration on 'Development Studies' (the study of Third World development) through technocratic school of analysis and design to soft systems approaches such as Multiview. His methodological development mirrors this movement, from hard technical specification to soft multiperspective. Areas of application range from East and West Africa to Asia.

A more conventional, business-orientated approach is shown in Table 3.2. The second model, which does not relate directly to

TABLE 3.2   *The chronological development of an accountant*

Frame	Intellectual framework	Methodology in use	Area of application/ problem context
Frame 1	Financial record keeping and accounts	Workaholic, work as a grind	Small electronics business
Frame 2	Corporate mentality	Team approach and team responsibility	Local government
Frame 3	Leaner and fitter, a predatory approach	Competitive edge to the team dynamics	Local government

information systems design, shows the key snapshots in the development of an accountant. She begins work in a small electronics company and works to the book of her accountancy training. The second frame shows her movement to local government. A team approach is important in a large company and with this comes what we call a corporate mentality. The mentality requires the accountant to concentrate on the aspect of the local government body she is working for and not the total situation – her experience when working for the electronics company. The third frame shows a switch in the direction of local government (such as that which occurred in the UK in the 1980s). Accounting thinking becomes much more 'predatory'. Costs are being cut and fiddles are being sought out. This in turn brings a competitive edge to team work and also introduces a 'dynamic' edge to the team concept.

3.4   Conclusions

As we have seen in Chapter 2, systems analysis and systems design is a highly complex subject incorporating many different 'flavours' – from the hard and scientific to the soft and holistically focused.

Along with the analysis of problem contexts we have to recognize that we, the analysts and designers, also come into the frame. We affect what we work upon. In order to be fully aware of the impact that we are having upon the work in hand it is quite useful to gain knowledge on two major areas of concern:

• First, where our own strengths and weaknesses are in the

problem context. We can get this information from a present self-analysis. The task in hand may require a shift in our present approach to analysis and design and may lead to further shifts in the light of the findings. This indicates a positive switch towards reflective practice and to a learning culture.

- Secondly, what our path has been to the present situation and therefore what our overall tendencies have been in terms of intellectual development and work methodology. We can ascertain this information from the chronology of self-development. Our current area of application may require a substantial change in intellectual framework or methodology.

All self-analysis procedures provide the analyst with an overview of his or her current state. This can be vital if problems arise with the analysis and design procedure and there is a need to rethink the approach. For example, there may be a situation in which the analyst favours the soft approaches, tending to focus on client/user self-help and workshops to discuss problems. The client, however, requires more leadership and drive from the analyst ('why ask us to think it out, that's what we are paying you to do'). This may require the analyst to shift focus to the hard tools in the methodology and to adopt a more managerial style or, more challengingly, to switch focus to a still more facilitating role thus involving the client in the planning process by illustrating for the client the potency of participation in the information systems analysis and design process.

As we shall see in Chapter 4, the methodology we apply here allows the analyst a certain amount of freedom in the selection of tools in the problem context. If problems arise due to the analyst's approach the analyst can substitute soft for hard tools (or vice versa) or can reschedule their use.

3.5   Exercise

Imagine you are the project manager, being paid by a major publisher in the following scenario. Read the scenario and decide what qualities you would require from a systems analyst.

Non-governmental organization (NGO) in London, UK

The NGO is involved in the provision of educational books to developing countries. Although quite a small concern the agency is well connected to major publishing concerns and gains substantial quantities of textbooks at no cost. The main work of the organization is to react to demand from other educational trusts and agencies working in the field. When a request for books come through the NGO tries to meet demand.

The NGO has been convinced by the main publisher it works with to place all its contacts, projects and stocks onto a central computer. The computer, analysis and design and staff training budget are all being donated by the publisher. The idea is being enthusiastically taken up by the NGO's director who is charismatic but who has no grasp for or interest in the details of the project. The senior administrator is hostile to the project because she does not have enough time or assistance to maintain manual systems – the organization is very busy and seems to lurch from crisis to crisis. There are three clerical staff who work part-time.

References and further reading

(For more reading on self-analysis and reflective practice see Checkland, 1984; Boud, 1985; Russell, 1986; Bell, 1991; Bell, 1992; Horney, 1994; Levin, 1994; Biggs, 1995; Wood-Harper *et al.*, 1996; Bell, 1996; Bell, 1997.)

Awad, E.M. (1988). *Management Information Systems: Concepts, Structure and Applications*. Menlo Park: Benjamin Cummings.

Bell, S. (1991). Systems Analysis and Systems Design in Developing Countries – present problems, various methods, self analysis, pre analysis and the need for professional humility. Paper presented at a meeting of the British Computer Society Developing Countries Special Interest Group, 14 October, London School of Economics.

Bell, S. (1992). Self-analysis and pre-analysis: lessons in the application of systems analysis in developing countries. In G. Cyranek and S.C. Bhatnagar (eds), *Technology Transfer for Development: The Prospects and Limits of Information Technology*. New Delhi: Tata McGraw-Hill.

Bell, S. (1996). *Learning with Information Systems: Learning Cycles in Information Systems Development*. London: Routledge.

Bell, S. (1996). Reflections on learning in information systems practice. *The Systemist*, **17**(2), 54–63.

Bell, S. (1997). IT training, personality type and Winnie-the-Pooh. *The Systemist*, **19**(3), 133–146.

Biggs, S. (1995). Contending coalitions in participatory technology development: challenges to the new orthodoxy. *The Limits of Participation*. Bedford Way, London: Intermediate Technology.

Boud, D. (1985). *Reflection: Turning Experience into Learning*. London: Kogan Page.

Briggs Myers, I. *et al.* (eds) (1994). *Introduction to Type* (fifth edition). Oxford: Oxford Psychologists Press.

Burrell, G. and Morgan, G. (1979). *Sociological Paradigms and Organizational Analysis*. London: Heinemann.

Checkland, P.B. (1984). Systems thinking in management: the development of soft systems methodology and its implications for social science. In H. Ulrich and G. J. Probst (eds), *Self Organisation and Management of Social Systems*. Berlin: Springer-Verlag.

Harvey, C. and Harvey, S. (1994). *Sun Sign, Moon Sign*. London: Thorsons.

Hirsh, K. and Kummerow, J. (1990). *Introduction to Type in Organizations*. Oxford: Oxford Psychologists Press.

Horney, K. (1994). *Self-Analysis*. London: Norton.

Levin, M. (1994). Action research and critical systems thinking: two icons carved out of the same log? *Systems Practice*, **7**(1), 25–41.

Morgan, G. (1997). *Images of Organization: New Edition*. London: Sage.

Myers, K. and Kirby, L. (1994). *Introduction to Type: Dynamics and Development*. Oxford: Oxford Psychologists Press.

Russell, D. (1986). How we see the world determines what we do in the world: preparing the ground for action research. Hawkesbury: University of Western Sydney.

Watson, H. and Wood-Harper, A.T. (1995). Methodology as metaphor: the practical basis for multiview methodology (a reply to M.C. Jackson). *Information Systems Journal*, **5**, 225–231.

Wood-Harper, A.T., Condor, S.V., Wood, J.R.G. and Watson, H. (1996). How we profess: the ethical systems analyst. *Communications of the ACM*, vol. 39, no. 3.

Chapter 4

TERMS OF REFERENCE AND SELECTING OUR PLANNING/ DEVELOPMENT TOOLS – SEQUENCE AND SCHEDULE

Keywords:

the project cycle, terms of reference, **human activity system**, **rich picture**, **root definition**, **conceptual model**, **information modelling**, **social and technical systems**, human–computer interface, **technical aspects**, tool selection, context.

Summary:

All planning or analysis and design begins with a set of terms of reference. Following these the analyst will have some idea as to what specific work is expected, under what conditions and with what resources. Following on from this, the analyst can select the tools that are appropriate within the context of the problem being reviewed and set out their sequence and schedule.

4.1   The reality of analysis: terms of reference

It would be pleasing to the ego and satisfying to the power hungry to believe that the analyst can be all-powerful in the problem context. Like Caesar, to cry 'Veni, Vidi, Vici' (I came, I saw, I conquered) would be a rather satisfactory way of concluding the analysis. This will not happen to you very often if at all if common experience is anything to go by!

Many systems analysis and systems design books set out as though the analyst's word were law and the specified logic of the analysis were always carried out to the letter. This is rarely the case and possibly especially so in situations of rapid change and risk. Financing agencies, be they banks or accounting departments, putting up the cash for analysis and design, tend to impose very strict guidelines or *terms of reference* upon the analyst, which will mean that a certain amount of prejudging of the situation will have taken place (sometimes by individuals carrying out feasibility studies with little knowledge of information technology, sometimes by managers who think that they already know the answer to the problem).

It is no good the analyst specifying a new, mini computer-based Management Information System and Intranet for an organization if the terms of reference restrict all further development to simple PC database functions. Sometimes you may feel disheartened when your analysis tells you very different things from the guidelines you have received.

The ability of the analyst to move freely within the context of his or her terms of reference and the associated budget and personnel limits will depend very much upon:

- the ability of the analyst to convince the funding body that more or less may be required (the latter is easier!)
- the willingness of the funding body to be flexible.

The golden rule is never to exceed the boundaries of the system as seen by the funding body without first convincing all the major stakeholders in the system that such a course is both right and necessary. This introduces a larger issue, the position of the analysis and design procedure in what is called the project cycle (see Figure 4.1). In this figure analysis and design is one element (item 6) of the cycle and depends for its integration on self-analysis and methodology selection and testing as described in Chapters 2 and 3. The

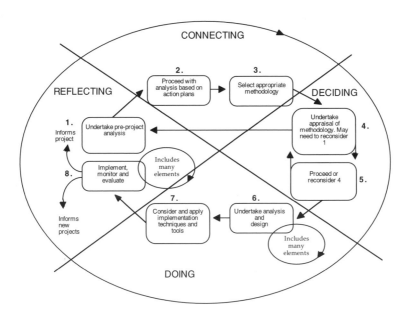

FIGURE 4.1   *A view of the project cycle (adapted from Bell, 1996)*

terms of reference are the principles that guide the pre-analysis (item 1). We have included the 'learning cycle' of Kolb (Kolb, 1984) in which all activity is based upon reflecting on what has gone before (e.g. terms of reference, previous analysis and design experience). This is followed by connecting (e.g. seeing what is relevant from other approaches and experiences). The deciding aspect is the final selection of the methodological tools and techniques and the doing is the analysis and design itself followed by implementation of the project. The learning cycle means that lessons from experience are gathered by the team and, as we saw in Chapter 1 in the Senge model (Senge *et al.*, 1994), by making use of systems thinking and mental models (in items 6 and 7) driven by shared vision achieved during the first four items of the cycle, various strengths arise including the development of team learning and enhanced personal mastery in analysis and design procedures as well as understanding the organization (identifiable in item 8).

4.2   The context of an analysis methodology – selecting the right tools

Thinking back to Chapter 3 and the need to select appropriate analysis and design tools, the first activity within our analysis is to select the tools that are appropriate to the situation under study, those that conform to:

- the conditions set out in the terms of reference, and
- the personal preferences set out in our self-analysis (outlined in Chapter 3 and highlighted in item 1 in Figure 4.1).

We have already introduced, in outline only, the methodology tools that we are going to set out in this text. These are shown in Figure 4.2. We now need to flesh out what these tools actually do.

4.2.1   Soft systems methodology

This comprises the analysis of what Checkland has defined as the **human activity system** (HAS). The HAS is the main element of our approach to soft systems methodology (SSM) and is in turn composed of three core items:

- The **rich picture**, which in our approach is devised to show the principal human, social and cultural activities at work in the perceived environment. The rich picture usually includes the structures and processes at work in an organization.
- The **root definition**, which by identifying the key customer,

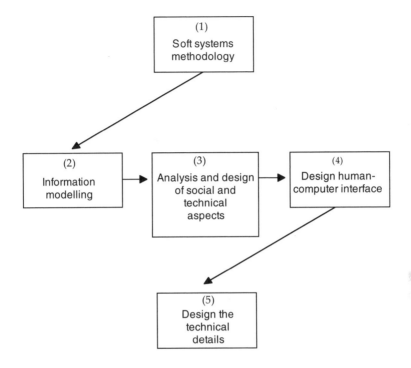

FIGURE 4.2   *Rapid planning methodology – Multiview*

actors, transformation expected, assumptions, problem owners and environments, attempts to structure the results of the rich picture analysis into a mutual (analyst and stakeholders) perception of 'what can we do about the problem?'.

- The **conceptual model** which is used in our approach as a means to set out the key systems and sub-systems involved in the new improved information system. The conceptual model (or maybe a **systems model** would be a better phrase) is an outline of what we are going to attempt to design.

4.2.2   Information modelling

The second phase of the analysis is information modelling. In this phase we adopt a more quantitative and technical approach. At this stage we want to develop the conceptual model, which by definition is an idea requiring structuring into a workable information system. In information modelling we attempt to draw together the:

- major **entities**
- **functions** of these entities

- **events** that trigger these functions to occur
- **attributes**, or discrete elements of the entities.

In applying this tool we are able to generalize the key systems identified in the conceptual model down to a set of data objects and information processing functions which can be the basic design of a new information system. Figure 4.3 shows an outline example of an information model.

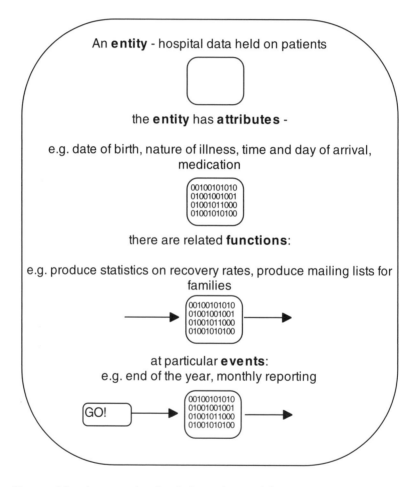

FIGURE 4.3   *An example of an information model*

4.2.3   Social and technical requirements

The third phase requires that the analyst bring together the right mix of social (human resources) and technical (information technology, other technology) aspects. Here the key hardware and identified human alternatives, costs, availability and constraints are married together to make the appropriate mix. This stage produces a combination of technology and personnel to implement the system outlined in phase 2. The theme of this phase is that the system to be devised it both feasible and **sustainable**.

4.2.4   Human–computer interface

The fourth phase deals with the human–computer interface (HCI). This involves thinking about the means by which the two aspects of the proposed information system (human-being and technology) can best communicate with each other.

4.2.5   Technical aspects

The fifth and last aspect involves the design of the necessary technical aspects that combine to produce the overall technical solution. The major technical aspects are shown in Figure 4.4.

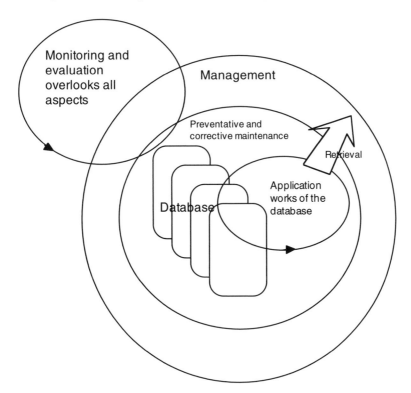

FIGURE 4.4   *Technical aspects of the information system*

The six major systems shown are arguably the core of any information system:

- The *applications* area deals with transactions within the computer (updating records, gathering data elements for output in digital or paper format).
- *Retrieval* deals with the output from the system.
- *Database* is the core structure containing entities of the information system.
- *Maintenance* covers both preventative and corrective.
- *Management* controls the overall information system process within the organization context.

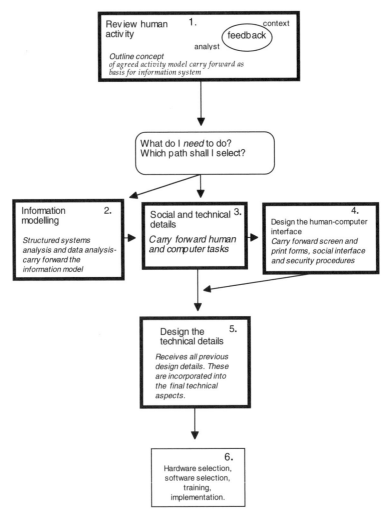

FIGURE 4.5 *Rapid planning methodology*

- *Monitoring* (and *evaluation* for the purposes of this book) deals with the effective performance of the system and ensuring that learning occurs when and if problems occur.

The current task is to select which, if not all, of the tools to use. The methodology as a whole can be set out as shown in Figure 4.5.

Again, do not panic about the complexity of this picture. Figure 4.5 gives us some more detail. First it is worth noting that the first stage of the analysis involves an iterative loop, or period of discussion and feedback between the analyst and the stakeholder group in the context. The second point to note is that the second stage of the analysis, information modelling, may throw up inconsistencies which we will need to rethink. This type of eventuality is impossible to foresee. An example would be where the conceptual or systems model requires two departments to share one common information product such as salary details but where in fact this idea is strongly objected to by staff. This would require a reworking of the model and most certainly the rich picture. The third point to note is that following the fifth stage of the process comes software selection, hardware selection and implementation strategy – a new sixth stage. These issues are not strictly part of the analysis and design but are general issues which will be dealt with in Chapter 10.

The major constraint on the use of analysis and design approaches is cost and time. With analysis and design this simplifies down to time. If we return to the overall picture of our methodology we can identify three separate ways (Figure 4.6) in which the approach can be adapted and adopted.

AUTHORS' ASIDE

This book is about rapid information systems design and we include the words 'imperfect world' in the title. The approach we set out here is based upon the fundamental beliefs that:
- non-specialists can and do undertake analysis and design
- a little analysis and design is better than no analysis and design at all
- that analysis and design approaches often have to be cut to meet the constraints of the context (but as we have already said, a little is better than none).

The three 'paths' shown in Figure 4.6 offer three different levels of analysis. They each contain strengths and weaknesses, opportu-

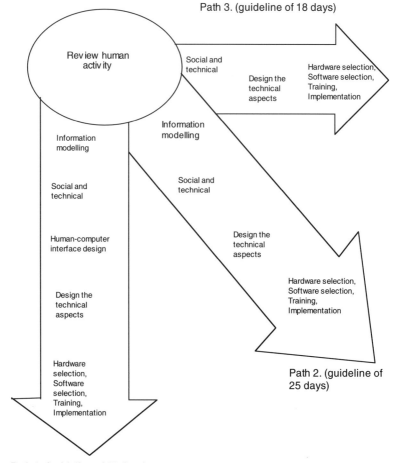

FIGURE 4.6   *Which path do I take?*

nities and threats (SWOT). SWOT analysis is a useful technique for thinking about an issue. We provide a SWOT for each path below.

Path 1, the six-stage path—*Strength:* it contains the complete methodology and we estimate that this can be completed in six weeks or 30 working days although this is only a guide figure (organizational size and complexity are major factors). *Weakness:* it requires that you become competent in a number of new skills and does take time to learn. *Opportunity*: the value of analysis and design within the organization as an opportunity to learn about organizational processes is enhanced. *Threat*: you may discover that there are deeper problems around than you originally thought. This may mean that the analysis and design is extended.

Path 2, the five-stage path—*Strength*: the ability to cover ground more quickly and as a guide can be completed in 25 working days. *Weakness*: the design of the human–computer interface. *Threat*: the analysis as a whole may be deficient in planning the manner in which the computer interfaces to the user. *Opportunity*: much IT comes with highly developed built-in graphic interfaces (e.g. Windows 95 and related software) and sometimes there is little need to consider additional items – the needs of your context will help you understand if this stage is necessary.

Path 3, the four-stage path—*Strength*: further cutting of time on the analysis and as a guide can be completed in 18 working days. *Weakness*: the loss of elements, in this case the human–computer interface (as with Path 2) and also information modelling. *Threat*: this loss is quite a serious omission and it will result in there being no clear planning of database structures (the core of most information systems) and the related programmes. *Opportunity*: information modelling is most specifically important where the client is concerned with writing software for a specific and unique purpose. Very often this will not be the case and the end of the analysis will be to propose the client purchase software off the shelf. In this case information modelling is not essential.

The following five chapters outline each of the stages given above. Your current task is to select the best path for your specific analysis. Your choice needs to be based upon the constraints of budget and time and the needs for a detailed analysis and design.

AUTHORS' ASIDE

A strength of all three approaches is that the review of the human activity system occurs first – we are approaching the context from the point of view of the people in the organization and not the data. This means we can build confederacies of interest and develop participation as a major feature of the analysis and design.

4.3   Conclusions

Following on from the review of the approach we are adopting set out in Chapter 2 and the self-analysis set out in Chapter 3, Chapter 4 requires us to select the tools which we have the resources to use in our analysis and design. Before going on to the analysis and design proper, be sure in your own mind that you know which of the three paths you think are going to adopt (you may change your mind in the light of reflection on learning but you need to have an idea of the right path at this point).

4.4   Exercise

Read through the scenario set out below and think about it in terms of its strengths, weaknesses, opportunities and threats as an information systems project. Which of the three paths do you think would be most appropriate?

Local Education Authority Management Information System

A Local Education Authority (LEA) is attempting to link up a number of schools to a central Management Information System (MIS) to share information on student and staff records. This is a pilot project which may well lead to extension to all schools if it works. The LEA has pres-elected an MIS package imported from software developers in the USA. The project has a proposed six-month cycle and the pilot schools are already selected for the pilot. Schools do not need more bureau-cratic intervention at present and the attitude of heads of schools is antagonistic. However, staff are well trained in the use of computers and some of the outputs from the system could help schools in applying for additional resources (e.g. the identification of children with special needs).

References and further reading

(There is a great deal of information on developing participation in information systems work: Land, 1982; Bjorn Andersen and Skousen, 1984; Heirs, 1989; Hirschheim, 1989; Knight, 1989; Reason, 1994; IIED, 1995; Koh and Heng, 1996.)

(The human activity system is dealt with in a number of good publications: Davies, 1989; Haynes, 1989; Checkland and Scholes, 1990; Macadam *et al.*, 1990; Ison, 1993.)

Bell, S. (1996). *Learning with Information Systems: Learning Cycles in Information Systems Development*. London: Routledge.

Bjørn Andersen, N. and Skousen, T. (1984). User-driven systems design. *Participation in Change: Readings in the Introduction of New Technology*. Canberra: Department of Employment and Industrial Relations.

Checkland, P.B. and Scholes, J. (1990). *Soft Systems Methodology in Action*. Chichester: Wiley.

Davies, L.J. (1989). Cultural Aspects of Intervention with Soft

Systems Methodology. PhD Thesis. University of Lancaster.

Haynes, M. (1989). A Participative Application of Soft Systems Methodology: an action research project concerned with formulating an outline design for a learning centre in ICI chemicals and polymers. University of Lancaster.

Heirs, B. (1989). *The Professional Decision Thinker: The Art of Team Thinking Leadership*. London: Grafton.

Hirschheim, R.A. (1989). User participation in practice: experience with participative systems design. In K. Knight (ed.), *Participation in Systems Development*. Andover: Chapman and Hall.

IIED (1995). *A Trainer's Guide for Participatory Approaches*. London: IIED.

Ison, R. (1993). Soft systems: a non-computer view of decision support. In J. Stuth and B. Lyons (eds), *Decision Support Systems for the Management of Grazing Lands*. Paris: UNESCO, **II**, 83–121.

Knight, K. (1989). *Participation in Systems Development*. London: Kogan Page.

Koh, I. and Heng, M. (1996). Users and designers as partners – design method and tools for user participation and design accountability within the design process. *Information Systems Journal*, **6**, 283–300.

Kolb, D. (1984). *Experiential Learning: Experience as the Source of Learning and Development*. London: Prentice-Hall.

Land, F. (1982). Notes on participation. *Computer Journal*, **25**(2).

Macadam, R., Britton, I. and Russell, D. (1990). The use of soft systems methodology to improve the adoption by Australian cotton growers of the Siratac computer-based crop management system. *Agricultural Systems*, **34**, 1–14.

Reason, P. (1994). *Participation in Human Inquiry*. London: Sage.

Senge, P., Ross, P., Smith, B., Roberts, R. and Kleiner, R. (1994). *The Fifth Discipline Fieldbook: Strategies and Tools for Building a Learning Organisation*. London: Nicholas Brealey.

Watson, H. and Wood-Harper, A.T. (1996). Deconstructing contexts in interpreting methodology. *Journal of Information Technology*, vol. 11, no. 1, pp. 36–51.

Watson, H., Wood-Harper, A.T. and Wood, J.R.G. (1995). Interpreting methodology under erasure: between theory and practice. *Systems Practice*, **8**, 4.

Chapter 5

WHAT IS THE PROBLEM? THE HUMAN ACTIVITY SYSTEM – MAKING A MODEL

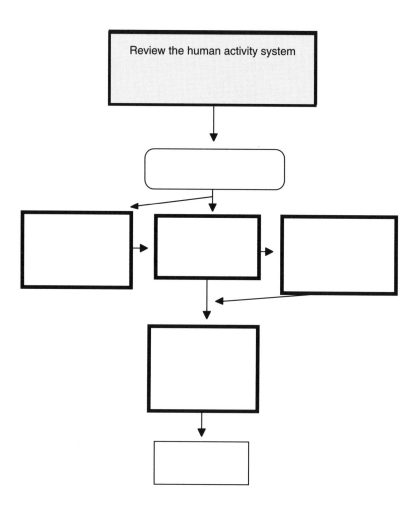

Review the human activity system

FIGURE 5.1   *Where are we in the process?*

Keywords:

human activity system, rich picture, context of the user, root definition, new systems model.

Summary:

To produce a useful analysis and design the analyst must clearly define the key elements of the situation and relate these to the terms of reference. The chapter makes this connection and develops the analysis within the context of the rich picture, the prime means for understanding the context for the information system in terms of issues and tasks. Having agreed the rich picture the major factors of the proposed information system environment are developed in terms of the root definition (who is doing what for whom, in what context) and agreed with the major stakeholders. Finally a systems model is produced which gives the outline of the proposed new system, this can then be fed into the next stage of the analysis.

5.1   Introduction to the human activity system

It should be noted that the development of the human activity system (HAS), as set out in this chapter, is the result of practice in a wide variety of contexts (e.g. developing countries, newly industrializing countries and industrialized countries). The version we give here is a reflection of our need to adapt methodology for context. If the reader is seeking the definitive text on the conventional form the book by Checkland and Scholes (1990) is recommended.

In most contexts of information systems development there is a need and a problem (at least one of each!). The perception of the problem situation and the resulting definition of the need for information is the nexus of this stage of analysis. Our job is to alleviate the problem by improving the information processing capacity of the organization.

AUTHORS' ASIDE

We should not confuse the concept of the information system with the more specific *automated information system*. Quite often the situation requiring analysis will already contain a manual information system and the result of all the analysis and design may be to prescribe a revised manual system. On the other hand, computerized information systems are very common and the result of analysis and design is usually to advocate an improved technologically based facility. The important point is that the analyst should not prejudge the context or the result of the analysis and design process.

With the key ideas of information needs and the problem situation in mind we can say that the problem as such will exist within the context of the HAS. The HAS can be seen as a view on the social/cultural/ethical/technical (etc.) situation of the organization. In outline we can see the process of HAS analysis as shown in Figure 5.2.

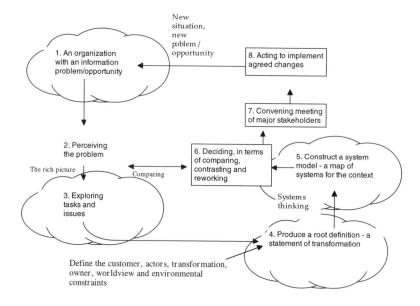

FIGURE 5.2   *Overview of the soft systems approach (adapted from Wood-Harper, 1989; Avison and Wood-Harper, 1990)*

Figure 5.2 begins from the standpoint of perceiving the new information problem situation. From this arises our first tool, the creation of the structures of the rich picture. This should define for us the major tasks and processes involved in the problem context. The next stage of the analysis, and the next tool to be used, is the root definition in which we make use of the CATWOE criteria (more on this later, but meaning who is doing what for whom, under what assumptions and in what environment) which sets out the fundamental features of the problem context. From this definition we can create a new model of the improved situation as we see it. This model is called a conceptual model in most of the literature. In the examples we develop here we make use of the term 'systems model'.

Do not worry about these phrases. For a definition of each see the Glossary in Chapter 11. Each will be developed in the next few pages or so. Like most new and jargonized sounding phrases you will find them quite simple concepts in themselves.

For now, let's return to our problem context, the organization. This organization may be a research institute, a government department, a training centre, a single office within some large organization or a non-governmental organization. It may even be just one person, a sole researcher wanting to keep research records, or a teacher recording student progress.

The purpose of this phase is to assist the analyst because he or she must understand the HAS in order to study the information flows involved in the organization. With this in mind the first job of the analyst is to help the major stakeholders in the organization define the situation and analyse what the problem is so that they can set about solving it. The analysis of the situation viewed as a human activity system as shown in Figure 5.2 consists of:

- Perceiving the organization's problem situation as defined in the terms of reference.
- By means of the rich picture identifying the tasks and issues.
- Identifying and noting key conflicts of interest.
- Coming to an agreed definition of the problem that is to be tackled.
- Setting out the outline of the improved system themes in the systems model.

The following sections will develop upon these themes.

5.2   The rich picture

5.2.1   Preparation

Often professional analysts will have very little knowledge or understanding about the range of issues involved in the target organization's information processing work. This book is intended for non-professionals and for those planning information systems for their own organization, so we do not assume that you will necessarily be new to the problem context. It can be an advantage to have little knowledge of the organization in which you are working! An outside analyst will have terms of reference, timescale and budget and an outline job to do. As an outsider the analyst will not have problems with existing staff relationships or subjective preferences concerning the way the organization is run. The analyst often needs to understand the problem context rapidly and in this process of understanding has a chance to bring a degree of *impartial and uncommitted* analysis. If, on the other hand, you are a member of the organization in which your analysis and design is taking place you probably will have developed your own ideas which will often be unstated and sometimes not consciously recognized. This can cause problems. For example, the analyst has a strongly held belief that department x is a better candidate for automation rather than department y. This belief may be based upon close familiarity with the one department and comparative ignorance of the other. New systems which in turn reflect this view may cause problems for the user community and ultimately for the analyst. Outsider analysts may also have problems e.g. imposing their expert opinion on situations of which they have little understanding (for a development of this see Antill and Wood-Harper (1985)). To reduce the likely problems that may arise from this type of subjective preference we have a series of analysis and design application tools which we will use throughout the following analysis:

- User/client (or more generally, stakeholder) participation is usually essential if the analysis is to be useful. The problem is not the analyst's property – it belongs to the organization and for this reason the individuals in the organization must be brought into partnership with the analyst designer as part of the problem-solving team. Some useful tools for doing this include:
  (i) A preliminary meeting with all those concerned with the analysis and design this can include setting out and discussion of the terms of reference. The stakeholders should be encouraged to comment on the task and to make any observations on the way in which the analysis and design might develop. A SWOT analysis by all those present can be very useful.
  (ii) Regular workshops throughout the analysis and design for briefing and sharing of views.
- Rigorous application of the agreed terms of reference. Many forms of systems analysis and systems design tend to spill over into areas that are not contained in the original problem. This is quite easy to do with systems work. Nevertheless the practical analyst needs to be able to focus on the issues that are of primary concern. This does not mean that other areas are to be ignored. If the new system impinges upon a large area recommendations can be made for a wider study at a later date.
- Reporting. All stages of analysis need to be adequately reported, primarily for the analyst's own benefit and also as an aid for the stakeholders. Information systems professionals are renowned for providing poor or no documentation.
- The use of interview techniques. Books have been written on the art of interviews (three particularly readable books are Bell (1983), Kumar (1993), and Gosling and Edwards (1995)). Key points for the analyst are:
  (i) Initial contact – dress and manner should be appropriate to the problem setting. It is surprising how many analysts

'lose' their object of study by appearing too glib, off-hand or conceited.

(ii) Sequence – it's a good idea to lead in your interview with some light and non-threatening conversation (especially with those who seem most uncomfortable with the idea of information systems). More detailed questioning can then follow.

(iii) Questions must be understandable. This may appear obvious but quite often computer-related questions are far from obvious to those being asked.

(iv) Caution is required when pushing into areas that are sensitive (internal audit, interdepartmental competition, etc.). A lack of tact can cause an interviewee to dry up.

(v) Always be neutral in your style.

(vi) Again a basic point – be sure to document the interview, you *will* forget much of the detail otherwise.

- Basic observation of site and behaviour. Many key factors for a successful analysis taking place in limited time are literally eye catching. By keeping eyes and ears open we do not neglect the vital clues (staff aggression, resentment, poor filing, shabby record keeping, etc.).

THINK POINT

How would you use these techniques in an analysis in your organization? Most particularly how might you make use of a general observation of site behaviour? In participatory approaches (for example see the work of Chambers (1997)) a technique called *transect walks* which are systematic walks with local stakeholders through the context. The walk through is accompanied with conversation about what we are seeing. The discipline is to note, remember and write up what is seen and experienced.

Quite often the analyst will discover that there has never been a prior analysis or review of the organization's information processing problems and capacities and there may be a fair degree of surprise at some of the findings of the rich picture. In terms of learning and the Senge five disciplines (Senge *et al.*, 1994), this stage of the analysis hits a number of major targets (see Table 5.1).

5.2.2   The primary components of the rich picture – structures

The way in which we produce rich pictures is composed of two elements – structure and process. These are divided into two key areas

TABLE 5.1   *Learning organization and HAS*

Discipline	Value in HAS thinking	Outcome?
Systems thinking	Essential, provides a view of the wholeness which is the context	Insight beyond what may be the **presenting problem**
Personal mastery	In the HAS stage there is the opportunity for the vision that drives the terms of reference to be questioned in context, and this in turn can be an opportunity for the team to develop their mastery of both the task in hand and the realities of the context	Ownership and control over the problem
Mental models	In the HAS stage the team gain a number of mental models of the problem context. The models range from an unstructured group perception, a focus on what transformation is needful and a vision of activities to bring about useful change	Clear, risk free analysis
Shared vision	The HAS is the main tool for developing this in the process of developing a shared view of the problem context	Improving clarity of purpose
Team learning	The team should begin to form in the participatory approach at this time	Consensus on the way forward

– technical 'facts' (hard areas) and social/ethical/cultural realities (soft areas). Throughout this book we will be working on one key example and several minor ones to explain the way in which the methodology works. Our first information will be a set of terms of reference. For the purpose of the example these are as follows:

TERMS OF REFERENCE

'Outline non-specialist functions that could be computerized in order to increase efficiency and timeliness in terms of day-to-day operations of a small government department in a developing country'.

Resources – One analyst
Time allocation – 30 days.

If you are using this book as an aid to your own analysis and design, then you will need to consider your own terms of reference before proceeding. Our example is selected intentionally to show how systems analysis and systems design tools can be used in the most hostile situations (in terms of cross-cultural analysis, tough climate, low access to expert skills, etc.) and still produce useful information systems and organizational (and personal) learning.

The conventional way to begin is to produce a map or cartoon of the major structures to be involved in the picture. These may be departmental boundaries, system boundaries, national borders, etc. as they are applicable to the problem in view. Working our way towards the eventual picture we begin the exercise by setting out the 'hard' structures in the context. Figure 5.3 shows our first stab at these.

We begin by depicting the major structures within the organization under study. Essentially we group the structures under two headings: soft and hard.

Immensely simplified as this view is it shows that the analyst is aware of various agencies at work both within and outside the focus of the analysis which in this case is a governmental department. Our hard structure tells us that the department is composed of several discrete sections or areas of activity and that there are three key structures operational outside the boundary of the department, in the world cloud, which will impinge upon the eventual system to

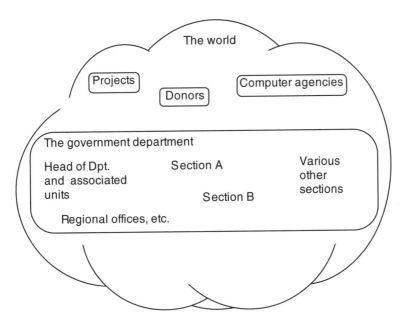

FIGURE 5.3   *Rich picture – major hard structures in the context*

be set up. Note: there will be quite a number of other agencies and groups at work within the context of the department. This initial portrayal of the major areas of interest already shows that we are beginning to focus on what the analyst believes to be the key areas of concern as expressed in the terms of reference – the major job of departmental management.

Our next task is to set out the less formal or 'soft' structures active within the overall problem context. The important feature of this stage is to set out structures which although we identify them as being essential for the eventual working of the system they are related more to cultural and ethical than technical points. Because of the sensitivity of some structures it may not always be possible to show these 'soft' structures in workshops with stakeholders and the final report. In our case the types of structure are shown in Figure 5.4.

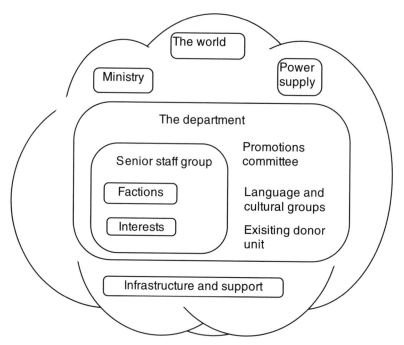

FIGURE 5.4   *Rich picture – major soft structures in the context*

THINK POINT

When is a structure 'hard' or 'soft'? (We provide one idea of the answer on page 69).

In the 'soft' picture we identify a range of structures some more formal (the promotions committee), some more informal (language and cultural groups) and some political (faction and interest groups). The reason all these structures are termed 'soft' may not be immediately obvious but it is because they are identified in our analysis to-date as having subjective and therefore to some extent unguessable effects. For example the promotions committee in most normal circumstances would be seen as having a hard, objective identity in the department. In this case we are not interested in the committee's function and purpose, we are interested in one of its informal functions which is to move staff around for political reasons. This could have a major impact on an embryonic computer or data processing unit. Another soft structure is the externally funded donor unit within the department. Again it is a physical unit with a task to accomplish not directly related to the work in hand. However, its presence is felt by most major actors in the department and for this reason it has a subjective (true or untrue) watchdog function. Most obviously soft are the cultural and language group-ings in the department. Any incoming system has to work with the dominant theme in terms of culture and will have to reach an accommodation with other interests. Almost subliminal to the outside, short-term consultant analyst but vital to note are the inter-est groups and factions within the senior staff groupings. These may not have a direct impact on the project as a whole but they do need to be understood and planned around. In the outside world we have a ministerial watchdog, problems of power supply failure and fluc-tuation and the lack of infrastructural support (hardware and soft-ware support).

As already noted, it will not always be advisable to identify all structures in reports and workshops. There are often good working reasons why an analyst wishes to keep clear of unnecessary con-troversy. This is part of the reality of understanding analysis and design in context. The result of the construction of a rich picture should be the identification by the analyst of what is possible within the problem context. What is and is not said and made explicit is a decision left to the discretion of the individual analyst.

5.2.3   The primary components of the rich picture – processes

Our next task is to identify hard and soft processes operating upon structures in terms of the overall work of the department. As above we can develop our thinking with two separate models. Figure 5.5 demonstrates the relationship between the structures and processes in the hard context.

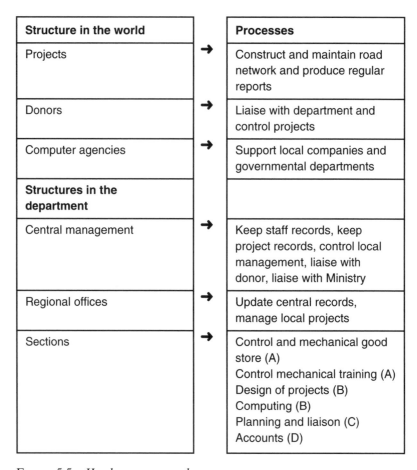

Structure in the world		Processes
Projects	→	Construct and maintain road network and produce regular reports
Donors	→	Liaise with department and control projects
Computer agencies	→	Support local companies and governmental departments
Structures in the department		
Central management	→	Keep staff records, keep project records, control local management, liaise with donor, liaise with Ministry
Regional offices	→	Update central records, manage local projects
Sections	→	Control and mechanical good store (A) Control mechanical training (A) Design of projects (B) Computing (B) Planning and liaison (C) Accounts (D)

FIGURE 5.5   *Hard processes and structures*

THINK POINT

One way to think about the question: When is a structure 'hard' or 'soft'? is as follows: the analyst is the final judge. What is hard to one person is soft to another although this is not always the case. Generally hard are fixed and formal, soft are variable and informal. As you see, arriving at a judgement is not always a scientific process.

The processes that we set against each structure are only part of the whole range of activities performed. This demonstrates again the subjective nature of the analysis (there is never a 'right' rich

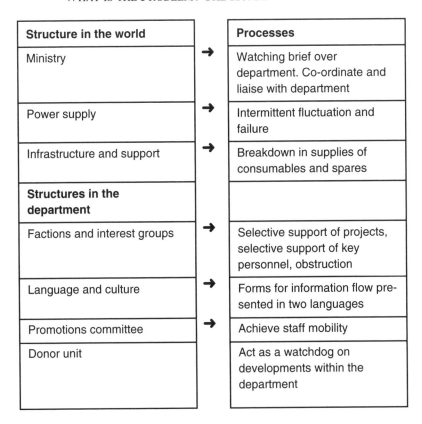

Structure in the world		Processes
Ministry	→	Watching brief over department. Co-ordinate and liaise with department
Power supply	→	Intermittent fluctuation and failure
Infrastructure and support	→	Breakdown in supplies of consumables and spares
Structures in the department		
Factions and interest groups	→	Selective support of projects, selective support of key personnel, obstruction
Language and culture	→	Forms for information flow presented in two languages
Promotions committee	→	Achieve staff mobility
Donor unit		Act as a watchdog on developments within the department

FIGURE 5.6   *Soft processes and structures*

picture in this sense as there will always be something missing) and the attempt of the analyst to stay as close to the terms of reference as possible. Figure 5.6 shows the parallel development of the 'soft' structures and processes model.

With the completion of the soft process and structure diagram we have completed the collection of information necessary for the final composition of the rich picture.

5.2.4   Constructing the rich picture

In one sense this might be thought to be no longer necessary. The foregoing demonstrates that the analyst has got a reasonable grasp of the various areas of the problem context and has sifted out technical from other issues. However, one of the major reasons for producing a rich picture is to visualize the problem situation at a glance. This cannot be achieved if the various elements of the analysis are kept as discrete diagrams.

Rich picturing first requires us to simplify reality. One method for doing this is to set out all the processes and structures, the most important characteristics of the major individuals involved and the terms of reference – see Figure 5.7.

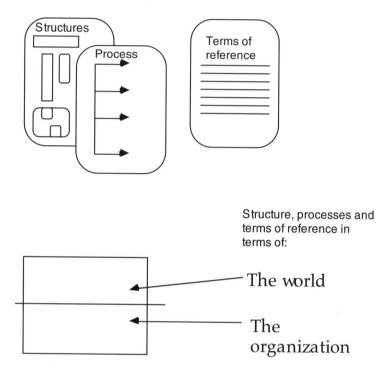

FIGURE 5.7   *Building the rich picture*

In Figure 5.7 the terms of reference, structures and processes are mapped onto one diagram. First the material is divided up into what is happening in the organization and what is happening outside the organization. This draws a boundary but does not inhibit the flow of information, power and resources through the boundary. Our next task is to set out the major groupings within these two components – see Figure 5.8.

We are beginning to bring together all the aspects of the situation into one frame. This in turn provides us with a core concept or **mindset** of the problem. One of the most common complaints that practitioners make at this stage is that they cannot draw, or they do not have a clever computer package to produce quality diagrams. Do not worry about this for now. We will give various examples of rich pictures in this chapter, some drawn without computers. It is, of course, useful if a rich picture can be attractive and pleasing to the eye – but of much more importance is the meaning of the content.

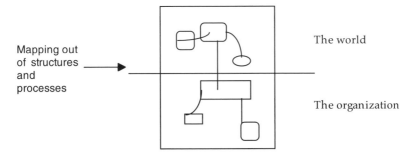

FIGURE 5.8   *Mapping out structure and process*

AUTHORS' ASIDE

The use of rich pictures is not terribly revolutionary as a way of capturing our thoughts. If we think back to ancient Egypt and the use of hieroglyphics we see the writing of stories in diagrams. In understanding the hieroglyphs the important thing to remember is that each image is symbolic, it represents an idea or a concern. Egyptian hieroglyphs are beautiful and, for those who can read the story, are dense with meaning, allowing Egyptologists to say a great deal about the nature of a society several thousand years ago. Our task is not so sublime, we are attempting to tell the story of a current organization.

To make hand-drawn pictures for overhead transparency it is of value to use a set of symbols that have a clearly defined meaning. In short, to make our final drawings more understandable it is useful to adopt some form of a grammar of symbols.

The symbols shown in Figure 5.9 are some that we use and like, you might think of more for your own situation.

The resulting rich picture for the government department is shown in Figure 5.10.

It may be useful to go back to Section 5.2 to be clear in your mind how this picture follows on from the process set out there. All the pictures on the following pages are simplistic and to some extent are superficial in their scope, leaving out some of the more contentious details of the previous diagrams. Without the rich picture there is little chance that we could structure into the analysis the type of personal and organizational problems that fall outside the scope of more objective, reductionist forms of analysis.

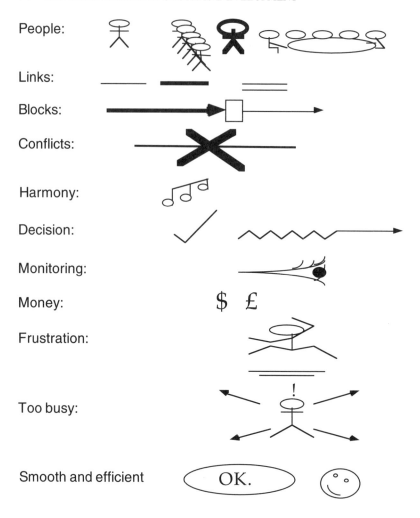

People:

Links:

Blocks:

Conflicts:

Harmony:

Decision:

Monitoring:

Money: $ £

Frustration:

Too busy:

Smooth and efficient

FIGURE 5.9   *Some symbols for rich pictures*

It should be noted that the rich pictures we develop here and the further analysis that follows are case studies drawn from experiences in various developing countries. They do not represent any particular department and do not reflect the experiences of any similar institutions.

Remember, the vital ingredient and assumption about the rich picture (and many of the phases that follow) is that they are worked through in collaboration and with the consent of the major stakeholders in the situation in so far as this is possible and that the information being gathered is not deleterious to the ultimate success of the project. The means by which collaboration and

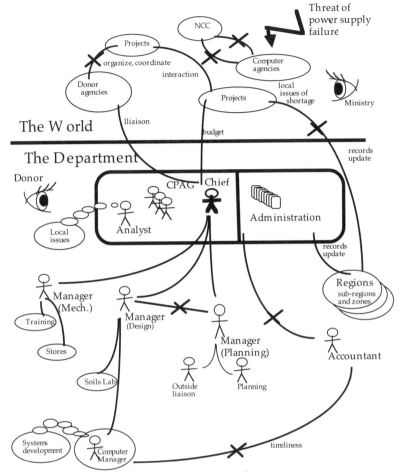

FIGURE 5.10   *The initial rich picture*

feedback are achieved are:

- regular reporting
- weekly/monthly (depending on the scale of the analysis) workshops with stakeholders
- regular (daily) discussions and feedback as you work through your thinking.

The examples shown here (Figures 5.10, 5.11, 5.12 and 5.13) illustrate what is required in the rich picture. The crosses on lines indicate conflicts of interest or conflicts of some kind between major aspects of the current situation. For example in the department of roads, the regional offices require rapid rebriefing on details of roadworks from the projects. At the same time the administration at central office also requires regular reports from the regional offices to ensure that records are kept up to date and the annual ministerial reporting procedure can occur smoothly. Poor communications infrastructure as well as different perceptions of priorities ensures that there is a constant level of friction. The thought bubbles show the main concerns of the major stakeholders involved. You can also see the way in which conflict and competition operate in organizations.

It may take many discussions, workshops and papers before the picture is agreed. However, this is time well spent because all further analysis work can be more surely directed towards the agreed problem. In this book we are concerned with rapid information systems design and so we recognize that this stage will need to be accomplished in the matter of a few days. Nevertheless, this time can be packed with interaction and discourse between the various stakeholders and yourself.

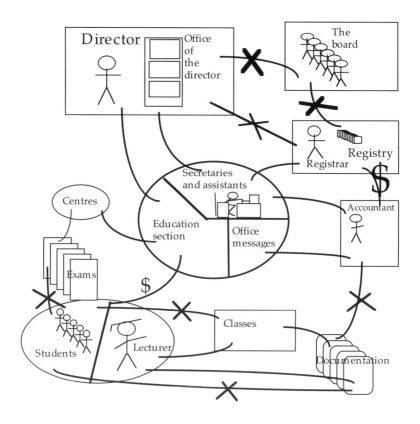

FIGURE 5.11 *Rich picture of a training institute*

Several new points arise from the rich picture shown in Figure 5.10:

- The importance of the power supply issue is re-emphasized.
- The centralized nature of the department around one key personality is drawn out.
- The internal conflict between two major sections is emphasized
- The peripheral nature of existing computing is expressed.

As a further example of a rich picture, Figure 5.11 is taken from a different context and is included to provide a further illustration of the variety of forms that the picture can take.

Just to show that this is not the only way in which a rich picture can be displayed, Figures 5.12 and 5.13 show a couple of other examples:

Figure 5.12 shows a training college. The main point made by the picture is the existence of an existing computer unit and the question of its value and relevance. This style of picture can be very helpful for display purposes for senior management. Because the

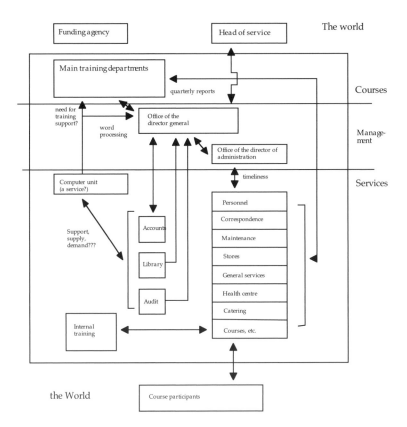

FIGURE 5.12   *An organogram-style rich picture*

picture is rigidly ordered and very 'neat' this may well have appeal. One word of caution. This type of presentation is often favoured by stakeholders because of its neatness. However, it fails to represent much of the soft, personality-based complexity that a true rich picture can encapsulate. We argue that even a badly drawn traditional rich picture offers the analyst more in terms of depicting problems in the situation being studied.

Our final example (Figure 5.13) builds on this last point, it is a working copy of a student's rich picture. This may look chaotic and incomprehensible but to the individual who produced it, it contains the essence of his view of his problem context. We show this rich picture in order to demonstrate that presentation is not the item of key importance. It is much more important to get the context and the meaning of the problem agreed to.

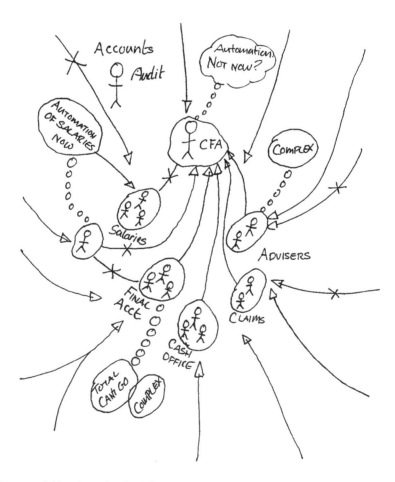

FIGURE 5.13   *A student's rich picture*

THINK POINT

Try drawing a rich picture now. Maybe produce one of your family or of your organization. Be sure to think in terms of soft and hard structures and processes.

The rich picture when drawn up and agreed should produce *primary tasks* and major *issues*. What do we mean by this? Primary tasks should reflect the most central tasks that need to be accomplished within the problem context. Any incoming information system is usually intended to support, develop and execute primary tasks. Issues are matters of dispute which can have a deleterious affect upon organizations achieving their purpose. In terms of the information system the issues are often much more important than the tasks.

In the rich picture of the government department we could say that primary tasks are: review the capacity and use of the existing computer unit and related staff, understand the nature of the relationship of the chief with senior staff, review the capacity of the context to support the MIS. The issues might be: internal feuding, poor track record regarding IT, communications problems.

It is usually not possible to resolve all issues and for this reason they should always be understood and recognized. In learning about issues and reflecting upon their causality we often discover important factors which we need to be conscious of in developing the information system. Issues are vital in making our analysis and design a learning process for the organization as a whole. Reality really is complex and the analyst should never approach a problem context with a conceited or inflated view of his or her own capacity. Not all problems can be mapped, discussed and designed away. Often the analyst will be required to develop a form of 'wait and see' towards certain problems that are either *imponderable* at the time of the analysis (given time constraints), or *too political*, in terms of the organization's capacity to express them openly and become involved in discussions about them. This does raise an ethical question for the analyst.

Situations can develop in which large numbers of insurmountable problems arise with issues that, in your opinion, are going to cause lasting impediments to the ultimate systems design. In cases of this type only you can decide which course to take:

• Design the system as best you can within these constraints.

- Say unpalatable things to the problem owners and set conditions for further work to be carried out.
- Ignore the problems and create the system as if they did not exist (we would never recommend this course).
- Refuse to continue the analysis until the issue is settled.

Each of these courses has quite serious implications. Only the analyst can make the decision concerning which is most appropriate within his or her own context. Generally speaking we have found that the first is suitable for 80 per cent of projects.

The bottom line for the rich picture is to provide the analyst with a means to move from *thinking about the problem* to *thinking about what can be done about the problem.*

AUTHORS' ASIDE

Throughout this book we will keep a tally of the number of days which we think each element of the analysis can be accomplished in. Of course, the tally we give is nominal and will vary with your context but we do feel that analysis can be made, in many situations, to fit a schedule.

Amount of time devoted to analysis so far:
Total for this stage (rich picture) = 3 days
Cumulative total update = 3 days

In most cases we feel that this stage of the analysis can be completed in less than three days, although we may need to recognize that rich picturing should not be artificially curtailed. In the minds of many people, this is the most important part of the systems analysis and sometimes considerably more time is required. If this is so in your case you may need to adopt either path 2 or 3 as set out in Chapter 4.

Keeping in mind the primary tasks and issues arising from the rich picture, we can now go on to look at the specific views of the major stakeholders as they are concerned with the new systems definition (what it is supposed to do). This should result in our tightening up the context of the job that we are to do and harmonizing the view of this job between stakeholders. The mechanism we use for this is called the root definition.

5.3   The root definition

5.3.1   Introduction

The assumption of the root definition is that the different stakeholders in the system will have different opinions about it. If you were to ask some of the members of a government department questions, such as: 'what is the main purpose of your department?', you will get different answers, such as: 'to carry out an efficient operation', 'to keep people employed', 'to provide a service for the national community'. These are all valid statements of aims, but they may have conflicting implications for the organization and the original terms of reference for the analysis and design into a new information system. Also they are much too vague to help the analyst produce a system that will help the organization in furthering its aims.

It is useful if a point of reference exists whereby the main tasks (in the light of the issues) discovered in the rich picture and produced by the analyst and stakeholders in the context can be tested to make sure that the perception of the elements of the terms of reference are being fulfilled. Therefore, at an early stage a careful definition of the required system (and therefore the change or transformation within the organization) is essential. Of course, this is going to be very general but in terms of our approach in this book the root definition contains six ingredients. In terms of the current issue: who is doing what for whom and to what end? In what environment is the new system to be implemented? To whom is the final system going to be answerable? In terms of the HAS these are known respectively as:

- *Customer*, the systems beneficiary or victim
- *Actor*, the individual(s) involved in the system
- *Transformation*, the change that the project is intended to achieve
- *Worldview* (or '*Weltanschauung*'), the fundamental assumptions that affect the proposed information system
- *Owner*, the eventual system owner, and
- *Environment*, the situation in which the system will be developed – this may also relate to the constraints that environment imposes upon any new information system.

This leads to the acronym *CATWOE*.

The definition of each of the elements, and the construction of a definition which encapsulates them all, is a matter of negotiation between the stakeholders in the situation, the analyst and the context of the terms of reference for the project. The forms of communication created during the rich picture stage of the analysis should be very helpful now. Depending upon the time available and the complexity of the situation you will need to carry out a CATWOE analysis of the major stakeholders. Again, you are the final decision maker in terms of setting out who needs to be questioned.

In our example the definition for the government roads department is shown, from the perspective of the:

- analyst
- donor
- chief of department

From the amalgamation of these with agreement on key items we can try to arrive at a consensus view:

- The learning team representing both departmental and non-departmental stakeholders (a consensus view)

The analyst is in the frame because it is very important to be sure that we are working on the same basic assumptions as the organization. There are cases where the analyst has undertaken systems analysis only to find at the end that the organization was under the impression that the research was being undertaken for very different reasons!

5.3.2   Three examples of CATWOE

The definition of each point of CATWOE can be as drawn out or as brief as you feel necessary. Generally a few words on each item will draw out the main features of each stakeholder's views. In our example sometimes only one word is necessary.

The analyst CATWOE

Customer: the donor and the department
Actors: the analyst, potential computer staff, actual computer staff
Transformation: an automated MIS
Worldview: departmental automation is an essential requirement for organizational development
Owner: the department
Environment: the department and regional offices – this includes features of climatic turbulence, very limited infrastructure and negligible technical support

The donor CATWOE

Customer: the department and also the ministry

Actors: the analyst and local staff
Transformation: an automated MIS in place for organizational development and increasing efficiency
Worldview: effective automation for management
Owner: the department
Environment: the department is the environment for the MIS

The chief of department's CATWOE

Customer: the department
Actors: staff and external consultants
Transformation: automation of major administrative functions
Worldview: to improve the efficiency of departmental operations
Owner: the chief
Environment: the department is its own environment for the MIS

These views were supplied during interview as were most of the details of the rich picture. They offer us a fair degree of agreement within the problem context. It is the analyst's job to assess the degree of differences between root definitions and to harmonize an overall view which all stakeholders can agree to. This will mean that differences in interpretation will not occur (or are less reasonably likely to occur!) later on. In some cases the root definitions can be seen as fixing together to form a cone focusing on the problem situation at the root of the exercise, as shown in Figure 5.14.

In this case the three levels of conceptual model can be seen as being focused on one agreed problem context and the transformation of that. The graphic presentation seen in Figure 5.14 indicates that differences in CATWOE relate more to the position of each party (remote or close to the problem context) in terms of local

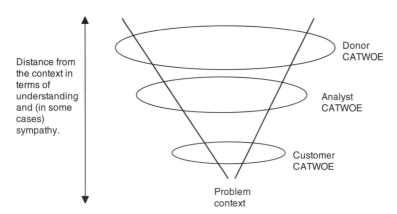

FIGURE 5.14 *Overlapping root definitions of the problem context*

understanding and sympathy rather than marked differences in opinion about the nature of the transformation sought. From this we can produce a consensus view such as that shown below.

The learning team of stakeholders (a consensus view)

Customer: the government generally and the department specifically
Actors: the analyst and local staff
Transformation: to improve departmental efficiency by use of an MIS
Worldview: the operation of an MIS in the department would sub-stantially enhance the productivity and efficiency of the department
Owner: the donor (as the remote owner) and the department (as the immediate owner)
Environment: the department as both a central office and (later) as the regional offices. The constraints will relate to power supply, climate and geography

This consensus view needs to be agreed to by all major stake-holders involved. Agreement may require a certain amount of flexi-bility by all parties and achieving this can be a matter of considerable skill. In developing the vision of the consensus root definition team learning is enhanced, the vision is shared and boundaries of agreement are being set out. The analysis and design is improving the internal learning of the organization.

The establishment of an agreed root definition takes us to the point where within the context of the situation as set out in the rich picture, and the agreed perspective of the root definition we can begin to design our new, improved systems outline. This outline is set out in the systems model.

Amount of time devoted to analysis so far:
Total for this stage (root definition) = 1 day
Cumulative total update = 4 days

In many cases the root definition can be arrived at in as little as one to as many as five days (depending on the complexity of gaining consensus). There can be exceptions to this. Figure 5.15 depicts a very different view of a root definition.

THINK POINT

Take a good long look at Figure 5.15. Would you think the outlook for the project is good, bad or average?

Director of a Research organization (RO)
Customer - Self and RO
Actor - Key staff in RO
Transformation - composite data translated into information, quickly
Worldview - 'we have the data not the information'
Owner - Self
Environment - RO

Head of of the research deprtment in the RO
Customer - 'Him' (the Director) - 'one of his whims'
Actor - 'All too likely to be me!'
Transformation - 'Create more bloody work when we cannot cope now!'
Worldview - 'I have data and information but no time'
Owner - 'Him' (the director)
Environment - 'As far away as is possible!'

Funding agency for the GIS
Customer - RO
Actor - Key staff in RO monitored by United Nations
Transformation - Improve effectiveness to forecast and act against drought
Worldview - 'we have the technology'
Owner - RO
Environment - RO

The analyst
Customer - 'Him' (the director), the United Nations and all departments
Actor - Initially me - to be all departments focused on IT unit
Transformation - Create more work and improve effectiveness
Worldview - Questionable technology - a 'test case'
Owner - The Director
Environment - The RO and Sub-Sahel Africa

FIGURE 5.15   *CATWOE for a geographic information system (GIS)*

THINK POINT

In this case there is very little agreement among the various stake-holders as to what should be done. The various views could be brought together into a rough consensus as shown in Figure 5.16. This example would appear to be doomed to failure. If this were so then the root definition has served us well, showing up major structural weaknesses in the new information system plan and stopping us from investing in a system which is so frail.

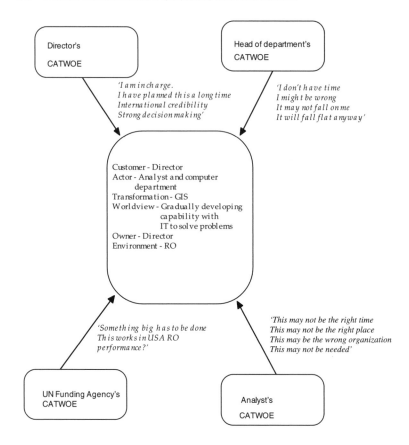

Figure 5.16   *Resolving the problem or papering over the cracks?*

5.4   The new system (in concept)

5.4.1   Introduction

The rich picture is intended to be 'rich' in terms of people, processes, ideas, conflicts, etc. Once one has a feel for the problem context we can begin the process of drawing out the aspects on which we now know we have to concentrate. The intention of this phase is to build a model of the system that we recognize as being a reasonable basis for the new information system. Two items which we must be aware of are:

- The desire to take elements of our methodology out of context. It is not our purpose here to specify exactly what the system must do, who will do it and how long it will take. This process might more usefully be thought of as arising in the second and third phases of the methodology which deals with information modelling. At this stage we are only concerned in separating out the main components of the system and to show how they relate to each other.

- Beware of the tendency to assume that we are modelling reality. All models are symbols of reality and represent the assumptions of individuals and groups. In this case the model will represent the shared perception of the activities of the ultimate information system as focused and presented by the analyst in collaboration with the major stakeholders. This is quite a different thing from saying that we are modelling reality.

Back to the modelling exercise. Ideally, and according to all the textbooks, we should remove personalities, though not their roles, from the picture, because we do not want to create a system around particular personalities. Frankly, this is not always possible. Many organizations are so designed around key personnel that to design any incoming system without taking them into account would be a nonsense (you will probably have identified whether this is so in your case during the phase of the rich picture). At best we can say therefore that at present we should, so far as is possible and useful, sideline personalities from our systems design. In phase three of the methodology we will be looking to integrate the information system into the lives of the people who will be using it. In the creation of system models we should recognize two key issues:

- It is not the job of the model to align existing sub-departments/ units with tasks. At present we want to set out the incoming system tasks irrespective of units and sections. The new system may well require the substantial reworking of such groupings.
- The model has to comply with the results of our *root definition* and our original *terms of reference*. It is quite easy to get carried away at this point!

If you are having trouble assessing the dynamics of the new systems design we recommend that you carry out a two-stage systems modelling phase.

- Produce a model that depicts the existing system (on context).
- Produce a model that demonstrates the transformed situation.

Note that this can only be carried out successfully if you are given the necessary time to do the work (you will know your own constraints) but if this is not possible go straight onto the second activity. The development of our systems model takes various stages.

1. Reassess the consensus root definition to form an impression of the type of system that will be necessary to carry out the transformation generally agreed to.

2. Put together a list of verbs that describe the most fundamental activities of the defined systems, e.g. record, liaise, purchase, report, inform, etc.
3. Thinking in terms of a simple system (input, process and output), structure what each component part of your system will have to do, how it has to do it, and how activity will be monitored. Try to describe the input and output where appropriate (see Figure 5.17).

FIGURE 5.17   *A simple input, process, output system*

This is a simple idea of a system. Usually systems are developed with regards the emergence of new properties as items are combined and the hierarchy by which these items are related. For our purposes in setting up information systems practically and rapidly we simplify the issue (for a fuller exposition of the theory see Checkland (1981) and Checkland and Scholes (1990)).

4. Structure similar activities into groups (e.g. day-to-day accounts, long-term budgets, short-term budgets could be grouped in a financial system). See Figure 5.18.

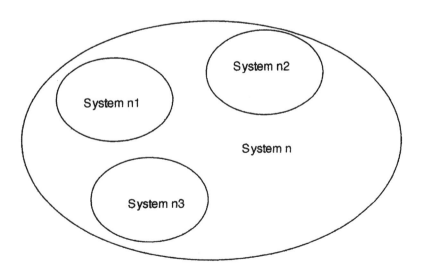

FIGURE 5.18   *Grouping the systems*

5. Use lines or lines with arrows to join the activities/systems together. The arrows symbolize information or energy or material or some other form of dependency. It is quite useful to use the arrows as representing the main flows of information between systems. The information output from one system is usually the information input for another (see Figure 5.19).

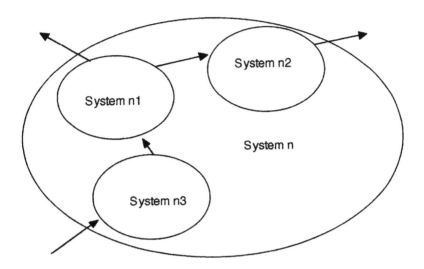

FIGURE 5.19   *Systems and flows*

6. Verify the model with the users of the existing system. This is very important. The relationships and major inputs and outputs need to be agreed with all major stakeholders in the system.

Figure 5.20 shows a system model of the government roads department. Note how it has been derived from the corresponding rich picture in Figure 5.10. The boundaries show the various subsystems within the overall organizational system.

In particularly complicated or large organizations (i.e. in most cases where an analyst is being used in the first place) there is often the need to produce various levels of model. Figure 5.21 is a level 2 model showing more of the details involved with the management and administrative system as shown within the level 1 model.

The level 2 model shows the central role of the chief of department and the immediate sub-systems which serve that office. Each of these would ultimately need to be further developed in a similar manner to give us the actual workings of each unit. The system

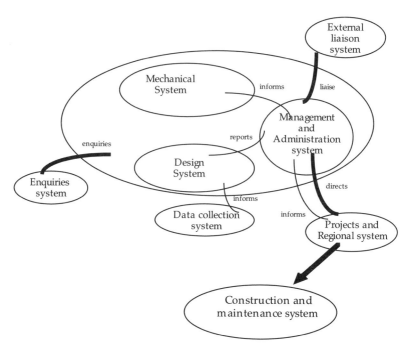

FIGURE 5.20   *Level 1 system model arising from the rich picture of the department of roads*

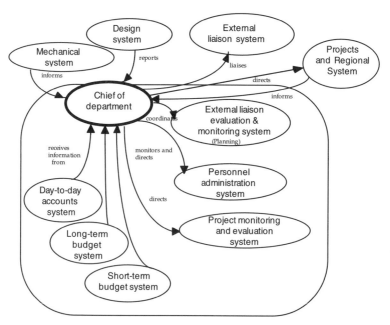

FIGURE 5.21   *Level 2 systems model: the management and administrative system*

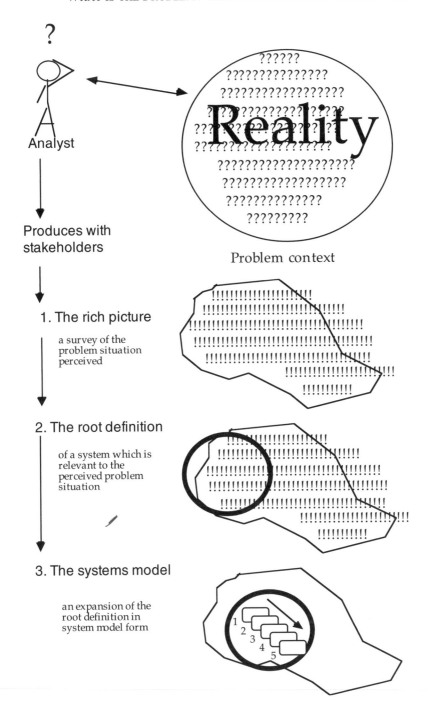

FIGURE 5.22   *Selecting priorities – the process so far*

model gives us a pad from which we can launch our detailed information modelling exercise.

Amount of time devoted to analysis so far:
Total for this stage (root definition) = 3 days
Cumulative total update = 7 days

The time schedule for the exercise can vary but *if no more is required in the early stages of a project than an understanding of the major systems*, a period of between two and five days should be sufficient.

Before we can do this, however, we must identify the items arising within the model which have priority in the development of our terms of reference. It is unlikely that we will initially be able to carry out all the exercises that would be required to set up a total system. For this process to be effective we need to identify our initial priorities. Figure 5.22 shows where we have come from and what we should be left with at the end of the first stage of our analysis. We can see the process of analysis as coming from a situation of ignorance. Through the information gathering and representation stage of the rich picture we build up an idea of what is/are the problem/s. The root definition further focuses us on an agreed perception of the major components of the work in hand, most importantly the transformation. Finally (at this stage) we produce a new model system which we wish to develop.

5.5   Final considerations

The terms of reference will make you very selective in your initial problem context identification. Thus, in terms of our CATWOE, the first person who has a say in this may not be the problem owner in the immediate sense but the more remote owner (if there is one in the case which you are dealing with) who is funding the overall operation.

The first job will be to define the boundary between the activities to be included in the analysis and design and those which are pertinent, may well be candidates for further phases within further projects but which are outside the short-term priorities of the terms of reference. The exact position of the boundary must be a matter for discussion between the analyst and the stakeholders. Often, however, the analyst will be asked to advise on areas of the organization's operations where a new information system could produce the greatest benefits. The area that the analyst selects may be the only one to be tackled, or it may be the first part of a phased study of information processing throughout the organization. However, we should keep in mind before we go into technical detail about what should and should not be computerized that often political and other interests will preclude the analyst from dealing with the real area of concern at all. All examples of management interference with the analyst's area of study, specifying certain areas out of bounds, demarcating 'priorities', etc. can be seen as political acts but as we have already noted these often have to accepted as facts of life to the analyst.

5.6   Conclusions

By the end of this stage of the analysis you should have moved from a position of seeking to identify the problem situation to having an organizationally shared view of the potential model of a solution. The rich picture gave the overview, the root definition defined the key issues and identified the primary task, the systems model has outlined the next step. We can now enter on a harder (in the sense of objective and quantitative) phase of our methodology and look at the process of information modelling. In this stage we will seek to indicate the major components of the proposed system in a manner which can be transposed into a working system.

5.7   Exercise

This is the first exercise in a series aiming at building an overall analysis and design. We are assuming that you have an existing organizational problem and would benefit from an exercise, set out in sequence of how to go about the process of analysis and design. Similarly, if this book is being used as a class text the following tutorial can be used for the core of an assessed exercise. A model approach to the problem is set out in Appendix C.

Exercise 1   The human activity system phase

You are a consultant reviewing the capability of a construction company in one of the poorer countries of southern Europe to make effective use of IT. Here are some details.

Personnel
Managing Director – M.R. Ario
Director – D.F. Badro
Director – A.F. Ario
Departmental Head (A, Policy) – G.T. Galio

Departmental Head (B, Works) – G.V. Ario
Departmental Head (C, Planning) – B.T. Tefri

The company employs 89 people in the head office, 656 people outside the head office.

Tasks
Preparing quotes and outline contracts (buildings, roads, emergency repair to river banks and sea defences, rail)
Dealing with sub-contractors
Drafting contracts
Project supervision
Deadline enforcement

National characteristics
Poor regularity of power supply
Poor road and rail transport
Difficult topography and seasonal heavy rains which cause further transport difficulties
Poor internal telephone service. Supplemented by radio communication
Scarce access to international currencies

Your brief is to look for likely departments within the company requiring effective MIS tools and which have a high probability of being able to maintain a new system. You have been able to glean other useful information on a series of transect walks:

- Company turnover has been static for the last three years, there has been a linked reduction in customer demand.
- The accounting section has been seriously undermanned for three years and has suffered from considerable staff loss (particularly younger staff).
- The senior accountant does not sit on several senior committees.
- There is a small computer unit using very old machines and turning out very poor pay-roll and costing information.
- Morale among senior staff can be seen as being fairly poor.
- One family has members in several senior positions. This family link tends to be the information/operational spine of the company.
- Junior staff are generally well trained and frustrated by poor promotion chances.
- The outlook is surprisingly good, contracts being negotiated and European Union grants would indicate that growth will increase at 7 per cent per annum for several years.
- The three major departments within the company – planning, policy and works show a certain amount of internal friction. Loyalty to family appears to be a bone of contention.

- The planning section deals with contractual details and some works design.
- The policy section exists to lead discussion with major customers (government departments, private companies) and contractors and set outline policy statements.
- The works section is the business end. It employs 75 per cent of staff, carries out and/or supervises construction and maintenance. Works is directed by one of the Ario family.
- The works section employees operate all regional offices.
- Your project donor/financier is an international bank. It is looking for an area to invest $300,000 initially in MIS activity.

Given this background, produce the rich picture for the organization. Prepare the rich picture as a brief for yourself and possibly as the basis of a seminar to brief the donor.

Some hints. You have three key areas – the world, the regional offices and the department. Obviously there is conflict in the department and the prominence of the Ario family cannot be overlooked. As this is a document for the donor you can be quite frank in your views of the scenario.

Don't attempt to appear to be all-knowing. There will be a lot of details that you will not have. For example, how does the organization's administration fit into all this? What role does the existing computer unit have and how well trained are its staff?

Be sure to make a list of items that you will require more information about.

Exercise 2   On root definitions and systems models

Working from the rich picture go on to prepare root definitions for:

- the analyst (you)
- hypothetical – for the donor
- hypothetical – for the managing director

Include all your own doubts and problems with the job in your own CATWOE. Remember, how do the terms of reference fit with what you have found out in the rich picture? Do the regions need help? Are they getting it? Should other individuals and agencies be questioned?

Presumably if (for example) the analyst finds that the regions could do with computer support in the line functions of the organization, whereas the customer and bank feel that the core concern is central office MIS detail, this will show up in your consensus CATWOE.

Outline the top level conceptual model of the initial MIS you would set about designing. Pay particular attention to:

- the limits of the initial MIS
- the products of the initial MIS
- the dangers of the initial MIS

Your existing work will probably have indicated that the organization contains numerous sub-systems (e.g. management, strategy, policy, planning and works). Your MIS will need to focus on these type of sub-systems. How will you deal with the 'issue' of the regions?

A model answer is given to the exercise in Appendix C.

References and further reading

Antill, L. and Wood-Harper, T. (1985). *Systems Analysis*. London: Heinemann.

Avison, D.E. and Wood-Harper, A.T. (1990). *Multiview: An Exploration in Information Systems Development*. Maidenhead: McGraw-Hill.

Bell, J. (1993). *Doing Your Research Project: A Guide for First-time Researchers in Education and Social Science*. Buckingham: Open University Press.

Bennetts, P.D.C., Wood-Harper, A.T. and Mills, S. (1998). The soft systems methodology as a framework for software process improvement. *Journal of End User Computing*, vol. 10, no. 1.

Chambers, R. (1997). *Whose Reality Counts? Putting the First Last*. London: Intermediate Technology Publications.

Checkland, P.B. (1981). *Systems Thinking, Systems Practise*. Chichester: Wiley.

Checkland, P.B. and Scholes, J. (1990). *Soft Systems Methodology in Action*. Chichester: Wiley.

Checkland, P. and Holwell, S. (1998). *Information, Systems and Information Systems: Making Sense of the Field*. Chichester: Wiley.

Gosling, L. and Edwards, M. (1995). *Assessment, Monitoring, Review and Evaluation Toolkit*. London: Save the Children Fund.

Kumar, K. (1993). *Rapid Appraisal Methods*. Washington DC: World Bank Publications.

Senge, P., Ross, P., Smith, B., Roberts, R. and Kleiner, R. (1994). *The Fifth Discipline Fieldbook: Strategies and Tools for Building a Learning Organisation*. London: Nicholas Brealey.

Wood-Harper, A.T. (1989). Role of methodologies in Information Systems Development. Norwich: University of East Anglia.

INFORMATION MODELLING: MAKING A WORKABLE SYSTEM

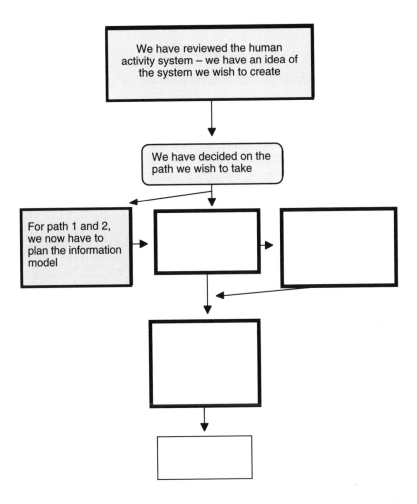

FIGURE 6.1   *Where are we in the process? The second stage of the rapid planning methodology*

Keywords:

entity model, functional **decomposition**, events, entity/function matrix, data flow diagrams, attributes.

Summary:

The systems model leads on to a harder systems analysis and design that is: information modelling. During this phase the subject of the problem is broken down in terms of entities, functions, attributes and events. The ground is prepared for the proposed information system in that entities correspond to things which we wish to keep information about. Functions are the tasks which these entities are involved with. Attributes are the qualities (or fields) that compose the entity and events are the triggers that cause functions to arise.

6.1   Introduction to information modelling

The second, more quantitative stage of our methodology is to structure our systems model of the new information system in such a way as to produce a workable information system outline for the major stakeholders. This stage is vital if we are going to build our information system for ourselves. As we set out earlier in Chapter 4, it is not so important if you are eventually going to purchase your software ready made.

Assuming that you need to work out exactly what your information system is going to be like in terms of files and functions, once the analyst and the stakeholders have reached agreement (even if this is quite tentative) on the overall picture of the situation and on the root definition of the system to be designed then information modelling can begin. This stage can be very long winded. To achieve a high measure of accuracy in terms of information modelling the task can take a considerable amount of time to work itself out in great detail. This is not the purpose of this book. Texts that offer a high level of academic accuracy are indicated in the further reading section at the end of the chapter (Everest, 1986; Korth and Silberschantz, 1986; Bowers, 1988; Avison and Fitzgerald, 1995).

AUTHORS' ASIDE

In this chapter we discuss the intellectual tools which non-specialists can use to model their information system. The tools described have a fairly lengthy and well-tried track record but other approaches do exist most notably object orientated programming (OOP). It is useful to look briefly at OOP but not all reviews are positive. David Avison has described object orientated information systems development as 'the latest silver bullet' (Avison, 1997). Wainright-Martin *et al.* (1994) describes OOP as follows:

> Objects are self-contained software modules that perform a given set of tasks on command. By connecting a number of these objects, a software engineer can create a complete, working application almost as easily as assembling a stereo system by plugging together a receiver, tape deck, and CD player.
>
> The difficulty arises in creating an object that works properly and is robust enough to be used in a variety of applications. ... the object orientated approach (is) ideal for the large-scale, team development cycle typical in the corporate setting (p. 190).

We will not build on OOP ideas in this chapter partly because we are more focused on developing non-specialist's intellectual tools for thinking about and describing information flows and partly because, as Wainright-Martin puts it the OOP is a 'quintessential black-box' and our task here is to increase the understanding of information flows not obscure them in functional black boxes. For further material on OOP see sections of Moreton and Chester (1997), or Tozer (1996) or Cats-Baril and Thompson (1997).

In terms of the present task *we do not want to spend our time on lengthy academic review, we need to think about what our information system is actually going to do and attempt to produce an outline system that is practical and workable.*

Figure 6.2 gives us the broad brush strokes to work from. We now need to identify (in liaison with the stakeholders of the system):

- What do we wish to keep records of data about (entities)?
- Of what are these entities composed (attributes)?
- What functions are carried out on the entities?
- What are the triggers or events that fire the functions?

Of course, at any one stage in the analysis and design process it is impossible not to think of the manner in which the current stage will affect those stages that follow. This is a very useful feature but one which analysts and designers in the past have undervalued. It can be argued that at each stage of the analysis it is best to attempt to banish all past and future analysis from your mind. This ensures that analysts do not attempt to take elements of the analysis out of context, e.g. to specify the hardware and software for a system before having carried out the information

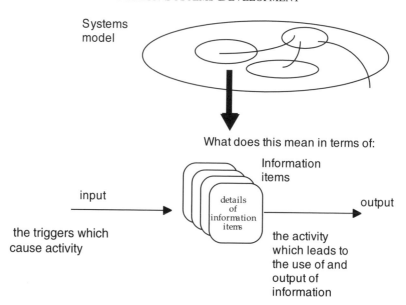

FIGURE 6.2   *The HAS/information model link*

modelling stage. The problem with not thinking about other
stages is that the links between stages are ignored and we end up
with a six-stage methodology, with none of the six stages interre-
lating with each other. Therefore our task at this stage, and at
every other stage is to keep a clear notion of the ideas that led
to the current analysis, keep in mind the main needs of the stage
to come and to concentrate chiefly on the work in hand (see
Figure 6.3).

To be aware of how our current work fits into our overall analysis is useful but to make any decisions concerning hardware, software and training would be to reduce the value of the entire
analysis exercise and would make a nonsense of the process. We
will eventually want to make decisions in terms of implementation
but this is not the time. There is great value in having a nominal
idea as to what combinations might produce the system we are
designing but these ideas should be held lightly until the final
stages of the analysis (whichever route through the methodology
we select). The reason for this is quite simple. Any joint discussion
of hardware and software with stakeholders can raise false expectations, unnecessarily bring pressure to bear on yourself to deliver,
and most importantly, rule out the possibility of making changes to
your planned system. If stakeholders perceive that the system that
they have so far agreed to is to be changed they may consider this

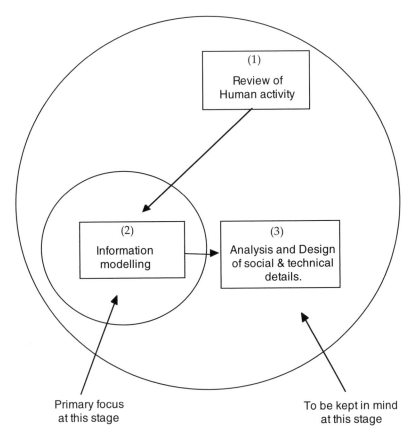

FIGURE 6.3   *The focus of our thinking*

to be regressive. This in turn can cause problems in the relationship between the analyst and the stakeholders. This stage of the
analysis also has meaning in terms of our learning. Table 6.1
shows the elements of the learning organization in relation to
information modelling.

With these thoughts in mind we will now look at the major features of the second stage of our analysis.

6.2   Entities, attributes, functions and events

We are going to try to reduce our proposed information system to
four features. In order for our analysis to be accurate we need to
spend a little time defining them.

- An *entity* is something about which records are kept. The definition is intentionally vague in its meaning. The need for a degree

TABLE 6.1   *Learning organization and information modelling*

Discipline	Value in information modelling thinking	Outcome?
Systems thinking	We can get away from this if we are not careful. This stage can become very focused on the parts of the system and not the whole. In thinking systemically we maintain our focus on the whole system	A system designed as a whole if the approach is truly systemic
Personal mastery	This stage develops the team mastery of the problem context and produces a model that can be made actual. In information modelling we gain mastery over the data and information detail of our organization	Ownership and control over the information system
Mental models	Each of the four main elements of information modelling includes mental models focused on data issues	Improving the accuracy of the eventual system
Shared vision	Because the process is participatory, the information model should be a shared vision of the eventual information system	Improving the clarity of the vision of the transformation
Team learning	The team continues to develop the participatory approach at this time	Consensus on the way forward

of flexibility is essential because the entities in a system can range from the major individuals who are working within the organization (e.g. senior managers, chief accountant, etc.) to operational and strategic information sources (e.g. staff records, sales records, pay-roll, land use data, profitability, research and development, etc.).

- *Attributes*, that is, the attributes of the entities. For example, if the entity is a land use planning system, the attributes might be rainfall, climate, percentage of the land use which is arable, percentage of the land use which is pasture, percentage of the land use which is urban, etc. Or if the entity is a management information system dealing with company performance, some of the attributes might be gross sales for years x to y, gross profit, net profit, number of staff employed, staff salaries.

- *Functions* are actions that take place within the information system and concern entities. Therefore some of the functions related to a small computer maintenance business might include: update the customer ledger, update the supplier ledger, keep inventory of the companies stock, register sales, register bad debts, register sales staff mileage. Functions set out in this form are fairly chaotic. To understand the web of functions that make up even a basic operation we make use of a hierarchy tree. For example the major function:

Update customer file

would contain such sub-functions as:
  - Receive sales data
  - Receive bad debt data

The first of these items might then contain sub-subfunctions such as:
  - Add new customer data
  - Edit old customer data
  - Delete archive customer data

This is a very simple example, and quite often you may need to go into quite a lot more detail. However, it is also true that in breaking down the core functions that are essential for the information system in its first phase the analyst often discovers that things are much more simple than was first envisaged. The breakdown of the functions or functional decomposition, will work its way out to a tree structure as shown in Figure 6.4.

- *Events* are triggers which make functions occur. For example in a training organization a potential participant wanting to enrol for a short course is an event that triggers the function 'process application'. This may in turn trigger off other functions – 'check vacancies' or 'assess sponsor'.

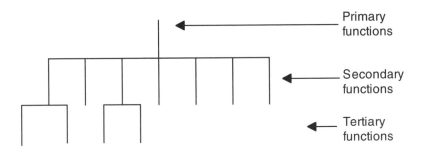

FIGURE 6.4   *A tree structure*

If we try to put the entire scheme together in one particular case it might appear as follows:

An ENTITY	Farmer

has

ATTRIBUTES	Reference number
	Contact date
	Farming type

Carries out

FUNCTIONS	Purchase
	Plough
	Sell

at specific

EVENTS	Seasonal events
	Financial events

This simple example shows the way the entire system fits together. We will now go on to look at each element in greater detail.

THINK POINT

Can you, for your own organization, think of three major entities, three major functions and then break down one of the entities into attributes and consider an event that will trigger one of the functions?

6.3   Entity models

Entity models are usually the primary components to look at. If we do not know what we want to keep records about then we have not got a system view to work from.

It is possible to start off the analysis with a review of functions or entities. We feel it makes sense to begin with the entity (the nouns of the system so to speak) rather than the function (the verbs or actions of the system). Also, for the purposes of the continuity of this multiperspective methodology, we feel that the clearest correlation between the HAS and information modelling is from system model to entity model.

What are the major items about which we wish to store information? It should be remembered that all entities will contain attributes and also have associated functions and we will eventually want to link all these items together. The process of arriving at a definitive mapping of entities can be argued to be a slightly academic exercise as there is room for judgement in the selection. Two things are vitally important and have been pointed to many times by other authors: getting a complete picture and at the same time not *flooding* the analysis with information. We will discuss this in greater depth shortly. The process of producing a map of entities and groups of entities (known as entity types) can be seen in Figure 6.5.

To model the entities...

- list all entities for the new system
- group related entities into blocks (entity types)
- For each block
  —draw the entities as boxes
  —link the entities together
  —show on the link line the nature of the relationship
- put all the blocks together
- link the blocks and indicate the nature of the relationships

FIGURE 6.5   *A procedure for organizing entities*

This is far from being a straightforward process. You may need to simplify your analysis down to one or two basic entities. There are a few basic rules that need to be understood concerning relationships and entities (see Figure 6.6).

One to one (e.g. in an veterinary practice one vet has one practice area)

One to many (e.g. one customer may make many visits)

Many to many (e.g. many customers may make use of many veterinary products)

FIGURE 6.6   *Entities and relationships*

AUTHORS' ASIDE

We realize that information modelling is a topic that is dealt with in great depth elsewhere and for mastery of the topic further study is necessary (for more details on entity relationship see Avison and Fitzgerald (1995)). In this book we wish to empower the non-specialist to create a model of the system that is to be produced. The model may not be complete and may not be entirely accurate but it should be the basis for later development. Our aims are for modest and understandable information systems.

Earlier on we mentioned being complete in terms of our entities while at the same time avoiding *flooding*. By completeness we mean that no major thing about which you wish to keep information is missing. Flooding refers to the potential complexity of the final model if we were to map out every single entity that comes to mind. At this stage we want to map out major entities only. In fact the process of reducing complexity down to the key components of study is an important lesson to learn. It will always be possible to increase complexity and even have levels of entity model later on. In Table 6.2 we list all the major entities for our department of roads MIS as set out by a team of non-specialists. In the table they have tried to keep in mind the main systems in the systems diagram set out in the previous chapter.

TABLE 6.2   *Main entities for the MIS*

Relevant system from the systems diagram	Entity	Links to other entities
Management and administration	Management	Employee database, heavy equipment inventory, roads register, accounting, planning
Management and administration	Accounting	Management, departmental finances, preliminary budget, final programme
Design	Soils test laboratory data	Roads information
Construction and maintenance	Roads information	Soils test laboratory data, regional and project data, roads register
Construction and maintenance	Roads register	Roads information, management
Management and administration	Departmental finance	Accounting
Management and administration	Preliminary budget	Planning, regional and project data
Design	Planning	Final programme, preliminary budget, management
Management and administration	Final programme	Accounting, planning
Management and administration	Employees	Employee database
Management and administration	Employee database	Employees, management, regional and project data
Regional and project data collection	Regional and project data	Employee database, preliminary budget, heavy equipment inventory, roads information
Mechanical	Heavy equipment inventory	Management, regional and project data

Table 6.2 does not demonstrate a complete picture of the data in the department but does indicate that there are a number of things about which we wish to obtain information and that these things (entities) are related to other entities. From this point we can link together certain groups of entities and then produce a final map showing all entities and their relationships with each other. In Figure 6.7 the team (including analyst and main stakeholders) have linked all the entities by means of lines and notes defining the relationship in a preliminary diagram. Figure 6.6 indicates what these relationships mean. If the line has a multiple line ending (crow's

feet) it shows a one-to-many relationship (e.g. the employee data-base contains data on many employees). As shown in Figure 6.6, there are three types of relationship between entities, one to one, one to many (or many to one) and many to many. Perhaps the easiest way to understand this is to look at an example. Figure 6.7 is the entity model for the government roads department.

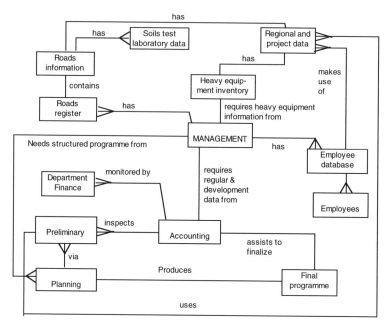

FIGURE 6.7   *A preliminary entity model*

Sometimes the analyst may find it helpful to make a note of the direction of the entity relationship, e.g. Departmental Finance *is monitored by* Accounting. The reverse (Accounting monitored by Departmental Finance) does not seem to be too silly so confusion might arise without this type of clarification. The name for this type of explanatory note is 'anchor point notation'.

The major insight that we can give concerning your entity model construction is that it may take many attempts to get the model clearly defined. Lines should cross as little as possible, and for most purposes you should be able to reduce the situation to about 20 enti-ties. If there are more than this you are probably dealing with a very complex problem and unless you have existing analysis and design skills we recommend that you try to begin by reducing the scope of your analysis to a subset of your original terms of reference. In our example here we have reduced our analysis to four key areas as derived from our conceptual model:

- Programme planning and finance
- Personnel records
- Roads register
- Equipment inventory

THINK POINT

Before going on, take a close look at Figure 6.7. Can you see a how we might construct a simpler entity model? Could we prune this one back to essentials? Have a good think about this before going on.

It is possible to reduce the entities still further. Table 6.3 provides one view.

When you are satisfied that you have:

- identified and listed your major entities, and
- modelled them in a manner that makes sense to you and to the major stakeholders

you are ready to go on to the next stage. It is quite important to realize that entities can change into other entities, e.g. in a training institution an applicant could become a student who in turn will become an ex-student. In the example we have above the accounting entity transforms information in the preliminary budget entity into information for the final programme entity.

TABLE 6.3   *A simplified entity list*

Entity label	Function
Management	This is the sink for all information, everything ends up here
Regional and project data	This is the source for all information
Preliminary budget	Secondary entity, drives information from regional and project data
Personnel records	Secondary entity, drives information from regional and project data
Roads register	Secondary entity, drives information from regional and project data
Equipment inventory	Secondary entity, drives information from regional and project data

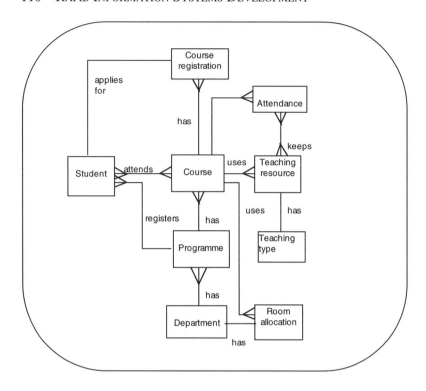

FIGURE 6.8   *Preliminary entity map of a training college*

Figure 6.8 shows another example of an entity map. This relates to a training college and shows the map for a project focusing on student records.

It is not the purpose of this book to go into considerable detail on these issues. Entity modelling (and all the following stages of this phase) can be developed in great depth. If you feel that you require greater detail we refer you to the further reading for data analysis. Our main theme is not to provide an academically polished model but to make use of existing analysis and design tools and produce practical and reproducible analysis and design products. In some fields such approaches are called 'reasonably quick and dirty'.

At this stage it is important that you keep a note of the potential size of entities – that is will they contain hundreds, thousands or more information or data elements and about how often the data changes in the system. For example, you might end up with a notion of a system with 60 data elements, 40 per cent of which you might expect to change each year. This information will be very important for the next stage of the analysis.

Amount of time devoted to analysis so far:
Total for this stage (entity modelling) = 2 days
Cumulative total update = 9 days

Working on the estimates of time we set out in the first stage of our approach we suggest that two or three days should complete this phase of stage 2.

For now we are assuming that you are ready to go on to mapping the major attributes as related to the entities.

6.4   Attributes

For the development of the system it is useful if we begin to identify key attributes of entities. Thinking back to our introduction to the chapter the reason for this is because the attributes we set out here should form the basis for the fields of our eventual database for the management information system (in the primary case we are using in this example).

One way of carrying out this exercise would be to create an entity/attribute matrix as shown in Figure 6.9.

That is, for each entity on the *x*-axis we list all the attributes on the *y*-axis to make a complete listing of attributes. One reason for *not* doing this is because if we have quite a lot of attributes related to any one particular entity the matrix would become rather ungainly. Ten or eleven entities would produce possibly hundreds of attributes. It is probably easier to just set out each set of attributes against each specific entity. An attribute listing is shown below.

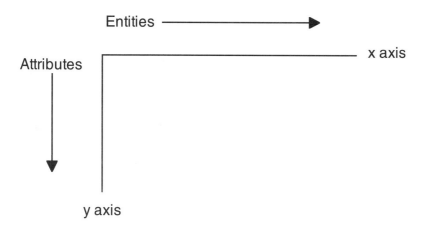

FIGURE 6.9   *Entity/attribute matrix*

Attributes for the roads register entity

Name of road
Date of construction
Personnel involved – engineers, overseers
Duration
Cost
Benefit as projected in original report
Source of finance – external, internal
Total quantities and costs of:
    cutting
    filling
    gravelling
    culverts
    bridges
etc.

We could go into much greater detail if time, resources and need demanded. The amount of detail is again your decision. It is not intended that at this stage you should be thinking of the actual database structures that might be required to accommodate the datasets that you begin to generate in outline. A rather different approach is seen in Figure 6.10, the attribute listing for the training college entity map.

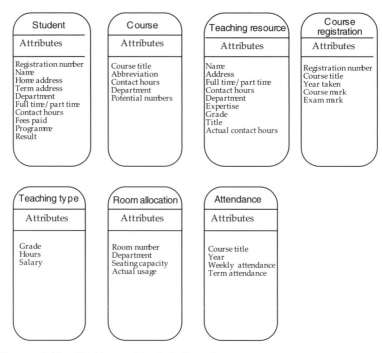

FIGURE 6.10   *Entities and included attributes*

This example of attribute mapping focuses on setting out the analysis as an aid to computerization. Each entity can be clearly seen as a record and a group of entities is a file. Each attribute is a field in an entity. Sometimes this type of approach is appropriate. For example, if the analyst knows that he is required to design a computer-based system and is familiar with database design there is little point in not setting out the attributes in this manner. However, if a manual system is required, or if there is some debate as to what the analysis is actually telling us, then it is better not to be thinking of the final system at this stage. Again we cannot over stress the need to resist the impulse to attempt to plan the whole system before carrying out the entire analysis.

As with the entity phase of this stage, keep a note of the likely size of the attributes for the entity, i.e. how many attributes are there, how many records will be kept in the system? One day should see this phase completed.

Amount of time devoted to analysis so far:
Total for this stage (attribute listing) = 1 day
Cumulative total update = 10 days

6.5 Functional decomposition

This may sound rather a mouthful, but as with so many analysis and design terms, the reality is quite straightforward. **Decomposition** as used here refers to a hierarchy of tasks broken down into their component and even subcomponent parts. This is used to show the major functions and the way in which these consist of other simpler functions. A simple example would be to demonstrate digging a hole in a road (see Figure 6.11).

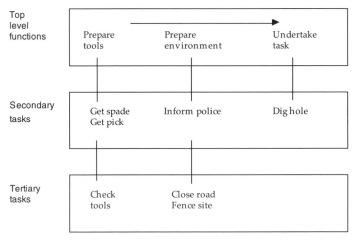

FIGURE 6.11   *Decomposition of digging a hole in the road*

You might think that this is a trivial example but it does demonstrate the way in which decomposition works.

THINK POINT

Try it for yourself. Take one of your standard tasks and see if you can break it down into a series of decomposed tasks. A major point is to try to get tasks of the same intensity or degree at each level. A great deal of modern project management relates to functional decomposition, that is assigning tasks and different levels of tasks to different individuals.

The breakdown of the whole into its parts is known as top-down decomposition. In Figures 6.12 and 6.13 we demonstrate the decomposition of functions at two levels for the department of roads.

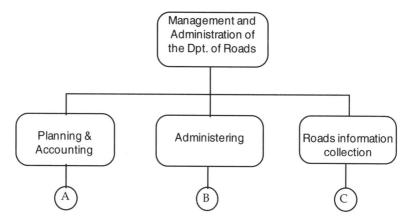

FIGURE 6.12   *Top level decomposition – the department of roads*

It is important to notice that there are three major functions – planning and accounting, administering, and the roads information collection. This does not mean that these are the only functions. It means that these relate most closely to the job we have been set in our terms of reference, the greatest areas of need as shown in the rich picture, the consensus view arrived at in the root definition and the new systems outline as given in the systems model. As a learning exercise, the information model has provided us the with opportunity to focus on three core areas, considered by the team and the stakeholders to be of primary importance. We need to restate that this is a subjective process and a different analysis and design team and different stakeholders would, in the same context, almost certainly select different information priorities. However, in this case it is not surprising to see that the major areas proposed functionally for a management information system in a government department are administration and major inventories. Also the planning and accounts areas are fairly clear contenders for new information systems design as invariably our priorities will be initially be focused on repetitious and well-structured tasks.

The level 2 chart shown in Figure 6.13 develops the decomposition of the planning and accounting function. A point to note on this chart is that there are two paths to 'receive programme proposals'. Ideally this should always occur following the 'report assessment' and 'evaluation' stages. However, there are times when this is not possible and an informal short cut is taken.

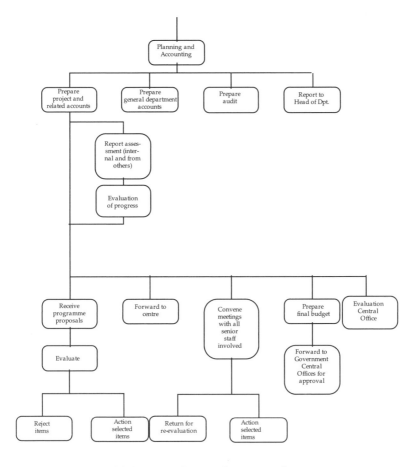

FIGURE 6.13   *Level 2 function chart – planning and accounts*

AUTHORS' ASIDE

This takes us into the area of the discretion of the analyst and professionalism again. In some cases it is the responsibility of the analyst to remove unwieldy pieces of activity and in others to conform the new design to some tried and tested (if 'informal') activities. The way in which the individual analyst deals with this type of 'informal' information processing reality entirely depends upon the specific situation in which he or she is working. Sometimes the problem owner may not wish to have this pointed out but will still require you to work round it. It is another example of the analyst having to sometimes make use of a subjective evaluation of an 'economy of truth' in terms of his or her actual reporting. In our view the discovery of informality of this type is important for the organization's self-learning and should normally be discussed and reviewed by the stakeholders – it is a learning benefit from analysis and design.

In our other example of a training college, functions were mapped out much more closely with the final computer system in mind. This does require a little explanation. The example shown in Figure 6.14 is very specifically related to generating information products (**performance indicators** or PIs) for a training college. Much of the detail is abbreviated (FTL = full-time lecturer), but it is not important to understand the detail of the example. The decomposition is dealing specifically with generating information PIs. In fact there are numerous PIs altogether but we show only four here. The purpose of this example is to show that functional decomposition can be very specific to a computer-based system, just as the entity map for the college that we showed earlier on. This functional decomposition is intended to provide the basis of the computer programmes that will run the functions.

6.5.1　Double checking on entities and functions

Even the simplest of information problems will by now have generated quite a complex picture of the work to be done. When complexity increases it is useful to supplement the analysis with a little double checking to make sure that the picture of the entities and functions that we are developing is sensible. One way to carry out such a check is to make use of an entity/function matrix. We have already mentioned entity/attribute matrices an entity/function matrix operates on the same principle (see Figure 6.15).

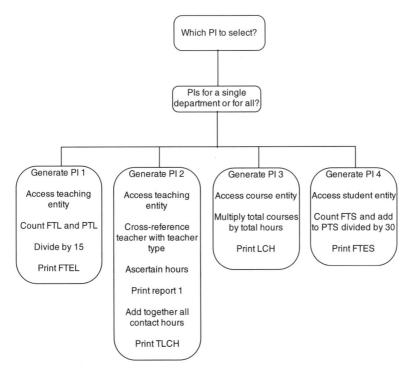

FIGURE 6.14   *Functional decomposition for performance indicators*

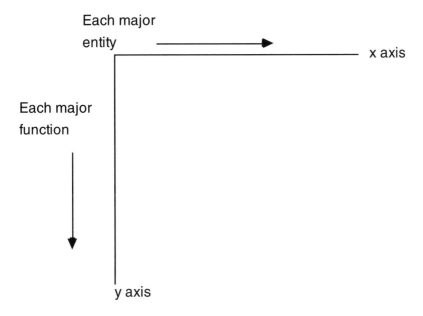

FIGURE 6.15   *Entity/function matrix*

As with our previous example, the easiest way to demonstrate this is to give an example (see Figure 6.16). The rule is, if there are any functions without entities or entities without functions, or – more difficult to check – missing entities or functions, this matrix should be able to pick up any problems.

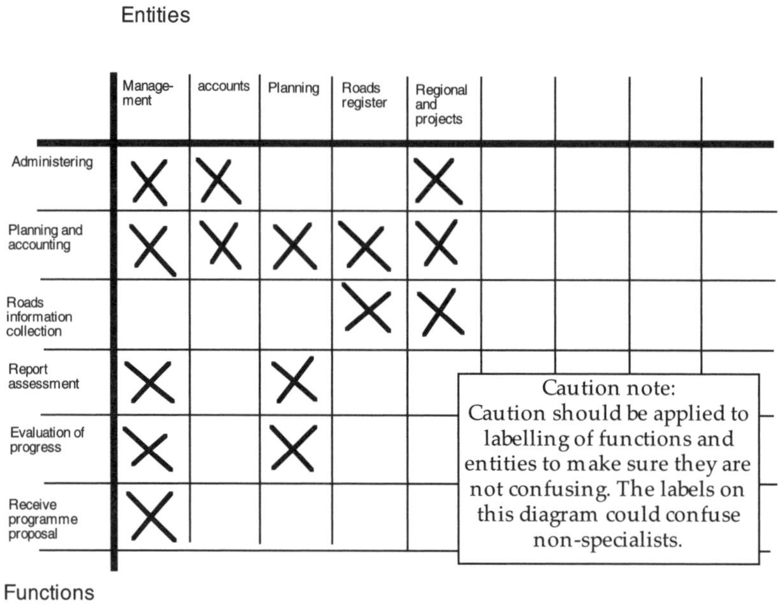

Entities

	Manage-ment	accounts	Planning	Roads register	Regional and projects				
Administering	X	X			X				
Planning and accounting	X	X	X	X	X				
Roads information collection				X	X				
Report assessment	X		X						
Evaluation of progress	X		X						
Receive programme proposal	X								

Caution note:
Caution should be applied to labelling of functions and entities to make sure they are not confusing. The labels on this diagram could confuse non-specialists.

Functions

FIGURE 6.16   *A semi-completed entity/function matrix*

THINK POINT

Are all these entities and functions legitimate? Do they all have corresponding entities and functions ranged against them? What would be the outcome of a functionless entity?

It is estimated that in many contexts this stage should take no more than two days.

Amount of time devoted to analysis so far:
Total for this stage (functional decomposition) = 2 days
Cumulative total update = 12 days

So far at this stage in the analysis we have:

- A clear, if preliminary entity model – enough for us to work from. We know what we want to collect data about.
- A listing of the key attributes or the exact types of data within the entities.
- An idea of the size and volatility (the rate of change) of the data in the entities.
- A correlation of the relationships of functions to entities and also have some understanding of how these functions decompose in the organization.

We can now go on to the next stage of the information modelling which is to build in the events whic will trigger the functions which will move and mould information within the entities which have the attributes ('which lived in the house that Jack built!').

6.6   Events

Here we will introduce another analysis tool that complements and completes the previous three, focusing on measuring and quantifying the information flow in the organization: the data flow diagram (DFD) type drawing. Note, in what follows we make use of an adapted DFD type of drawing. The reason for the adaptation is to provide the non-specialist with a tool which we feel is more consistent with the rapid approach we advocate. Our label for this variant of DFD is simply a flow diagram (FD).This is a useful tool for modelling the input of events which will trigger functions in the system.

Again you should realize that the issue of DFDs and other types of flow diagrams is quite a major subject in the science of analysis and design and if you want to develop this aspect of the analysis and other elements of information modelling we again refer you to the appropriate structured systems analysis and design texts in the further reading section at the end of this chapter (some useful general texts are CCTA (1988), Downs *et al.* (1988), Ashworth and Goodland (1990), Avison and Fitzgerald (1995)). Considerable practice will be needed for a really detailed and professional understanding. For now we will continue with our theme – an introduction to useful tools that can be applied rapidly.

The flow diagram examines and demonstrates how information flows in functional hierarchies. Within the diagram the information flows from left to right through the functions. The functions are shown in boxes. Events come in from the top driving the functions (see Figure 6.17). A key item to be aware of is the avoidance of ambiguity in terms of terminology, e.g. what 'entities' behind the functions are referring to at any one time? In this case we are looking at a shortened outline of the events that trigger the functions in the planning and accounts major function as related to the management, administration and planning entities. Ideally the flow diagram will provide the analyst with another element of learning about the organization:

- Where have events that trigger functions arisen?
- Do these events as modelled check with the realities of the present situation?
- Has the team missed out any major functions in the analysis to date?
- What is the degree of risk of an unlooked for or unwelcome event arising?

Generally, it is necessary to produce flow diagrams of major or complex areas. It is not usually essential to model the events for all functions. Figure 6.17 shows that it is useful (and possible!) to put concrete dates to the events.

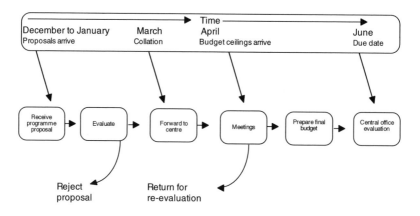

FIGURE 6.17   *An example flow diagram linking into the functions*

In terms of the second phase of our rapid appraisal approach we have completed the analysis when we have mapped out the events for the major functions that will form the core of our new information system, as mapped out in the systems model in stage 1. Stage 2 of our analysis can be set out in total as shown in Figure 6.18.

At this stage much of the concrete detail of the eventual information systems has been produced. It may be that much of what the team has discovered is partial and limited. Nevertheless, a view of the information model has been achieved and this will (at the very least) help the team in dealing with systems suppliers and developers later on. The process of stage two has continued the vital process of the team gaining ownership and confidence over the information and data flows within the organization.

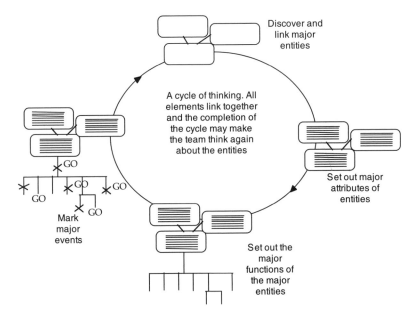

FIGURE 6.18   *Information modelling in rapid information systems development*

A further two days should be sufficient to prepare the data flow diagrams as and when necessary (it is not envisaged that all aspects of the analysis will need this stage).

Amount of time devoted to analysis so far:
Total for this stage (events) = 2 days
Cumulative total update = 14 days

6.7   Tying it all together

The finalization of the information model should not take place without the overall schema being presented to all major stakeholders for agreement. For this procedure the analyst will need to produce the information model in such a form that is readily understandable to non-specialists (see Figure 6.19).

It may be that the outcome of such a consultation process will be the need to rethink the systems model, ownership of the information model extends beyond the analysis team. The information model should provide a good basis for understanding the likely extent of the system. This in turn will have repercussions for the cost of the system. It may be necessary to think in terms of several phases to

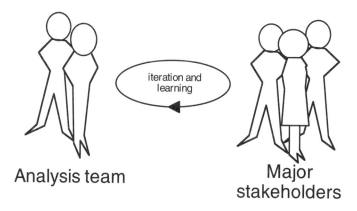

Analysis team   Major
                                    stakeholders

FIGURE 6.19   *Information modelling requires agreement*

eventually produce the system that the model shows. This is also useful thinking to surface at this stage of the analysis. When the stakeholders of the system are content (or at least are willing to sign off) this stage, the third stage of the analysis can take place.

6.8   Conclusions

The information model provides quantifiable details for the insights of the systems model. During this stage the team may have to rethink the systems model. It may be that implications of the model are unworkable, too expensive or too wide scale in terms of their implications. *This is all right.* One of the purposes of this approach is that the information system can be adjusted in reaction to further study, that the approach is a learning approach encouraging a learning organization. Between human activity stage and information modelling there should be a feedback loop allowing for further refinement of the proposed system.

When the information model is complete it can be put to one side although never forgotten – it is the basis of the system to come (on paths 1 and 2). We need to keep references of the amount of data and the number of entities that will need to be planned for. This information can be carried forward to the next stage of the analysis.

6.9   Exercise

At this stage we are assuming that you have compared the results of the exercises at the end of Chapter 5 with the model answer set out in Appendix C. Having arrived at a systems outline of the new system the crunch has come. We now need to turn our systems model into the outline information system. The way we shall do this is to set out major entities, attributes of key entities, functions and triggers or events. You need to:

- Make an entity map of the company as described in your top-level conceptual model. Only focus on key entities. Try to keep it simple (KISS – Keep it Simple Stupid).
- Related to your entity modelling work, set out the major functions related to a primary entity. Think about how many of the functions might be coped with by an automated system and how many of them could not.
- Set out the triggers/events that will be most important for the system.

Some hints. Entity model construction. If there has been any discussion about the situation for regional offices this must be put behind us now. The terms of reference are explicit and therefore we need now to break down the systems model into the entities about which we wish to store information. Primary entities might include planning and administration. These two will in turn be served by others. The top end of the entity spectrum is the issue of strategy for the company. Once you have drawn the entity model take a look at the model answer in Appendix C.

In listing attributes for the entities only concern yourself with the primary items.

When working on the functional decomposition focus on the key issue of strategy. Work out the preparation of strategy function with particular emphasis to the hierarchy of sub-functions which help to provide the strategy formulation necessary for effective management. A key issue here will be understanding what the competition is up to. Feel free to go down two or even three levels in the decomposition. When you have completed take a look at the example worked out in Appendix C.

When you come to look at flow diagrams, again focus on an element of the strategy formulation (for example, the events that could contribute to the effective monitoring of major competitors).

References and further reading

A number of good texts exist which are consistent with information modelling (Lucas, 1973; Lucas, 1976; De Marco, 1979; De Marco, 1982; Lucas, 1982; Lucas, 1985; Kozar, 1989).

For more material on management information systems see Gory and Scott-Morton, 1974; Davis, 1984; Awad, 1988; McLeod, 1989; Bush and Robbins, 1991; Romm *et al.*, 1991; Wainright-Martin *et al.* 1994; Avison and Fitzgerald, 1995; Bell and Minghze, 1995; Lederer and Salmela, 1996.

Ashworth, C. and Goodland, M. (1990). SSADM: *A Practical Approach*. London: McGraw-Hill.

Avison, D. (1997). The discipline of information systems: teaching, research and practice. In J. Mingers and F. Stowell (eds), *Information Systems: An Emerging Discipline?* London: McGraw-Hill, pp. 113–136.

Avison, D.E. and Fitzgerald, G. (1995). *Information Systems Development: Methodologies, Techniques and Tools* (second edition). London: McGraw-Hill.

Awad, E.M. (1988). *Management Information Systems: Concepts, Structure and Applications*. Menlo Park: Benjamin Cummings.

Bell, S. and Minghze, L. (1995). MIS and systems analysis applications in China: a case study of the Research Institute for Standards and Norms. In M. Odedra-Straub (ed.), *Global Information Technology and Socio-Economic Development*. Nashua: Ivy League, pp. 153–160.

Bowers, D. (1988). *From Data to Database*. London: Van Nostrand Reinhold.

Bush, C. and Robbins, S. (1991). What does 'MIS' really mean? *Journal of Systems Management*, June, 6–8.

Cats-Baril, W. and Thompson, R. (1997). *Information Technology and Management*. Chicago: Irwin.

CCTA (1988). *SSADM – the Open Standard for Information Management*. Norwich: CCTA, Information Systems Engineering Division.

Davis, G.B. (1984). Challenges in the Management of Information Systems. Paper given at International Conference on Information Systems, Tucson.

De Marco, T. (1979). *Structured Analysis: System Specifications*. Englewood Cliffs: Prentice Hall.

De Marco, T. (1982). *Controlling Software Projects: Measurement, Management and Estimation*. New York: Yordon Press.

Downs, E. *et al.* (1988). *Structured Systems Analysis and Design Method – Application and Context*. Hemel Hempstead: Prentice Hall.

Everest, G. (1986). *Database Management: Objectives, System Functions and Administration*. London: McGraw-Hill.

Gory, G.A. and Scott-Morton, M.S. (1974). A framework for management information systems. In R. Nolan (ed.), *Managing the Data Resource Function*. St. Paul: West Publishing Company.

Korth, H. and Silberschantz, A. (1986). *Database System Concepts*. London: McGraw-Hill.

Kozar, K.A. (1989). *Humanized Information Systems Analysis and*

Design: People Building Systems for People. New York: McGraw-Hill.

Lederer, A. and Salmela, H. (1996). Toward a theory of strategic information systems planning. *Strategic Information Systems*, 5, 237–253.

Lucas, H.C. (1973). *Computer Based Information Systems in Organizations.* Palo Alto: Science Research Associates.

Lucas, H.C. (1976). *The Implementation of Computer Based Models.* New York: National Association of Accountants.

Lucas, H.C. (1982). *Coping with Computers: A Manager's Guide to Controlling Information Processing.* New York: Free Press.

Lucas, H.C. (1985). *The Analysis, Design and Implementation of Information Systems.* New York: McGraw-Hill.

McLeod, R.J. (1989). *Introduction to Information Systems*: A Problem Solving Approach. Henley-on-Thames: Science Research Associates, Pergamon.

Moreton, R. and Chester, M. (1997). *Transforming the Business: The IT Contribution.* London: McGraw-Hill.

Romm, T., Pliskin, N., *et al.* (1991). Identifying organizational culture clash in MIS implementation. *Information and Management*, **21**, 99–109.

Tozer, E. (1996). *Strategic IS/IT Planning.* Oxford: Butterworth Heinemann.

Wainright-Martin, E. *et al.* (1994). *Managing Information Technology: What Managers Need to Know.* New York: Macmillan.

Chapter 7

TECHNICAL NEEDS, SOCIAL NEEDS – GETTING THE RIGHT BALANCE

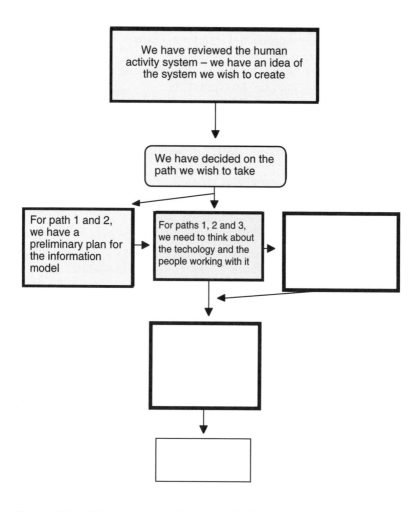

FIGURE 7.1   *Where are we in the process? The third stage of the rapid planning methodology*

Keywords:

socio-technical systems, future analysis, social objectives, technical objectives, social alternatives, technical alternatives, best-fit solution participation.

Summary:

This section covers the development of the implementation of the information system. We have learned a lot about the organization both in qualitative and quantitative terms. If we have pursued paths 1 or 2 we have gained insights into the information flows and stores as well. At this stage, common to all three paths we are interested in considerations of hardware, software and people used to operate the outline system. The integration of a variety of alternatives in terms of their costs, resource implications and constraints leads to the expression of the actual tasks that will be accomplished by the various human and computer aspects of the system.

7.1 Introduction to socio-technical systems

It is not essential that the third aspect of the methodology should directly build off the information modelling stage. The main reason for this relates to the various ways in which our approach can be used. If you are using path three you will not have undertaken information modelling at all. On the other hand, if you have undertaken information modelling this will have provided you and your team with an outline of the structure which the eventual information system can make use of. We could even go so far as to say that the process will have identified for us a database structure:

- entities = files and records
- attributes = fields
- functions = menus of necessary actions to take
- events = the triggers that prompt the functions.

The items which might be of most importance for this stage of the analysis are:

- details of entities
- details of number of attributes
- details of potential number of records.

If you do not have this information don't worry. Following the third path you have an idea of the transformation which you wish to achieve and of the systems that will contribute to this transformation. In this stage you will generate a plan of the mixture of technology and training that will provide the transformation. The third aspect of the total methodology can stand alone. It is a holistic systems analysis and systems design process in itself.

Stage three, the design of a socio/technical system, allows us to specify the nuts and bolts of the actual system itself in terms of human and computer tasks, and human and computer requirements. After all, a system which is beautifully designed but is completely inappropriate for the people who are available to use it or the environment that will support it is not much use at all. Therefore it is essential to consider the way in which people carry out their work, the vested interests and politics of the local situation and the way in which the new system can best be fitted into it. What we set out in this chapter is based upon the work of Enid Mumford and the ETHICS approach (e.g. see Mumford and Weir (1979), Mumford (1995, 1997)).

The process of the socio-technical design stage includes the outlining of:

- job design
- specification of human and computer (if appropriate) tasks
- specification of decisions about staffing and training requirements
- a detailed technical computer specification (if appropriate).

The analysis depends for its background context on the rich picture (especially for issues such as local power supply, availability of spares/servicing, etc.).

The job that the analysis team is called upon to perform is to outline the various alternatives available to the stakeholders to provide decision makers with relevant and sensible plans for action.

The overall structure for the stage is shown in Figure 7.2.

The outline set out in Figure 7.2 demonstrates a seven-stage process:

- First, predict future environment analysis – this is the attempt of the analysis to build into any new information system some redundancy in terms of the system being able to deal not only with the issues of the context of the present moment but the situation as it continues to develop.
- Secondly, outline the social objectives and technical objectives – this stage sets out the general social needs of the system (improving job satisfaction, increased professionalism, etc.) and technical objectives (improving the timeliness of operations, holding and analysing data efficiently, etc.).
- Our third task is to outline the social and technical alternatives – the measures in the social and technical fields that can be taken to meet the social and technical objectives.
- The fourth step is to generate a number of 'mixes' by putting

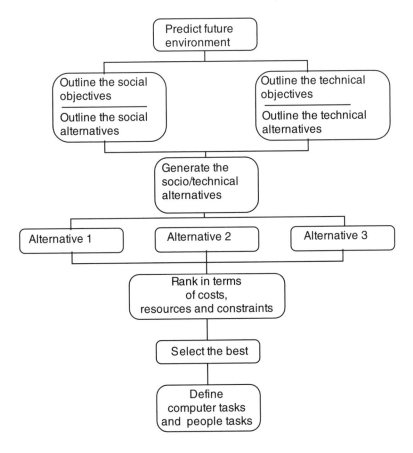

FIGURE 7.2   *Principles of socio-technical design*

together the social and technical alternatives into different options. Here we show three. There should be at least two but there could be many more.

- Fifthly we rank the alternatives in term of their costs, resources, constraints and benefits.
- Sixthly we select the best alternative mix – the 'best-fit' solution. This is an important point. Our mix and match of social and technical alternatives to meet our needs will rarely appear to be ideal. We will select the best and not the perfect alternatives.
- Finally and seventhly, we work out the human and computer tasks to meet the best-fit solution.

In terms of the learning organization, this process helps us in a number of ways (see Table 7.1).

Taking the outlines of Figure 7.2 and Table 7.1 as our starting point the analysis begins to develop as follows.

TABLE 7.1 *The learning organization and socio-technical systems*

Discipline	Value in socio-technical thinking	Outcome?
Systems thinking	This stage encourages holistic thinking within the boundary of the transformation we wish to make. All our linking of people and technology relates directly to this wholeness	A system designed as a whole if the approach is truly systemic
Personal mastery	Socio-technical modelling provides the opportunity for teams and stakeholders to define both their technological requirements and their work practice	Growing ownership and control over the detailed social and technical aspects of the information system
Mental models	A difficulty identified with much information systems work is the focus on a 'solution' to deal with a problem. This concentration on a solution can lead the problem-solving team to believe that there is only one answer to any specific problem. In this stage of the approach the team gains a map or mental model of a range of alternatives that can be applied to the context	The identification of choice is a powerful outcome. Developing the coherence of the socio-technical plan
Shared vision	Stakeholders are drawn in here again. They need to be in agreement about what is expected of them, what resources they will have to do it and what problems they might realistically expect	Improving the clarity of the vision of the transformation
Team learning	The team continues to develop the participatory approach at this time, again there is a switch of focus and different qualities will be needed	Consensus on the way forward

7.2 Predict future environment analysis

To review social and technical resources and constraints for the development of efficient information systems without thinking about the future of such systems would be a short-term attitude. Of course, we cannot know exactly what the future will bring but we can make some speculations on the nature of changes (see Figure 7.3).

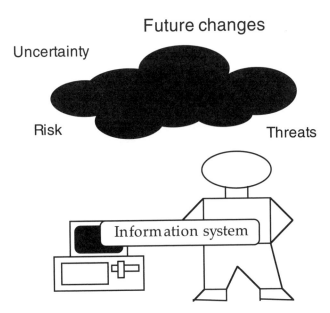

FIGURE 7.3   *What does the future hold?*

The consideration of future conditions may well help us to avoid some of the problems identified in Chapter 1. The study of future environments and conditions is expressed in the 'future analysis' phase (Land, 1982, 1987). Essentially the analysis we use here has four major foci:

- Prediction of the kinds of change that are possible (are they technological, legal, or economic?). This requires us to look at the context and situation of the organization in which we are working and, possibly with the help of structure plans (if they exist), predict the mid-term development of the institution (3–5 year plan). This analysis stage should give us some idea of the type of expansion, contraction, change that will occur and which the incoming system will have to deal with.
- The likely outcome of the system in the future – what will be the effects of an improved, possibly automated, information system? There are all kinds of disruptive and/or constructive events which may be related to the development of a new system (laying off staff, employment of computer professionals, development of new grades to cover computer staff, etc.).
- What features of the proposed system are more susceptible to change? – where would you expect the new system to change first? Can this be planned for? For example will data collection procedures change, will the existing departmental structures be maintained?

- What is the extent and horizon of the system? – this requires a long-term view (5–10 years). This will comprise enlightened guesswork but it gives one a sense of humility in the initial design and requires us to speculate as to how what we plan today may be the building block for further developments in the long-term future.

The end of the stage is to set out the new system within the context of continuing development in the organization. The study allows us to see the system in the context of one moment in time. This type of study can be quite detailed. Generally, however, it is quite a short procedure. In our case study of the governmental department our findings were:

- Prediction of the kinds of change that are possible. Major issue – fast growth for the department for the next five years; major investments in infrastructure (running to over 10 per cent of the department's annual budget). It is expected that the investment will lead to increases in employment within the department in terms of technically competent personnel. At a more political level, it is expected that the department will have a widening national responsibility in terms of existing roads.
- The likely outcome of the system in the future. The greatest efficiencies should occur in terms of finance and staff administration. More specifically there should be a reduction in unskilled staff employment and a tendency towards widening automation. The project is linked to related investment in improving communications.
- What features of the proposed system are more susceptible to change? The assumption is that the core management will feel the changes first, fairly widespread disruption and unsettling for several years to come. This will require training and motivational support.
- What is the extent and horizon of the system? Eventually the system will extend beyond the narrow centralized system to all the regional and district offices (again, this links to the communications investment).

The analysis can be far more detailed if time and circumstance (and need!) demands. This type of information can be drawn from a rich picture such as we drew in the HAS stage of the approach. Similarly a SWOT analysis, such as that discussed in Chapter 4 could provide the insights to deal with the above questions. However, you and your team go about answering the questions concerning the future and no matter how hesitant and preliminary the findings, all following analysis and design will need to keep in mind these considerations. They should be built into our planning and influence our choices in terms of the needs of the organization to cope with a new information system and the capacities of technology to cope with developments.

The next job is to agree and set the outline social and technical objectives of the system being created.

7.3 Outline social and technical objectives

Social objectives refer to the expectations of employees and major stakeholders. The technical objectives refer to capacity of the organization as a whole to react to key issues. For our case we can set out the twin objectives as follows:

Social objectives

- To be relatively self-sufficient
- To provide a quick service
- To provide job satisfaction
- To provide professional satisfaction
- To improve professional status of the department

All these objectives are arrived at following consultation with all major stakeholders. This is a vital point. The social objectives of a system – broadly to be seen as the expectations of the system in terms of the human beings who are going to be working with it, will vary from site to site. No two information systems being planned for organizations will have the same objectives. Often the social objectives of a system are undervalued. Management do not tend to feel that the social needs of a system are as critical for system development as technical issues. Thinking back to the systemic/reductionist arguments of the earlier chapters we cannot over stress the need for social issues to be adequately planned for. Having outlined the social objectives, the next task is to return to our systems model and information model to set out the technical objectives for the incoming system. In the case of our example these are as follows:

Technical objectives

- To inform management
- To improve timeliness
- To improve communication
- To increase information processing capacity
- To provide a long-term facility

These are the primary tasks which the stakeholders are expecting the system to undertake. In our example the objectives are quite brief and broad. They could be very specific, for example the single technical objective of a management system for a large trading company:

> To provide daily commodity movement statistics – in the form of 34 agreed performance indicators on 15 key commodities for all managers above grade 10.

As we have said before, your own position will indicate the depth of detail you will need to go into. There may be need for the analyst to grade objectives, particularly if interviews generate quite a lot of them.

THINK POINT

Consider your own organization. Could you outline the range of social objectives that your colleagues might expect from a new information system? Would you expect the objectives of different colleagues to change with different sections of the organization (the lateral dimension of the organization) or seniority (the vertical dimension of the organization)? What types of variation would you expect to find and why?

7.4   Generate social and technical alternatives

The social alternatives refer to the description of different ways of organizing individuals to undertake the work required for the system while at the same time achieving the social objectives. Technical alternatives should offer a range of means of meeting the information processing requirements. The issue of technical alternatives does require the analyst to understand the basics of what each type of alternative might mean. For example, one view of the range of technical means to work an information system might be as follows:

- An entirely manual system.
- A manual system with computerizable aspects (for example those produced by the Kalamazoo company).
- A mixed manual system with some microcomputer aspects. Microcomputers installed on a **standalone** basis.
- Information system based on standalone microcomputers.

- Microcomputers **networked** together.
- Microcomputers networked onto a minicomputer.
- A minicomputer system.
- A mainframe computer system.

If you are not familiar with hardware and software options don't worry – you are in good company. With the incredible continuing development of computer power it is almost impossible even for professionals in the industry to keep up with developments. As a very general briefing Table 7.2 provides an overview.

Each option offers benefits and costs. You will need to consider in some depth what your team is ready and able to provide analysis for and what it would be confident to recommend (as well as what the organization can cope with). The organizational team and self-learning you have achieved by this point in the analysis will be vital. The warrior type of analyst (first described in Chapter 3) is often over-stretched at this point and has a tendency to select systems that are either organizationally inappropriate or too demanding on the limited skills of the non-specialist analysts (or both). In our example the alternatives worked out as follows:

Social alternatives

S1 – In-house training of existing staff and organizational change to provide the complete computer service

S2 – In-house staff trained to supervise newly employed, pre-trained staff

S3 – Trained new staff employed

S4 – Make use of short-term agency and contract consultants – **outsourcing**?

As you can see the social alternatives are ranked from S1 to S4. Essentially we are looking at ways of staffing a computer-based system. The range of options ranges from the use of existing staff, trained in the skills required, to the use of short-term consultants (or even outsourcing). The technical alternatives are as follows:

Technical alternatives

T1 – Minicomputer-based system

T2 – PC network

T3 – PC standalone

Note that we have not included in our logical alternatives the possibility of using a manual system. This is because the alternative was not relevant following discussions with the funding agency (and thinking back to our root definitions in Chapter 5). This is a real-time limitation on any analysis and again reiterates the importance of the terms of reference on analysis and design routines.

TABLE 7.2 *Some generalized observation about different information processing systems*

Information systems	Selected features
A non-computer, manual system	By definition a manual system will have very limited processing power Subject to basic analysis errors (the human factor) Often these systems have been around since the organization began and they are well understood by their 'guardians'
Manual but computerizable	Often these are new systems, breaking with the traditional pre-computer systems Basic error avoidance through methodical practice Partially understood by some members of the organization, well understood by a small minority on the 'inside'
Mixed manual/PC	Old practice and new – often the worst of both worlds Basic software employed on standalone systems Thousands of records processable by the basic software and the PC Reduction in analysis errors over manual systems but often confusion between the two systems running in parallel. This reduction in analysis error will be true for all the computer-based systems Increase in input errors because, although the software is usually error-free (if it is well-tried and tested software) the input of data to the computer can be laborious and raise numerous new errors – this will also be true for all the systems set out below
Standalone PC-based system.	Maintenance required for the PCs and for all the following computer systems PCs have been around for a long time now and they are not usually seen by staff as new or threatening in themselves. What they do can be quite threatening, however, and they often require new practices every time the software is changed Basic software employed of the 'office' variety (word processor, spreadsheet, database, communications) Thousands of records processable Potential adoption problems if the technology is seen to take people's jobs Training needs to be developed at this stage. Mixed manual/PC systems have a parallel system to fall back on if the PCs fail. In this case there is dependence on the PC and this in turn means skill levels must be raised and spread among a wider number of staff
Networked PCs	Networking can often constitute a substantial change and development in practice within the organization. A network using inter or intranet technologies means that information is shared and that the organization can develop greater transparency and internal learning in its processes

PCs linked to minicomputers and higher systems

Basic software supplemented by some quite complex networking packages

Potential adoption problems resulting from the social implications of the network set out above

Training needs can become very high here most specifically for those entrusted with the maintenance and management of the network and the related shared files

Substantial changes in practice can result again. PCs, once trained for and introduced, tend to be used by the majority of members of an organization and they are inclusive, encouraging participation and thinking about how the system can be improved by all. Once the computers become more powerful they also become more remote and there can be a return to the days of the computer guardians or high priests, keeping the uninitiated away

Specialized software is often used by such systems

Hundreds of thousands of records processable

Large potential adoption problems as the organization gears up to a computer priesthood and the interface problems this can cause

Training needs can be very high especially for the programmers and managers of the system

Sometimes these systems require specialized, protected environments

Considerable maintenance needed

TABLE 7.3 Ranking the alternatives

Alternatives	Social costs	Technical costs	Social resources	Technical resources	Social constraints	Technical constraints	Totals
S1 T1	4	4	3	3	1	1	16
S3 T1	8	8	7	8	6	9	46
etc.							

7.5   Rank the alternatives

The next stage of the analysis is to mix and match the various alternatives together and then to list all the alternatives and reject any that are immediately not feasible. For example:

S1 T1   reject out-right on grounds of cost
S1 T2   proceed with analysis
S1 T3   proceed with analysis
S2 T1   reject out-right on grounds of cost
S2 T2   proceed with analysis
S2 T3   proceed with analysis
S3 T1   be wary of costs
S3 T2   proceed with analysis
S3 T3   proceed with analysis
S4 T1   proceed with analysis
S4 T2   proceed with analysis
S4 T3   proceed with analysis

AUTHORS' ASIDE

Of course, one can be much more sophisticated than the example we have discussed here. For example you may have set out the initial alternatives so that multiple social and technical combinations could be selected. In this scenario S factors could relate to training, management change, reduction in organization hierarchy, introduction of lifelong learning package for staff. On the other hand, the technical alternatives might relate to T issues such as digitize data, produce organization intranet, develop **web site**, use fast modems for communication between different sites. In this type of scenario there would be complex mixes of S and T alternatives (e.g. S1,S2,S5,T1,T4 as one set).

Working from our example we now need to find the optimum combination of alternatives. We need to consider each pairing in terms of their implications for *costs*, *resources*, *constraints* and if needed (although not usual) *benefits* (if thought necessary). These factors can be assessed using one of many methods, three of which are outlined below.

They can be arrived at by a process of cost/benefit analysis – whereby each alternative combination is costed and its benefits assessed. This can be a lengthy process and provides a purely economic framework for the consideration of the system. This is not an approach that fits in with the holistic approach adopted by the authors of this book.

They can be set out on a table and graded against each other on a ranking of 1 to 9. This is a qualitative and subjective approach but a team can try to arrive at a consensus view. For example we set the number values as follows:

1 = very good
2 = good
3 = quite good
4 = better than average
5 = average
6 = worse than average
7 = quite poor
8 = poor
9 = very poor

Our alternatives could then be set against each other as shown in Table 7.3.

The idea being that the alternatives with the lowest totals would indicate the more appropriate choices. This procedure can also be quite time consuming especially if undertaken by a team.

An even simpler rule of thumb would be to just set out the major factors against each aspect, For example:

S1T2 In-house staff and PC network

social costs – training in use of software and network
technical costs – software, hardware purchase
social resources – some trained staff
technical resources – some existing PC hardware
social constraints – none of real importance
technical constraints – power supply, climate.

S3T1 Trained new staff employed and minicomputer-based system, S4T1 Make use of short-term agency and contract consultants (outsourcing?) and minicomputer-based system

social costs – high cost new staff, training in use of software and network
technical costs – very expensive software, hardware
social resources – none available at present
technical resources – none available at present
social constraints – introducing new staff to practices
technical constraints – power supply, climate.

By using this method we can rapidly peel off the most expensive alternatives. We might still have trouble, however, if we have very close alternatives to compare. In this case we might feel justified in falling back on the second method of assessment. The result of this phase will be a ranking of the alternatives in order. Our ranking from our exercise were as follows:

First – the best alternative **S1T2** – In-house staff and PC network
Second – S1T3
Joint third – S2T2, S2T3
Joint fourth – S3T2, S3T3, S4T2, S4T3
Joint fifth S3T1, S4T1

For the purposes of this exercise we will work with the best combination and in applying the limitations which it will inevitably provide, attempt to relate it to our information model arrived at in the last section.

7.6   Human and computer tasks

The final stage of the socio-technical specification is to outline the new system:

7.6.1   People tasks

The people tasks that your team sets out must deal with the wide range of issues and potential problems that you thought of in your future analysis as well as the range of data tasks that were implied by the information modelling carried out in phase two of our approach (if you undertook that stage). These tasks can be broken down along a number of lines but for our purposes we provided a four-way division, i.e. management tasks, input-output tasks, training tasks, and maintenance and support tasks. In general terms we might structure these as follows:

- Management tasks
  - overall management of the system
  - management of an effective reporting procedure
- Input-output tasks
  - data input to the system
  - selective output from the system
  - specialized report generation
  - interpreting the output
- Training tasks
  - training senior management in familiarization
  - training assistant managers and administrators in use
  - training clerks in operations
  - training technicians in IT maintenance

- Maintenance and support tasks
  - repairing faulty items
  - regular servicing

Several points can be made concerning this type of checklist. As a rule, in our practice we have observed that training should always begin with the top management. If undertaken effectively this ensures that the system will be supported. One problem that is constantly recurring is the potential alienation of managers through assuming their commitment without training. Information technology is generally seen as being pretty threatening to those who are on its margins. If a system is planned and the senior staff are not given strong support in its uses and values it can often happen that the system is under used by other staff and lacks the political support to really gain thorough acceptance. Secondly, the outline which we prepare now will not be worked out in detail at this point. It will be the task of the final stage of our approach actually to set out the major aspects of the configuration in its final form. Here we are attempting to provide ourselves with the overall guidelines for the coming system. Thirdly, we need to gain the assent of all major stakeholders at this stage to the tasks that we outline. All such tasks will have immediate and recurrent costs on the organization and the donor. There may be need for the analyst to reduce his or her expectations in the light of what is financially feasible. This point also is true for the next stage, computer tasks.

7.6.2   Computer tasks

These will tend to be rather easier to structure at this level. Generally two levels need to be considered, the data and the equipment.

The data. This refers to the actual items that will need to be accommodated. The type of data that our government department needs to be stored and retrieved is as follows:

- roads register data
- heavy equipment inventory
- employee records.
- project data
- accounts data
- other items (miscellaneous), e.g.
  - word-processed documents
  - spreadsheet matrices
  - database files
  - graphics files
  - road design files.

The equipment. At this stage the equipment prescribed can be set out by general function rather than actual hardware and software. Thus, with our department we could specify:

- networking of data to key personnel (approximately 16 units) – multiple access to files
- quality output as required
- draft output as required
- equipment to deal with power fluctuations and power down (potentially hours)
- capacity and facility to archive (approximately 40 megabytes in year 1).

This stage could be completed in six days.

Amount of time devoted to analysis so far:
Total for this stage (socio-technical) = 6 days
Cumulative total for paths 1 and 2 = 20 days
Cumulative total for path 3 = 13 days

7.7   An example – a university information system

For your consideration we include here a total socio-technical analysis for a university management information system. We present the example as a rapid analysis produced by a three-person team. This is the kind of 'back-of-the-envelope' approach which is certainly not perfect but does produce good results in terms of thinking about the system and learning about the organization.

First we try to predict the future environment analysis. This is very subject to error. The task requires a look into the crystal ball on four levels:

- Predict changes possible? These can be listed as follows:
    - A national authority is required to handle funding for regional as well as national universities.
    - There are a growing number of universities.
    - There is an increasing need for good planning information, e.g. sophisticated budgetary information (fiscal planning).
    - There is an increasing student population.

All the above factors produce a growing pressure on any incoming system in terms of disk space, processor speed, rapid response. Other future changes might include:

    - Political uncertainty (general election imminent).

– Danger of loss of skilled staff to the private sector.
– **UNIX** minicomputer system.

The above seems to indicate extreme flexibility and volatility of this situation. The analysis can be closed by stating that the net result is to indicate a situation of rapid change potential skills shortage and high uncertainty. In the light of this it should be recognized that any incoming system is initially (at least) vulnerable.

• What is the likely outcome of the proposed system in the workplace? Our initial survey indicates:
  – Increased information for planning.
  – Increased timeliness of information.
  – Increased access to key information.

Therefore, the opportunity exists for either increased efficiency or for institutional paranoia! This worry (created by most new systems) is most likely to be felt in the financial area. In particular there is evidence that conflict may well arise between university financial managers and academic planners vying for the same information for decision autonomy.

• What aspects of the new system are most likely to change first?

On the positive side:
  – The information demanded will develop and grow in complexity.
  – Managers will become increasingly reliant upon rapid information to support decision making.

But, on the negative side:
  – Information systems will increasingly be seen as having to be computer based.
  – Computer-based statistics may be trusted without due care of data validation or verification.
  – Redundancy of the hardware and software.
  – Uneven national development between universities.

• What is the long-term extent of the system?
There is considerable interest and enthusiasm among the more technically literate for a wide area network (**WAN**).

The second task was to set out the social and technical objectives of the system. Briefly we give these as follows:

Social objectives
An improved information service (emphasis on the idea of service)
Improved professionalism in the university sector as a result of MIS
Improved funding choices for universities

Technical objectives

More accurate information, more rapidly
Internal self-sufficiency in maintenance
Initial system viable for future growth

The resulting social and technical alternatives are set out in a preliminary fashion as follows:

Social alternatives

Train internal staff – S1
Train internal staff and employ new – S2
Employ new trained staff – S3
Use contract workers plus internal – S4

Technical alternatives

Standalone **DOS** systems – T1
Ethernet network – T2
UNIX system with DOS applications – T3
UNIX system – T4

The next task was to rank the alternatives. As a rule of thumb in situations where there is very little time to carry out a detailed analysis (e.g. cost/benefit analysis of each alternative), we assume a scale of 1 to 9, where 1 is very good and 9 is very poor. The ranking covers the analysis team's perceived understanding of how each alternative scores in terms of its costs, resources available and constraints within the system (see Table 7.4). Usually all the details for each alternative are argued out. Here we deal only with the details of the top three alternatives. It should be remembered that the analysis is taking place against the background of our earlier future analysis. This assumes certain long-term trends which make simple, single user systems on DOS very redundant in the longer term. The analysis should ideally be carried out for the short, medium and long term. Here we are assuming certain long-term trends identified in the futures analysis will remain but we are focusing on the medium term.

These labels hold true where:

Social costs = introducing new staff, learning new skills, fitting in, etc.

Technical costs = learning new systems, supporting new systems, redundancy of old systems, replacement costs, etc.

Social resources = high levels of awareness, low number of skilled staff, high reluctance, etc.

Technical resources = existing equipment, existing software skills, no existing equipment, etc.

Social constraints = acceptable work practices, managerial support, etc.

Technical constraints = long-term viability, organizational capabilities.

TABLE 7.4 *Alternatives ranking*

Alternatives	Social costs	Technical costs	Social resources	Technical resources	Social constraints	Technical constraints	Totals
S1 T1	**2**	**7**	**3**	**3**	**3**	**9**	**27**
S1 T2	6	8	7	8	6	7	42
S1 T3	6	8	6	8	6	6	40
S1 T4	9	8	8	8	8	8	49
S2 T1	**4**	**7**	**4**	**5**	**3**	**8**	**31**
S2 T2	5	6	5	6	3	5	32
S2 T3	**5**	**6**	**5**	**6**	**5**	**4**	**31**
S2 T4	6	9	8	7	5	3	38
S3 T1	7	7	7	2	7	6	36
S3 T2	7	6	7	4	7	4	35
S3 T3	7	7	7	7	7	3	38
S3 T4	7	9	8	7	7	3	41
S4 T1	9	6	9	2	8	6	40
S4 T2	9	6	8	4	8	4	39
S4 T3	9	7	8	5	8	2	39
S4 T4	9	9	9	7	8	3	45

The analysis, however imperfect and subjective, indicates three options which fit one total implementation pattern given the future analysis. The pattern is as follows:

- S1 T1 which leads to:
- S2 T1 which leads to:
- S2 T3

This might be seen as constituting a development plan:

S1T1 – Initially the system comprises internal staff using standalone computers. This is low risk in terms of investment and discouraging staff. The situation changes when staff have been made familiar with MIS concepts on the new equipment by bringing in new, trained staff ready to adapt to the third phase. S2T1 – The second phase can be seen as a period in which existing staff and new staff get to work together. S2T3 – Phase three brings in the UNIX network but using, in the early stages at least, existing DOS applications. The new staff should have some UNIX awareness and this will hopefully be transferred to existing staff. In the long term there is the capacity to upgrade to a full UNIX system.

Having selected a development path we can go on to set out the computer systems and human systems

Human tasks

The incoming MIS requires the development of a range of skills including:

1. System needs
    (i)   network management
    (ii) system management (system security, hardware maintenance)
    (iii) computer hardware architecture
    (iv) database design
2. Management needs
    (i)   project management
    (ii) analysis and design
    (iii) project implementation
    (iv) monitoring and evaluation
    (v)   principles of data collection, validation and verification
3. Operational needs
    (i)   supervisory
    (ii) keyboard entry

Some of these items are already in evidence. Training will need to reflect these areas. In particular each computer unit will require:

- A computer unit manager to deal with day-to-day running of the system.
- A computer unit technician to deal with preventative and corrective maintenance.
- Several clerks for data input. There will be a seasonal fluctuation in this activity and at times the team believes there will be a considerable flow of data for the system.
- Ideally each unit should also possess a systems analysts and a programmer to make alterations and pursue software problems as they arise.

Computer tasks

Any incoming system will have to deal with some considerable number of records. The database forms which the team has been shown are quite large and some considerable storage will be needed in order for data analysis to take place comfortably. Any incoming computer system will need to be able to cope with entities of 50 to 60 fields, possibly related to several other entities at the same time, potentially containing thousands of records. The success of the system will depend upon the effectiveness of the training in the short run to allow the development path to progress as described.

7.8   Conclusions

The example set out in section 7.7 is taken from an analysis and design team's notes. There are various points that it and the previous sections of the chapter demonstrate and which we would like to express in general conclusions.

- At this stage the analysis and design team do not need a detailed knowledge of the technology. This can be sorted out later on either by the team making use of the numerous trade magazines or with the assistance of computer sales companies (more on how to deal with these characters later on in Chapter 10).
- The alternatives can be arranged in any type of order. Analysis will be subjective and no doubt different stakeholders and members of the team will have different preferences at this stage. The ranking of the alternatives provides the opportunity to set out in a more democratic fashion those alternatives that are more or less appropriate.
- Always bring the stakeholders into this stage of the analysis. You will need to explain and justify the socio-technical combination that you finally recommend.

The end of the stage should be a clear and agreed overview of the technology and social requirements for the system in question. This provides the third 'view' of the system. In the HAS stage we perceived the needs for the system and set out its main components. In the information modelling stage we worked on the data and the information which such a system will work with. In this third stage we have set out the technology we will use and the social requirements. Following this stage, depending upon the path you are using you are either ready to go onto the human–computer interface or technical subsystems (For further reviews of how socio-technical systems analysis and design can be undertaken see Avison and Wood-Harper (1990) and Bell (1996).)

7.9   Exercise

We have outlined the development of the social and technical systems that will make up our final system. Your task is to do the same.

First, working from the example you have to date, set out the range of social and technical alternatives that will meet the information system you have modelled. Remember your terms of reference and your budget. Then, work your way through the analysis. Give reasons for arriving at your conclusions.

Some hints. One way of simplifying the social and technical objectives outline is to set out some of the larger social objectives (as first set out in the CATWOE stage of the HAS) and set against each the related technical objectives, e.g.

Social objective	Related technical objectives
Improve planning	Technical skills
	Automated features
	Networking decision making

The alternatives arising from the objectives might be fairly standard (e.g. ranging from retraining staff to adding new staff on the social side, and manual to networked PCs on the technical).

Resulting ranking is probably best carried out by using the table method – comparing costs, constraints and resources. It would be best to set out all the details of the table here. When you have finished compare your answer to those set out in Appendix C.

References and further reading

(In the area of socio-technical systems, the authors would like to draw the reader's attention to the work of Mumford. There are numerous references but these are particularly helpful: Mumford, 1979; Mumford and Weir, 1979; Mumford, 1981a; Mumford, 1981b; Mumford, 1983; Mumford, 1985; Mumford, 1986; Mumford, 1996; Mumford, 1997.)

Avison, D.E. and Wood-Harper, A.T. (1990). *Multiview: An Exploration in Information Systems Development*. Maidenhead: McGraw-Hill.

Bell, S. (1996). *Learning with Information Systems: Learning Cycles in Information Systems Development*. London: Routledge.

Land, F. (1982). Adapting to changing user requirements. Information and Management, **5**, 59–75.

Land, F. (1987). Is an information theory enough? In D. Avison (ed.) *Information Systems in the 1990s: Book 1 – Concepts and Methodologies*. Armidale NSW: AFM Exploratory Series No. 16, University of New England, 67–76.

Mumford, E. (1979). *A Participative Approach to Computer Systems Design*. Associated Business Press.

Mumford, E. (1981a). Participative system design: structure and method, systems, objectives. *Solutions*, **1**(1), 5–19.

Mumford, E. (1981b). *Values, Technology and Work*. Martinus Nijhoff.

Mumford, E. (1983). *Designing Human Systems*. Manchester: Manchester Business School.

Mumford, E. (1985). *Research Methods in Information Systems*. Amsterdam: North Holland.

Mumford, E. (1986). *Using Computers for Business*. Manchester: Manchester Business School.

Mumford, E. (1995). *Effective Requirements Analysis and Systems Design: The ETHICS Method*. Basingstoke: Macmillan.

Mumford, E. (1996). Risky ideas in the risk society. *Journal of Information Technology*, 11, 321–331.

Mumford, E. (1997). Requirments analysis for information systems: the QUICK ethics approach. In A. Stowell, R. Ison and R. Armson (eds), *Systems for Sustainability: People, Organizations and Environments*. London: Plenum, 15–20.

Mumford, E. and Weir, M. (1979). *Computer Systems in Work Design* – The ETHICS Method. Associated Business Press.

Chapter 8

THE HUMAN–COMPUTER INTERFACE

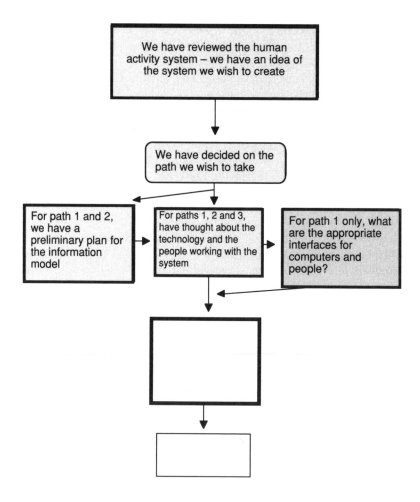

FIGURE 8.1 *Where are we in the process? The fourth stage of the rapid planning methodology*

Keywords:

technical interface, social interface, security interface, design procedure, priority access.

Summary:

It is essential that the user be able to work and communicate effectively with the computer. This chapter works out some of the details of the tasks that were discussed in the previous chapter. Various potential problem areas are reviewed including work styles, sources of discontent in terms of new work practice, **dialogue systems** (the way in which computers communicate with users) and the security of different user groups. Security can be seen as a way of protecting the system from the user as well as a means of safeguarding valuable and sensitive information.

8.1   Introduction to the human–computer interface

If you are using this book to assist you in analysis and design as set out in Chapter 4 you will have arrived at the human–computer interface following the three previous stages of human activity system, information modelling and socio-technical system design. By this stage you may feel that there is still more you don't know rather than do know concerning the information system that you are planning. One thing you must be clear about by now, however, is whether the system that you are planning will contain computers. If the system does not require a computer system, this stage still has value in terms of thinking about the interface that your manual system will have but the focus and detail of your work will be different. If you have decided that computers will be required then this stage provides you with insights into effective design. We assume that you have a fairly clear understanding of the tasks which the computer and the various users in the system are going to undertake. We do assume that you know that the computer systems are going to communicate to users and that users will need to be assisted in what can appear to be an unequal struggle. Our next job is to:

- explain what an interface is
- look at the principles of good interface design
- review examples of design.

The human–computer interface refers to the environment in which the user and the hardware come together to perform the information system operations. The range of functions that can be carried out include:

- the input of data

- checking data for errors
- making enquiries concerning information items
- producing reports at certain events (remember our information modelling?)
- management, security and monitoring.

However, the manner in which these tasks take place and the social implications involved in different work practices need to be understood if the system is to work well. Key issues pertaining to work practice should have already been described in the human activity system stage in Chapter 5. If they were significant they will have also been structured in terms of alternatives in the socio-technical stage in Chapter 7. Quality of work life is an important aspect of the total design. The interface set up here needs to provide end users not only with a technically sound system but also with a work situation that maximizes work interest at the same time as minimizing the negative aspects of technology (e.g. the potential for deskilling and reducing job satisfaction).

Therefore, when dealing with the human–computer interface we are dealing with a wide range of issues, such as those set out in Figure 8.2.

Always keep in mind one golden rule, you are thinking about information systems for users not for computer experts. If your system is to be used it has to be not so much 'friendly' as recognizable and useful to those who are going to use it. This may seem a simple idea but it is one which appears to be profoundly illusive to 80 per cent of those involved in information systems planning.

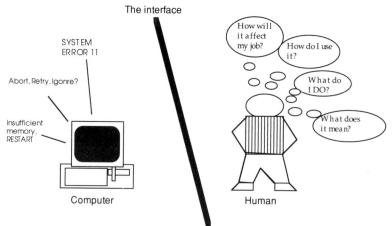

Task - to bring together the two parts of an unequal struggle

FIGURE 8.2   *The interface and the two parts of the struggle*

The contribution that this stage can make to a learning organization is set out in Table 8.1.

TABLE 8.1   *The learning organization and the human–computer interface*

Discipline	Value in human–computer interface thinking	Outcome?
Systems thinking	The challenge of this stage is to keep the vision of the whole despite needing to focus on very specific issues. The manner in which we address a number of different views of the interface should encourage a holistic overview	Interfaces that are designed with the organization as a whole in mind while providing for the needs of groups and individuals
Personal mastery	This mastery will now extend to the way in which technology and humanity interface with each other	Systems that people can feel in charge of. Sharing the ownership of the system
Mental models	Each interface must be modelled and tested in the organization context	Clear boundaries assigned to each level of the interface
Shared vision	As with the previous stage, stakeholders are encouraged into this stage – the interfaces have to be 'theirs', they have to drive the creative element of this stage	An agreed and participatory vision of the system
Team learning	The team learning of this stage is often within the context of worries and concerns of workers and users with technology. The learning is often related to understanding that apparently benign systems can be very worrying to those who do not share in their vision and creation	Insight into the organization and its use of technology

8.2   The nature of the interface

At root the computer has to be able to deal with any of the range of tasks which have been identified in Chapter 7 and give a response which is understandable and useful. For this to occur smoothly the designer must plan around the three major interface aspects of computer systems:

- Keyboards and computer **mice** are used for handling all aspects of data input and manipulation.

- Monitors in many forms (different resolutions, different sizes, flat and conventional) are for the display of information and data. The first device for output from the computer.
- Printers and plotters for **hard copy** of reports, etc. The second output device from the computer.

Depending upon your situation (e.g. the capacity of your organization to fund information technology related work, the skills of colleagues, the extent of the system that you are planning, etc.) you will require support in the development of the interface. Usually programmers would set up the nuts and bolts of the interface mechanisms. These mechanisms are designed in outline by the analyst in an interactive process with the range of ultimate end users of the proposed system. As we have already indicated the object of the analysis is to bring together two apparently contradictory and divergent themes:

- To provide the computer with clear, concise and unambiguous data and commands, and yet
- Provide the wide range of different users with appropriate interfaces which, while being clear and unambiguous, are also 'friendly' (or at least not hostile) and provide facilities for dealing with mistakes and accidental entries as well as the correct ones.

The latter theme involves the second, social, aspect of our system. In outline this means the way in which we deal with the potential problems arising from what is often seen as a confrontation between the users and the computer. One starting point is to look at existing communication forms (standard data collection forms, reports, etc.) within the organization and attempt to copy those that are most appropriate. The purpose of the exercise is to allow the user and the computer to 'understand each other'. To make this possible from the user's point of view we will need to try to facilitate understanding of what is going on inside the 'box'. Much initial user training is often required in this area.

8.3   Some interfaces

8.3.1   The technical interface

Information systems can only be flexible up to a point. Despite the fact that in recent years the technical interface has been 'humanized' with the advent of graphic interfaces (first on the Apple Macintosh and then more recently with Windows on the PC) and computers with speech recognition facilities, it is not possible to have a system which can be adaptive to any type of user that happens to come along. However, this level of flexibility is not usually required. The team designing the information system will normally be involved in looking at certain types of user, their basic requirements and then trying to match (by a process of interaction and participation) the right interface for the right user.

It is not difficult to think of examples. Data entry staff, will probably have very specific, fixed needs from an incoming system. They will generally be familiar with existing manual input too (registers, ledgers, etc.). The basics of these operations should be well known and so our interfaces can be matched to what is already understood. Researchers, managers or planners on the other hand are likely to want to talk about targets, aggregates, trends, etc. They will probably want to be able to manipulate large volumes of data quickly and may well be uncomfortable using limited interfaces. The sorts of interfaces you plan for these different categories of staff ought to reflect those differences.

THINK POINT

Before going on, if you were setting out the specification for an interface for managers, clerical staff and information users what sort of things do you think would be important to include in the introductory screen? Similarly, what do you think you would need to avoid at all costs?

Figure 8.3 shows a representation of the initial monitor input screen to a management information system. As you can see there are three key options – clerical, managerial or MIS products. Put yourself in the position of the users of this system. Three broad bands have been planned for:

- clerical workers inputting data
- managers for controlling the system
- information consumers needing to know things.

Clear and easy to understand? Maybe but complaints about this type of interface include:

- General – too vague. Users would like to know more about what option they want. 'Tell us what to do and where we ought to go next!'
- Clerical comments – generally OK but, 'not what we are used to'.
- Managers' comments – resentment about sharing a system, would rather be physically unconnected to the clerical and information

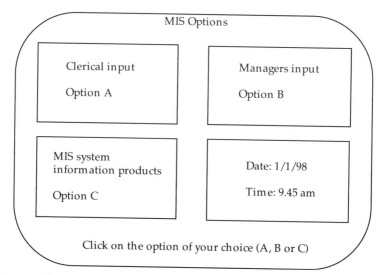

FIGURE 8.3 *An example of an introductory screen to an MIS*

product aspects, need less guidance and menus and more control.
- Information users – the system throughout gave information that was pre-planned, there should be less 'patronizing' menus and more capacity for users to formulate questions.

Some of these comments go outside the scope of this single menu display but it does go to show that even a simple introductory menu can have problems. One attempt to improve the system is shown in Figure 8.4.

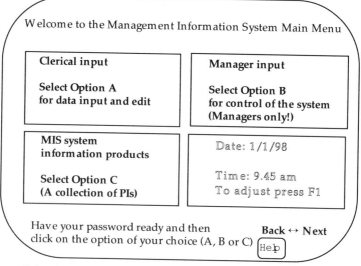

FIGURE 8.4 *An example of an improved introductory screen to an MIS*

The main criticism of Figure 8.4 is that the designer had gone too far! This screen is too busy, too full. It tries to say too much and still does not segregate out manager from clerical functions or really tell users what to expect from decisions. Possibly a better approach would be to start off by asking each user if they want one of the three options as shown in Figure 8.5, and then proceeding with the relevant options for each group.

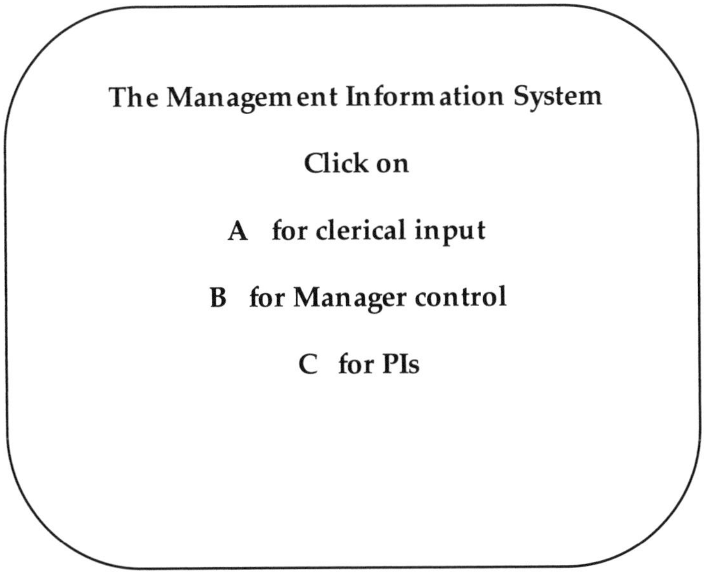

The Management Information System

Click on

A for clerical input

B for Manager control

C for PIs

FIGURE 8.5   *Yet another example of an improved introductory screen to an MIS*

However, variations in what users require from the interface should be seen as only part of the dynamic operating between the two aspects (human and technical) of the proposed working system.

8.3.2 Social issues

Automation will tend to radically change the nature of work itself often concentrating decision making in the hands of a few managers while simplifying work procedures for other groups. Willcocks and Mason (1987) have attempted to structure the impact of technology on jobs by use of a matrix. We develop a version of this matrix in Figure 8.6.

The matrix demonstrates the manner in which a variety of jobs can lose skill content because of higher levels of automation (the assumption being in this case that cleverer computers and systems are taking the place of an existing installation).

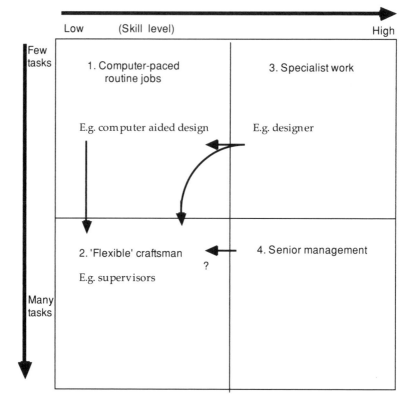

FIGURE 8.6   *IT and work (adapted from Willcocks and Mason, 1987, pp. 94, 96)*

AUTHORS' ASIDE

Anecdotally, and as also shown by Wilcocks and Mason, from our own experience we might argue that the reverse 'flow' is also possible in certain cases (see Figure 8.7).

Therefore, individuals can make use of incoming technology to improve their situation within the organization. Whether information systems can lead to job expansion or contraction the overall need is for the social impact of computer systems to be understood prior to installation. Willcocks and Mason (1987; pp. 94–95) argue that a series of implications follow automation when this is related to a 'scientific management-based approach':

• The division of mental and manual tasks

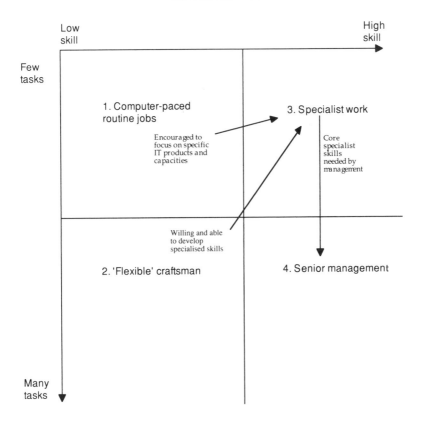

FIGURE 8.7   *Alternative impacts of IT on work?*

- Maximization of specialization in skills
- Minimize skill requirement
- Minimizing training and learning time
- Achieving full work-load
- Minimizing variety of work
- Creating short-cycle, repetitive jobs.

To determine whether all or part of this list of implications occur requires the analyst to consider the human–computer interface in terms of job interest and job content. There are a number of strategies which can be adopted so that deskilled work and relatively dull computer work can be improved. These include such approaches as:

- Goal-orientated working procedure – whereby the staff are given a sequence of short-, mid- and long-term goals to enhance job interest.
- Working teams – to share a series of low interest tasks.

- Vertical work groups – to distribute a range of working procedures around a group, rotating the higher value tasks to encourage interest.

The design of the social interface will usually require the analysis and design team to think about what the information system will mean to the end users and what strategies might be best considered to deal with potential problems. We shall return to this in section 8.5.

8.3.3   Security

The final interface issue we deal with here is that of security and the issue of user exclusion from certain aspects of the automated system. The issue of exclusion arises because *an inexperienced, unauthorized or malicious user allowed free access to a computer-based information system can cause intentional, wilful or unintentional harm to that system.* Two apparently contradictory positions need to be reconciled:

- To allow users to make the most use of the system.
- To protect the system from the user and others (e.g. the global issue of piracy (Gold, 1997)).

This is dealt with in more depth in section 8.6.

Working on all three interfaces provide the analysis and design team with rich learning opportunities and further potential for understanding the way the people in the organization work with, and react to, technology.

8.4   Considering the technical interface

At this stage we are setting out the design of the overall system and should not be too concerned with implementation and the problems that may well arise at that stage. It is quite important that we feel free to design the 'right' system rather than the one that is most practical. The two things may be identical or it may be that we will need to gradually work towards the system that your team believes to be best.

The provision of information to users requires us to look at the manner of the dialogue that will take place. Willcocks and Mason (1987) suggested a range of methods for implementing dialogue. These methods are shown in Table 8.2. The table shows at least eight ways in which the technical interface between user and machine can be handled. It is quite possible to have several different interfaces for different types of user, for example in section

8.3.1 we identified three different system users – clerks, managers and information consumers. A single menu-based system was planned. Possibly a better system might have been to provide:

- clerks with the highly controlled menu system
- managers with natural language so that very precise commands can be given
- information consumers with a graphic interface.

TABLE 8.2   *Ways to implement dialogue between user and computer (adapted from Willcocks and Mason, 1987, p. 126)*

Item	Dialogue type	Meaning
1.	Form filling	Form displayed, blanks to be filled by user
2.	Menu list	A set of options displayed, user keys in choice
3.	Question and answer	Computer displays a range of questions
4.	Function keys	Multiple function keys, some programmable by users
5.	Natural language	Dialogue in the user's natural language
6.	Command language	Limited number of commands available
7.	Query language	User requests in specified language
8.	Graphic	Icons and symbols used to convey meaning

Each of these options requires separate programming and therefore designing and implementing this type of technical interface design will be quite costly.

The first point in any interface design exercise is to be sure that the analysis team have identified the range of users working in the system. In the case of the example shown in section 8.3.1 method 2 (menu system) was universally adopted despite the problems identified by the users. The reasoning behind this approach was that menu-driven systems are one of the *safest* methods, boxing users into limited options within the system. To get round potential problems with three user groups being supported by one system the menu system was supplemented with method 6 (command language) because there were a variety of user groups, each needing a distinct information product from the MIS.

Another point to keep in mind when selecting the right interface for the right user is that any specific operation will involve the system in a number of exchanges. For example to provide an administrator with staff information involves several different dialogue exchanges:

- a review of the staff/division listings
- determining whether a required individual is still employed
- confirmation of department
- confirmation of priority to look at sensitive material.

And this structure does not take into account the problems of accident, incomplete information listing, forgetting the staff member's registration number or incorrect spelling of his or her surname. Without becoming unnecessarily concerned the analyst must realize that the potential for errors to arise in any system are almost countless. Systems should be provided with facilities to deal with such issues as:

- incorrect initial data entry leading to problems with search and retrieval
- incorrect retrieval information
- insufficient data available for specific request.

At this stage it is worth noting where potential errors can enter the system (e.g. basic data entry by clerical workers), the types of expected error (e.g. misspelling, double entry), and the type of error checking that will be required (e.g. random checking of spelling – one record per 100, computer check of record to see if it already exists, etc.) and the action to be taken (e.g. prompt to edit).

8.4.1   The case example: specific issues

In the case of our government department there were a number of special items that had to be covered in our analysis. An initial concern was that almost all computer software is written in the English language. In our case although much of the internal information in the department is in English, much of the input and the output is produced in the local languages. Moreover, many of the junior staff have only a very limited grasp of English. However, following a further stage of analysis the team were satisfied that the system would mainly be used by senior staff who tended to work most closely with the English language and that the manual system would run side by side with the incoming system so the facility to support information integrity (in case of loss or damage) would be available from that manual system. The junior staff acting as operators on the incoming system would be selected in terms (partly) of their good grasp of English. So the team could design our dialogue working on the valid assumptions that:

- English is the language medium
- there will be various levels of interaction
- interfaces will need to be designed for each level.

The levels of user we identified were as follows:

- senior managers
- computer unit staff
- clerical staff.

The next problem was to set out the principles of the user interface most appropriate to each user level. Computers tend not to be too friendly in this area. For example one very standard microcomputer system on sale throughout the world would give you the following message if there was a problem with the computer system:

```
Abort, Retry, Ignore?
```

This is not a very informative message. Today things are improving but basic systems still come up with messages such as:

```
Error 11, RESTART
```

What is error 11? What will happen when the restart happens? The user does not know what the result of any particular action in the context of the problem will be. For the three groups in this case the team now need to think about the types of dialogue that will be most appropriate.

The senior managers   This group should not require a detailed knowledge of the system as such. They will require information 'summaries' upon which they can either formulate further enquiries or make decisions. With this brief in mind the team can specify a design for the interface to be used:

- menu driven
- access via code number
- summary screens of data
- urgent request facility.

Note the code number refers to the security of the system and the issuing of code numbers which are to be confidentially held by all users. We will be looking at this area in a little more depth in section 8.6.

AUTHORS' ASIDE

We will go through the details of this design stage by stage but it is useful to explain the basis of a menu-driven system. For most of the specialized work that will be carried out on the databases of information it will be possible to pre-write menus of commands from which the user can select a function. For example, on logging in, a senior manager might see something like Figure 8.8. In this case the manager is not required to know any more than which function he or she requires. This menu will lead to another and so on.

DEPARTMENT MIS

Choose your information source.

- The roads register
- The heavy equipment inventory
- The register of projects
- The accounting systems
- The administrative system
- The urgent requests system
- To quit the system

Click on your choice

FIGURE 8.8   *The manager's MIS menu*

Computer unit staff   This includes all the individuals who are working directly with the computer system in terms of its day-to-day running and operation. The group might include:

- the computer manager(s)
- computer advisers
- computer trainers
- computer operators
- computer technicians.

The group is diverse in terms of responsibilities and activities, however, for the purpose of our exercise we assume that they should not require sophisticated intermediary dialogue devices between them and the computer. There must be some form of priority system whereby junior or untrained staff cannot gain access to sensitive material (e.g. access to details concerning salary, etc.).

Clerical staff   This group is not included under the general heading of computer staff because they will usually be involved with the inputting of data from specific sections of the department and therefore are not under the direct control of the computer unit. It is the responsibility of this group to enter data into certain systems such as the employee database, the heavy equipment inventory, the accounts system, soils laboratory data, word-processing, databases, spreadsheets.

The reason why the analysis team chose in our example to delegate the work to discrete sections of the department is threefold. First it conforms to the overall methodology of user-driven systems that we outlined in Chapters 1–4. Secondly, the sections mentioned already run manual versions of these systems. Thirdly, the data in these bases may be sensitive and should not be widely known outside the confines of the section itself, senior management and computer management sections.

In your examples you may decide that there is good reason to keep all data input and edit operations initially under the control of a central data-processing unit. This may be appropriate in the early stages of implementation specifically if the system is quite new and does not build upon existing manual practices.

AUTHORS' ASIDE

If you do want to do this you might be overridden by offended section managers who see their prestige as threatened by the removal of certain even quite mundane activities to the new computer unit.

Clerical operators will require facilities from the computer such as:

- menu driven
- access via code number
- summary screens of certain limited types of data
- help facility
- urgent request facility.

This may look similar to that which we prescribed for senior management, however, this will not take the same form. The level of help will be of the same type but the clerk is only supposed to be inputting data initially and possibly editing selected data later. No other access to the files is provided. The urgent request facility will operate to allow the clerk to forward notification of potential errors to the computer manager.

8.5   Considering the social interface

We have already identified the probability that an incoming computer system will have a range of impacts on staff moral, job mobility and staff seniority. The system you are planning may lead to massive social upheaval in your organization. Not all change can be known in advance but a range of measures should be set out to ease the implementation of the new system.

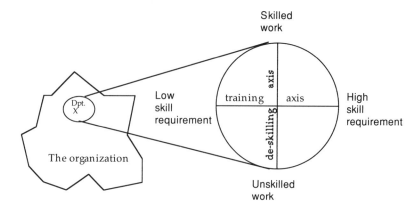

FIGURE 8.9   *Social issues – deskilling and underskilling*

There are many issues which the analysis and design team may need to confront but here we will focus on de-skilling and under-skilling (see Figure 8.9).

- Deskilling – the capacity of computers to reduce the expertise of an individual.
- Underskilling – the capacity of an organization to fail to recognize the importance of training existing staff in the use of computers.

As we see in Figure 8.9, the two forces can be seen as operating on linked axes. For each section of an organization which is adopting a new information system the planned system can be evaluated in terms of:

- The likely impacts on existing skilled staff in terms of deskilling.
- The need of the new system for existing staff to be trained in new areas.

Ideally any deskilling tendency should be countered by those staff being retrained in the new technology. This is not always possible.

8.5.1   The case example: specific issues

In our case the impact of the new system was generally seen as being positive. In the short term a certain amount of staff displacement would be encountered but this would run to no more than approximately four per cent of the total workforce. The perceived wisdom from meetings with stakeholders in the new system was that this level of disturbance was well within the tolerance level of the organization. Measures undertaken were as follows:

- Maximizing pre-installation briefings to provide workers with as much detail concerning the new system as possible prior to implementation (thus spreading understanding and ownership of the system at an early date).
- Detailed and long-term training inputs for all levels of staff. A core staff was identified which would be the focus of the new system. This core to be provided with relevant training and longer term outlines of potential future training.
- A degree of sensitivity to be agreed with senior managers concerning the displacement of existing staff. Sensitivity measures might include:
  - offers where possible to work with the new system
  - reallocation to other, similar departments
  - 'generous' redundancy.

8.6   Considering the security interface

We will look again at security measures for the system as a whole in the next chapter but for now we will focus on the essential work security of discreet user groups.

The focus for the interface is to balance usability with security. As Figure 8.10 shows in the form of a glass tube filled with fluid, it is very difficult to increase security without decreasing usability and vice versa. Sometimes, as systems become better protected they can become harder for users to gain access to.

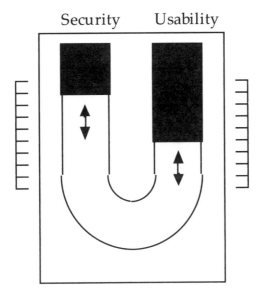

FIGURE 8.10   *Trade off between usability and security*

Therefore, the security that any one system requires will be a function of the level of hazard in the operational environment as assessed by you. If systems are locked in offices with physical access restricted to key staff then security within the interface can probably be quite slight. If, on the other hand, systems are in open office space where anyone can gain access then quite stringent interface procedures might be needed to protect the systems from casual access and/or abuse. 'Stringent interface procedures' generally imply password systems.

8.6.1   The case example: specific issues

In our case study we required a certain amount of security, although it was not thought necessary to physically lock computer systems away. When a manager first enters the system, the computer might inquire as shown in Figure 8.11. *This screen might protect, but it might also deter. Security is thus a compromise between safety and use.* The user will get no further unless his or her name and user code match up with those that the computer is expecting. If this is not so the potential user might, after several attempts, see something like Figure 8.12 – even if there is no monitoring procedure available at all! Often a severe message will put off most of the unwary. For example, most PC systems can easily be adapted to use basic menu systems. Also, many basic database packages come with menu systems available.

The code will also indicate the type of user (e.g. manager, technician or clerk). The summary screens of information will appear at the end of the process of working through the layers of menus. For example the senior manager may wish to see if a certain road project is running to schedule. He or she could select the roads

```
 WELCOME TO THE DEPARTMENT MIS

   Enter your user name: [                    ]

   Enter your user id:   [                    ]


   [Help]              [Back]       [Next]
```

Figure 8.11   *Entry screen*

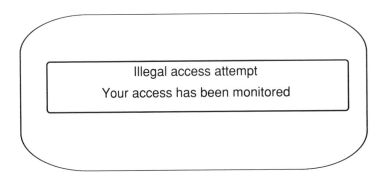

FIGURE 8.12   *Illegal access screen*

register in the first menu, within the roads register another menu would give details of the services available one of which might be:

INSPECT PRESENT PROGRESS?

Having selected this the computer would request details of the particular road by region, district and project and could then give the manager the most recent project report.

As a final note – the *urgent request facility* mentioned for managers refers to a method for diffusing potential frustration as well as providing the manager with a direct means of communicating, via the computer-based information system, with the people who run the computer. With this facility the manager can be provided with means whereby he or she can enquire about certain details which may be causing confusion and require further explanation. This could easily be expanded on most available computer networks to allow the user to send messages to other users of the system as well as to the computer staff.

8.7   Implementing the interface design

It is not usually the responsibility of the analyst to create databases and become involved in processes of database **debugging** although the analysis team may well find itself in this position. All we can suggest here is that if the team find themselves dealing with database set up/installation as well as analysis and design then read on to the database aspect in the next chapter; see the specific texts dealing with databases in the further reading section of Chapter 9; and follow all database manuals closely in terms of set-up procedures.

The analyst's brief normally runs to suggesting likely software packages which can carry out the types of operation as outlined in Chapters 3 and 4. In situations where computers are being brought into an environment for the first time there is often a degree of flexibility in the adoption of the results of the analysis, and often systems are designed at the point of contact in direct response to the user's wish – this type of approach is known as **prototyping**.

The interface can take quite some time to get right for all users but we feel that the major principles for interface design in the problem context can be outlined in five days.

Amount of time devoted to analysis so far:
Total for this stage (human–computer interface) = 5 days
Cumulative total for path 1 = 25 days
Cumulative total for path 2 = 20 days
Cumulative total for path 3 = 13 days

8.8   Conclusions

The interface as set out here has three major aspects:

• The technical interface – what is seen and how information is put in.
• The social interface – how the organization copes with new systems.
• The security interface – how systems are kept secure and at the same time used!

As with the previous chapters all recommendations in these areas are by way of rules of thumb for incoming systems. However, if these three areas are planned the final system has a much higher chance of success than might otherwise be the case.

8.9   Exercise

• Set out the range of impacts that your information system will have on the existing working relations within the company. Who will be deskilled, where may there be staff conflict?
• Set out a series of measures that you feel will satisfactorily deal with these conflicts.
• Set out the security procedures that you feel will be appropriate for the new system.

- Set out examples of ideal screen interfaces for your system.
- What measures would you plan to ensure reducing staff resistance to the new system?

When appropriate take a look at the model answer given in Appendix C.

References and further reading

(A good text on prototyping is CCTA, 1993.)
(Some texts of more general interest for the issues raised in this chapter are as follows: Korth and Silberschantz, 1986; Awad, 1988; Bush and Robbins, 1991; Wainright-Martin *et al.*, 1994; Avison and Fitzgerald, 1995; Bell and Minghze, 1995; Andreu and Ciborra, 1996; Bell, 1996; Yeoman *et al.*, 1996; Oz, 1993; Smith, 1997.)

Andreu, R. and Ciborra, C. (1996). Organizational learning and core capabilities development: the role of IT. *Strategic Information Systems*, **5**, 111–127.
Avison, D.E. and Fitzgerald, G. (1995). *Information Systems Development: Methodologies Techniques and Tools* (second edition). London: McGraw-Hill.
Awad, E.M. (1988). *Management Information Systems: Concepts, Structure and Applications*. Menlo Park: Benjamin Cummings.
Bell, S. (1996). Reflections on learning in information systems practice. *The Systemist*, 17(2), 54–63.
Bell, S. and Minghze, L. (1995). MIS and systems analysis applications in China: a case study of the Research Institute for Standards and Norms. In M. Odedra-Straub (ed.), *Global Information Technology and Socio-Economic Development*. Nashua: Ivy League, pp. 153–160.
Bush, C. and Robbins, S. (1991). What does 'MIS' really mean? *Journal of Systems Management*, June, 6–8.
CCTA (1993). *Prototyping in an SSADM Environment*. London: HMSO.
Gold, S. (1997). Global piracy continues to skyrocket. *Secure Computing*, June, pp. 5–6.
Korth, H. and Silberschantz, A. (1986). *Database System Concepts*. London: McGraw-Hill.
Oz, E. (1993). *Ethics for the Information Age*. London: McGraw-Hill.
Smith, A. (1997). Human–Computer Factors: *A Study of Users and Information Systems*. London: McGraw-Hill.

Wainright-Martin, E. *et al.* (1994). *Managing Information Technology: What Managers Need to Know.* New York: Macmillan.

Willcocks, L. and Mason, D. (1987). *Computerising Work.* London: Paradigm.

Yeoman, I. *et al.* (1996). Effective group knowledge elicitation through problem structuring methodologies. *Systemist*, **17**(2), 79–91.

Chapter 9

TECHNICAL ASPECTS – WHAT IS NEEDED?

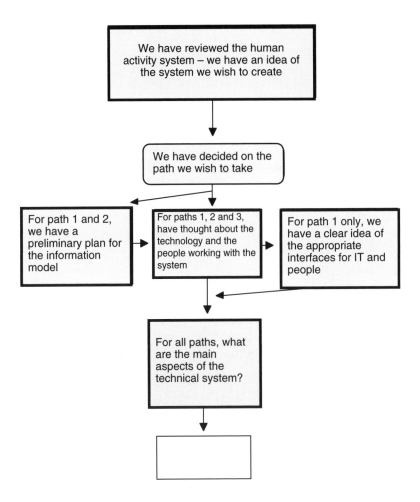

FIGURE 9.1   *Where are we in the process? The fifth stage of the rapid planning methodology*

Keywords:

technical aspects, applications, database, retrieval, maintenance, management, monitoring and evaluation (M&E).

Summary:

At this stage of the analysis we begin to design the various component parts that will make up the final information system – we gain a vision of the whole. The components that we deal with here concern the way information activities are coped with by the system, the database structure that contains information items, the production of reports and other output, the management and maintenance of the system and finally monitoring and evaluation.

9.1   Introduction

So far you will have undertaken one of three paths to arrive at the technical design stage. As an aid memoir take another look at Figure 4.6 (in Chapter 4). No matter which of the paths you have adopted you will arrive now at the stage of technical design (there is no escape!).

Technical design refers to the stage that is concerned with outlining and then combining key components of the information systems that can usefully be planned independently. The six areas that we will focus on here are:

- applications
- database
- retrieval
- management
- maintenance
- monitoring and evaluation.

The components link together to produce what we might refer to as a 'technically workable system' as seen in Figure 9.2. The figure shows that this stage is ideally based upon the results of previous stages, for example the application area is based upon events identified in Chapter 6, information modelling; the socio-technical system identified in Chapter 7 and the human–computer interface worked through in the previous chapter.

Before we look at each of the items in detail we can begin by discussing what each of the six areas actually involves (our interpretation here will be different to previous interpretations by other authors).

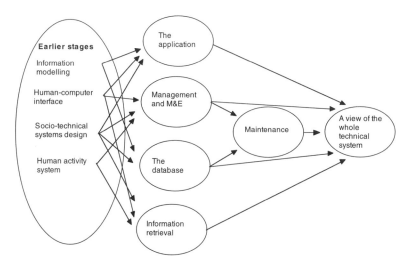

FIGURE 9.2   *The technical aspects – the 'whole' technical system (adapted from Avison and Wood-Harper, 1990, p. 200)*

AUTHORS' ASIDE

This raises a problem for teams who have taken paths two and three through the methodology. Will this stage be irrelevant for you? The human activity system reviewed in stage 1 and the socio-technical systems design are informative for all stages and provide some basis for all the six aspects. Even if you have taken the third, minimal path through the analysis and design procedure you will be able to make effective use of the rules of thumb which we apply in this stage of the design process.

Application   The application is the core aspect of the system that you are implementing – e.g. management information system, decision support system, geographic information system, accounting system, etc. The application is the 'to do' part of the system, it is all the functions that we wanted carried out on entities (if you undertook stage 2, information modelling) or at a higher level, it relates specifically to the transformation we set out in the human activity system. Generally this means that application refers to activity within the system to provide the information desired.

Database   The database is also central to the new information system. All information systems are centred on a database some-where or other. If you have taken paths 1 or 2 through this book you will have structured the basics of one or several databases already and you will be familiar with the ideas of 'entity' and 'attribute'. If you have taken path 3 then this may be a new idea. The database for your system will be the thing (or things) that store information that your application will work on to produce the key information prod-ucts (e.g. reports, etc.) as and when required. Going back to the human activity system stage, databases are implicit in the systems set out in the systems models.

Retrieval   The retrieval aspect is the component of the system that produces the information products be they maps, reports, perfor-mance indicators or whatever. These will have been indicated in several stages in the methodology so far.

Management   Management controls the overall system. It deals with security, backing up and all stages of activity within the system. Importantly, management also has the responsibility for maintaining user ownership and interest in the system and for being responsive to user initiatives for change. Management must *learn* as well as manage. Management is usually in overall control of both of the following areas.

Maintenance   This keeps the system going. Under the general title of maintenance we include the planning of preventative and corrective maintenance procedures.

Monitoring and evaluation   Central and often ignored or under-represented in information systems implementation, monitoring and evaluation will increase the odds that a working system stays working. Monitoring and evaluation, or M&E provides both man-agement and maintenance subsystems with vital information with regard to the overall health of the system. It is also the main tool that management has for learning and inducing participation in the ongoing system. Figure 9.3 sets out one hypothetical combination of these aspects.

Having introduced the area we will now go into the details of planning each of the six aspects and linking them in one overall schema ready for implementation. In terms of the learning organi-zation, this stage of the analysis and design process can enhance the development of learning in the ways shown in Table 9.1.

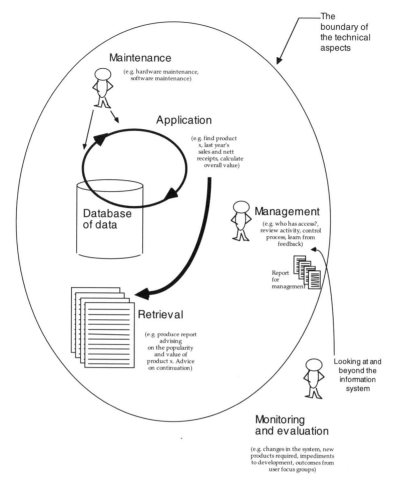

FIGURE 9.3   *The technical aspects*

THINK POINT

Take another look at the six aspects of this stage of the methodology. Now think about the information processing within your organization. Under the six headings can you set out some examples from your own context? Who is the manager? What is the application? How many databases? What is the form of retrieval? Who does the maintenance? Is there effective M&E?

In answering these questions you should quickly see that the six aspects can be applied rapidly as a means to think about the information systems you already have. To take the next step and apply them as mental leavers to think about the information systems you are planning should not be such a major step.

TABLE 9.1   *The learning organization and technical aspects*

Discipline	Value in technical aspects thinking	Outcome?
Systems thinking	The technical aspects are a technical system when combined. Here the team can develop a strong vision of boundary and (therefore) an understanding of what is in the system and what is outside	The clear demarcation of the new system boundary. If the team is going to submit this plan to a professional IS company at this stage, they should be sure of what they want the system to contain and do
Personal mastery	In our approach this stage deals with the user interface as a social, technical and security issue. Not only should the process of considering the 'humanization' of the information system be an empowering process for user and analysis team alike but also the result should be that the user will have a greater sense of control over the work environment	A real sense of individual and shared ownership over a complex technology
Mental models	Both analysis team and user community can gain valuable insights into what can often appear to be an information systems 'black box' if the stage is completed with discussion and participation	Consensus thinking about the roles of each technical aspect
Shared vision	The development of the M&E aspect should encourage the team to think about sharing learning, ownership, authority and responsibility among IS users	The beginning of procedures for 'bedding in' the information system with and by users (not imposing it on them)
Team learning	As above, the M&E stage helps the team to develop the view of extending ownership and learning throughout the organization	The organization becomes part of the team even as the analysis and design team is part of the organization

9.2   The application area – what we want to do

This element is concerned with the development of what the information system has to do, these are the 'transactions within the system'. One example of the outworking of this part of the process comes from Chapter 6. In the information modelling stage we suggested that activity could be set out, even at that early stage as a computer programme. If you are not familiar with this take a quick look at Figure 6.14 in Chapter 6, it will either serve to remind you or introduce the concept.

The figure shows the manner in which four performance indicators (PIs) are produced by a software package. The package does not interest us at this stage nor is it important to understand what is going on in detail. The important feature to recognize is that the PIs are the key information products that we want, the diagram shows what is required to generate each of these PIs and what information databases (or 'tables') need to be open to allow the applications to work effectively. PI1 produces information on full-time lecturers (FTL), PI2 on total allocatable lecturer contact hours, PI3 on lecturer contact hours and PI4 on full-time equivalent students.

If you have undertaken the work effectively a programmer could take your application outline and prototype (or using the rapid application development – RAD form of prototyping) a software structure that could do the job. Alternatively, a prewritten package, off-the-shelf, could be purchased and rapidly adapted to do the job required (e.g. the Sun Accounts package is used by numerous organizations as the key application in the accounts department or, ARC INFO is a geographic information system applied in numerous locations. Small contextual differences between organizations are not important when purchasing applications that have a general value).

AUTHORS' ASIDE

The previous paragraph demonstrates that this stage of the methodology can be used in at least two different ways:

- As a means to plan out the aspects of a new system which is to be written, as a one-off by a programmer or more usually,
- As a requirements list to be built into a specification for a software package already written. In this latter case the work during stage 4 on the HCI will also be important. The interface specification is already produced and should be developed as software is selected – more about this in Chapter 10 – software purchase.

The main skill to develop for this phase is to think through the applications sequentially and hierarchically, e.g. *How many applications do I have and what shall I call them?* Within the overall application of MIS I have:

- Application A – Product listing
- Application B – Relative product value in terms of return
- Application C – Best performers in the last x months

etc.

What does each application involve? Application A:

- open product database
- index the database on product name
- produce listing of products including present gross return for financial year
- print out listing.

This process can be developed to a high degree of detail if required. In this book we assume that the team will want to gain the overview.

9.2.1 The case study

For the department of roads the application of key concern was the roads register. For this register particular applications outlined were:

- Present cost status. This referred to the running cost of a particular section of road. The figures would need to be comparable between different regions.
- Amount of use. The physical amount of traffic that a specific road has to cope with.
- Environmental impact. What effect has road x had on the surrounding countryside. Details would need to be given in terms of specific indicators such as – physical factors (land slips, etc.), economic factors (economic inequality between different regions connected by the road(s), etc.), social factors (migrant labour in and out of region, etc.).
- Present maintenance status. The maintenance record of a road or section of road. Current tasks required to be undertaken.

Tasks for each of these applications were set out and agreed with stakeholders.

THINK POINT

For your own organization think again about the main applications. What is the main 'to do' element of any existing information system? If it is an MIS it is probably the bit of the system that produces the PIs or major information products. How might the application be improved in your view?

9.3   The database area – the data store

If the application is the centre of the system to the user, the database is the core to the computer people. Without it there can be no applications or reports. Although the database is central it can be quite simple to outline so long as you have a complete listing of all the information items that should comprise the final system. If you have undertaken information modelling you will have a list of entities and attributes that can be carried forward, if you did not complete that phase you will need to consider:

- What are the things that you want to keep information about? (registers, listings, people, contracts, etc.). These are entities.
- What are the main features of these entities? (for example a student register might contain – surname, first name, term address, home address, past marks, disciplinary records, etc.). These are attributes.

Rather like the applications area there is no great mystery concerning the expression of this stage, it requires you to think through what the major entities are and then give as complete a listing as possible of the attributes required, keeping in mind that this stage is intimately linked to the applications. The application aspect cannot undertake work if key attributes of key entities in the database subsystem are missing.

9.3.1   The case study

Continuing the theme from the applications subsystem, the major entity was agreed as being the roads register. Some of the working out of attributes was as follows:

Attributes for the roads register entity
Name of road
Date of construction
Personnel involved – engineers, overseers
Duration
Cost
Benefit as projected in original report
Source of finance – external, internal
Total quantities and costs of:
    cutting
    filling
    gravelling
    culverts
    bridges

Maintenance costs
Total cost to date
Current condition
Secondary developments along road (shops, camps, etc.)
Evidence of environmental degradation
   land slip
   pollution
etc.

THINK POINT

Can you set out 10 or so attributes (or fields) of one of the major databases in your organization's information system?

   Constructing and testing databases should not be trivialized and in this book we are careful to explain that we are seeking to gain understanding of new information systems in a rapid way for non-specialists – the view and the detail can always be developed and improved upon. However, non-specialists gain in understanding of IT-based systems if they have an understanding of what data is important to make this system work well.

   Of the 10 or so attributes which do you think are the most vital data items for the system to work well?

9.4   The retrieval area – what we want from the system

The retrieval area provides the team with the opportunity to:

- Structure the content of reports and other output.
- Agree the timing of reports and other output.
- Prepare the presentation of reports and other output.

   There will be key events when certain information products are required:

- end of the financial year
- enrolment of new staff
- completion of a project
- marketing of a new product.

   At these events information of certain types will be required. The form and presentation of the information is also important. One of the most powerful functions of modern computer-based information systems is that retrieval can be automatic and fairly effortless (from the point of view of the user anyway) if planned for. On the other hand, if a system has not been properly planned the production of reports can be almost as time consuming as undertaking the process manually. The retrieval area should link in closely with the application and database areas but can be planned as a separate function. The planning process requires the following action:

- Assess which reports are required. Make allowances for reports required at a given time (e.g. end of the financial year) and those which are required at any time (e.g. the current activity of staff in a design agency). List these reports and indicate when they are required.
- For each report set out key information which should be included. This can comprise a listing. When producing the list keep in mind the applications area. Applications should produce all the workings for these reports. There should never be a report or other retrieval operation without a link from an application. Similarly there should never be an application that does not produce, or combine to produce some form of report.
- When you are sure that your listing of all retrieval products is complete and that the content of each of these is similarly set out think about design. There are two golden rules in the design process:
  – clarity and simplicity
  – recognizability – resemblance to existing reports.

Reports can contain far too much information. Reports can be highly unstructured. For the clarity of a report it is advisable to work with an agreed template. A template is a structure that all reports in a given context will obey. For example a promotions record report taken from a personnel register might be as follows in template form:

Surname:

First name:

Home address:

Work address:

Grade:

Pay-roll number:

Last three promotions:

But, do you need to know sex and age? Does 'Work address' mean 'name of department'? What does 'Grade' mean. Does a promotions report need to contain details of the pay-roll number?

Certainly this form is short but will it tell a manager what he or she needs to know?

The retrieval system should be planned to provide information at a time and in a form that is useful. The caveat to this is the need to produce all designs in cooperation with the major stakeholders who are going to make use of the reports.

THINK POINT

Think about the kinds of reports that you get in your organization. Are any of them computer generated? Could any of them that are not so generated be so? What do you get from reports that you do not need? What do you not get which you could usefully apply? In the university sector we get lots of information but it is often not digestible. A pile of print outs is no substitute for one well-produced pie graph.

9.4.1   The case study

Following discussions with the major users of the applications it was decided that existing report forms would be copied and reproduced by the system. There was a certain degree of inflexibility concerning reporting. The computer-based information system was seen largely as a way of speeding up the existing process, the range of new options in terms of reporting was largely ignored and/or not seen as being important. This is a situation that occurs quite regularly. A popular response to this is to design reports around the existing documents but to leave provision in the system for change and further development. Most software packages allow the user to continually add reports.

9.5   The management area – how to control the system

Management covers a wide variety of issues (see Figure 9.4) for our purposes we will focus on:

- Controlling the information system with an operating system.
- Job priority control – what to do and when (issues of continuous workload and seasonal workload).
- Security – access, debugging and backup.
- User support – including mutual learning.

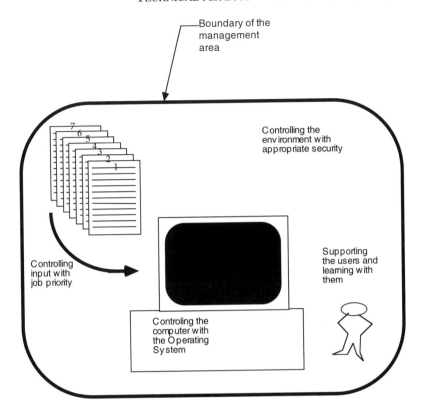

FIGURE 9.4   *Management issues*

9.5.1   Controlling your system with the operating system

This section will not teach the use of the operating system. The object is to point at needs for good management and suggest ways to achieve these needs.

Inevitably understanding the operating system is the bottom line for good management of the hardware and software. Yet training in the use and control of operating systems is a component left off many training schedules. This is a point worth noting and carrying forward to your plan of training needs at the time of implementation. The operating system allows the user to:

- Control the computer itself effectively
  - understand **error messages**
  - **partition** hard disks
  - check disks for errors
  - control output
- Handle software properly

- **install software**
- **backup files**
- **backup disks**.

Although the operating system can be laborious and difficult (in fact it can often be the source of many problems for new and old users alike) it is essential if your system is to work effectively. What problems can arise without it?

- Computer error
  - overloaded **hard disks**
  - **fragmented files**
  - **lost clusters**
- Software error
  - incorrectly installed
  - incorrect screen/printer driver
  - **software/hardware mismatch**
- User error
  - files lost – no backup
  - disks lost – no backup
- Cost
  - unnecessary use of potentially expensive outside agencies
  - lost time
  - lost work

Effective training or literature are the major means of avoiding problems. For most purposes a good book is good enough if you already have some experience. For the new manager – look to a good training programme to start off.

9.5.2   Job priority control

That is – what to do and when (issues of continuous workload and seasonal workload). Priority is often a balance between four factors:

- the job being done
- staff seniority (more senior staff tend to expect quick access)
- limited computer time available
- computer frailty.

These four factors can be balanced by the following rule of thumb method:

- Arrive at an agreed working day for the machines. A standard applied in many locations is 16 hours/day.
- Review all existing work. Assess for seniority of demand in terms of: seasonal cycles of work, continuous workload and freak loads.

AUTHORS' ASIDE

Seasonal work (e.g. annual accounts) cannot be moved around. There is need to schedule computer availability for key times of the year. Continuous workload such as order entering, inventory updating, etc. can be slotted in on a more casual basis. Freak loads cannot be planned for. This is the percentage of time that you build in to deal with unexpected eventualities. One way of dealing with this is to make public that the computers are available for 12 hours/day and to hold the extra 4 hours as a buffer against need.

When you have assessed the workload produce weekly, monthly and annual schedules indicating on and off computer times. Most importantly, circulate the schedule with a note indicating the need for discussion and agreement on your plan. It is best if the schedule is known by all users (even if they do not all agree with it). Once agreed, an annual review is useful but otherwise – never deviate! It is always a good idea to hold back some computer time in the event of emergencies. This should be time that you do not mind seeing the computer being used but is generally not available for the user.

9.5.3   Security

A most important aspect which includes access, debugging and backup. As we indicated in the last chapter when dealing with software security at the level of the user interface, as you improve access, so you can loose control! Loss of control of the system is to be avoided at all costs. As you increase control so the user has less and less access! This is also highly undesirable. Most security involves us in coping with a paradox.

The individual manager sets his or her own balance. Three major aspects of security are hardware safety, software safety and user safety.

Hardware safety

Computer rooms need to be protected from a variety of enemies including:

Excesses in climate   Climate is of particular importance. Hot, dry, dusty spells in rooms with no air conditioning can be fatal to micro-

188 RAPID INFORMATION SYSTEMS DEVELOPMENT

computers. Humidity can be a danger. Basic precautions include the following:

- Rooms with many PCs in them should have doors that make a good seal. An anti-room is a good idea.
- Air-conditioning in computer rooms removes problems of over-heating. Keeping blinds and windows closed is an even cheaper option.
- For very sensitive equipment ensure that air-conditioning provides a positive air pressure so that air will rush out of the room if a door is opened.
- Carpets on the floor remove dust from the atmosphere. But care needs to be taken when vacuum cleaning the carpet.
- During very humid periods, moisture extractors can be fitted in the room.

Power supply   This refers to irregularities in power supply and its criticalness will depend upon firstly your location and secondly the sensitivity of your equipment. Some software is very prone to problems with power supply cuts, for example some database software will corrupt files if they are open when the power goes down. Obviously you must assess your own risk but there are three levels of protection you can apply:

- Total – an independent generator designed to cut in when the mains supply goes down.
- UPS or Uninterruptible Power Supply, these are battery based and will guarantee you 30 minutes or more work time after power goes down.
- Voltage stabiliser – this will regulate any peaks and troughs in your supply. If you are in doubt, get an electrician in to check on your supply.

Theft   Local conditions will again prevail, but unfortunately hardware and software are attractive to thieves. Levels of protection include:

- Situation of the computer room on the second floor of the building.
- Electronic burglary devices.
- Bars on windows.
- Security staff.
- Searching of staff on entering and leaving the work rooms.
- Access to key holder only.
- Securing all computers and peripherals to desk surfaces.
- Providing user identity disks.

Accidents   By their nature these are difficult to plan for. The computer manager should get to know the level of risk in the environment. Some of the favourite items to guard against include:

- Tea and coffee being used to irrigate computer systems!
- Disks being erased.
- Keyboards being dropped on the floor.
- Keyboard being hammered by over enthusiastic typists!
- Computers being left on overnight.

Most of these items are dealt with if the manager obeys some basic systems maintenance disciplines:

- Ensure that all operational staff know what they are supposed to be doing and are kept up to date with systems development. This means that staff training and workshops for users to discuss problems and learning areas should be continual.
- Ensure that all software is copied and protected prior to release. Copies of software should be periodically examined for corruption.
- Ensure that all hardware is kept in a good state of repair. Measures to provide for this include monthly checking for keyboard failure, **screen burn**, **drive alignment** and general trouble-free operation.

Servicing (annual)   Be careful in your selection of agency! Many servicing agencies are not all that they seem to be. It is worth getting a number of quotations for work and then taking a look at the servicing department of the short-listed companies.

Software safety

We have already mentioned keeping the software in a state of physical safety in terms of regular backing up. Another issue is that of selecting software which offers a clear upgrade path. Often it is difficult to see if software products will still be around in several years' time. The best indicator is to go for products that are well supported and have a strong existing customer base. This will be an item that will attract growing attention as software continues to grow as a percentage of the total cost of an information system. Two other items arise:

- Staff taking liberties. Bringing in their own software and working with it on office machines.
- Sabotage.

Both these items are hard to deal with. Physical protection includes vigilance of staff and threatening notices. Software protection includes the use of lockable keyboards and passwords. Some software does now come with software password control. Also packages can be purchased. These come with their own password protection which can be used to keep away the non-expert. But beware: on PCs there is no complete software protection as yet.

Another software threat comes from computer **viruses**. These are small software packages, written by people who either have nothing better to do with their time or who wish to disrupt computer processes. Viruses can attack any computer system and are transported onto systems (generally) in the form of copied software. Viruses are preventable if you do not copy software. If you get a virus there are quite a number of potential symptoms:

- The temporary interruption of key jobs. This appears to be a common problem. No sooner does an agency or department become dependent upon an information technology assisted system then the system becomes corrupted and ceases to function. The implications are particularly worrying where decisions are delayed in such critical areas as health care, agricultural planning and product profitability. Close to the root of this problem is the inability of manual practices to cope when the computer fails.
- The closing of information technology departments. Again this seems to be becoming increasingly regular. In one case an information technology department in a university was closed to students because it had just been cleared of viruses for the third time and staff did not want to have to go through it again!
- Unnecessary and expensive hardware replacement. Sometimes hardware is replaced mistakenly when the real fault lies with the software. On several occasions fixed disks have been replaced, and even thrown out when the real fault lay with a virus.
- Slow and/or faulty data presentation. Too often computer output is seen, by computer people it must be said, as being adequate in itself. Results of calculation are not checked effectively and the garbage which eventually comes out can be used, unknowingly in management decision making. With the proliferation of management information systems based on computers and the related spread of viruses decision making is threatened. One of the primary indications of the presence of many boot sector viruses is the slowing down of computer processes.
- Project failure. This is the bottom line. Computer facilities can produce tremendous value, they can also be the weak link that cause projects to fail partially or completely, in the short or long term. (Lots of examples of this but, for a cross-section of failures see Lyytinen and Hirschheim (1987), Bicknell (1993), Collins (1993), Sauer (1993), Collins (1996), Davies (1996), Dickinson (1996), Lambeth (1996), Schein (1996), Bicknell (1997), Collins (1997) and Kaye (1997).) Without efficient local data collection,

verification, validation, storage and processing the risk of some form of failure is increased. This is so with manual systems, the risk is even greater when systems are computerized.

What can we do? First and most important – effective management of information system facilities needs to be focused on. There is evidence that at present absolutely minimal attention is being focused on the management of resources. Secondly, culturally and politically sensitive analysis and design should precede all installation. Overly technical approaches to analysis and design produce admirable technical systems. These, however, often break down when put into the social context. Analysis and design needs to understand the context for information systems and recognize that information systems are social systems. Thirdly, planning should be central to precomputerization and manual systems can often be strengthened and run parallel with incoming information technology based systems. This is a matter of common sense. Any information system requires a degree of contingency planning to ensure that systems can be provided in the event of major breakdown.

User safety

We will deal with user support shortly. User safety is improved by:

- Priority access being in place. Users need to know when and how much access they have.
- Passwording in place. A hierarchical structure of passwords can be set up in most systems.
- Training is sufficient and maintained. Training schedules for all staff should be outlined. Users often have a better idea about what they need to know than computer 'experts'. We shall return to the need for a mutual listening and learning processes to be in place between users and IT staff.
- Unauthorized use is guarded against.

9.5.4 User support

User support as we deal with it here has four major themes: access, control, backup and feedback. We have already dealt with access.

Control

This includes:

- Control over unauthorized physical access.

- Control over unauthorized access to sensitive software.
- Control over access to other users' **workspace**.
- Control over user files. If the application which the user is working with is producing data for a third party and that data is critical for decision making (e.g. MIS information) then the user should be guided in appropriate security measures such as always working with copies of files and regular backing up of files.

User backup

The manager needs to provide:

- Supervision to hands-on users.
- Training in the use of new packages. This will probably mean at some time the computer unit will need to provide the users with a curriculum of training activities including basic introductory programmes, advanced programmes and programmes in specific applications. Further, training will need to be differentiated between basic operator skills, advanced operator skills and expert user skills.
- Regular updates on latest developments. This is a great way of keeping the curious happy, e.g. with a regular newsletter or a weekly/monthly bulletin.

User feedback

There is little point in providing users with support if there is no capacity for the user to provide the computer manager with feedback as to the success or otherwise of his or her endeavour. Throughout this book we have been focusing on the additional value which the analysis and design process and the subsequent information system implementation can provide an organization in terms of learning (about core business and organizational well being). The emplacement of learning mechanisms is vital if a new information system is not to fall foul of the types of problems that we identified in Chapter 1. To this end, useful facilities include:

- Regular team meetings – the team being defined as all 'users and suppliers of the system'. **Focus group** forums are a good mechanism for drawing out learning and problems.
- A regular, formal user committee attended by the manager.
- A well-advertised complaints procedure.

9.6   The maintenance area – keeping the system going

The lifetime of IT equipment is not a subject that encourages universal agreement. A computer committee might advocate seven years for minicomputer hardware, a microcomputer manufacturer might expect 18 months for the desk life of a fixed disk. Much will depend upon the wear and tear that the equipment receives and upon the level of maintenance provided. Generally speaking computer maintenance has two major components: *preventative* and *corrective*. Precise details of maintenance procedures can only be given when firm information is available concerning the location of the system and the type of hardware and software to be used. However, in practice we can set out the major requirements of preventative and corrective maintenance as shown in Figure 9.5.

9.6.1   Preventative maintenance

Taking as our theme the idea that all information systems are set up in situations of hazard, a preventative 'shell' is essential to provide

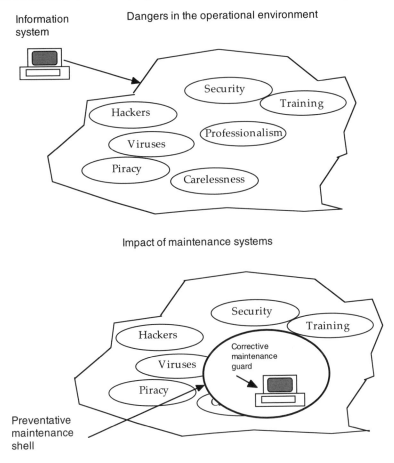

FIGURE 9.5   *Preventative and corrective maintenance*

the system with the bare chance of survival. Features of the shell might include:

- Daily supervision of the users – this includes the development of appropriate security measures set out in the management sub-system.
- Regular, quarterly servicing of all hardware.
- Annual servicing down to computer component level.

9.6.2 Corrective maintenance

Within the preventative shell some unexpected problems will arise. To deal with these problems rapidly and with minimum disruption to users a corrective 'guard' is useful. The guard might include the following aspects:

- In-house understanding of basic fault finding. Operators and supervisors can be trained in fault identification.
- In-house maintenance technician or a 24-hour call-out procedure agreed with a local maintenance company.
- Security procedures linked to monitoring and evaluation of key indicators (e.g. wear and tear on machines, incidence of disk theft, incidence of new, software appearing on machines).

9.7 The monitoring and evaluation area – learning about the system

The working system is never static: changes constantly occur. The way to plan for the events is to implement effective monitoring and evaluation (M&E). M&E in a project cycle can be seen in Figure 9.6. Monitoring and evaluation is our primary means for making sure that the system is producing the information users require when required and also that this is occurring at a cost that is proportional to the benefit. Although M&E is a detailed subject in its own right (see Further reading), there are at least three levels of rapid M&E that we can plan for in our rapid planning approach, namely rule of thumb. key indicator and logical frame-work.

9.7.1 Rule of thumb

Monitoring This comes before and complements the mainte-nance of the system. Monitoring should be constant and refers to the wear and tear on the computer facility as well as the opera-

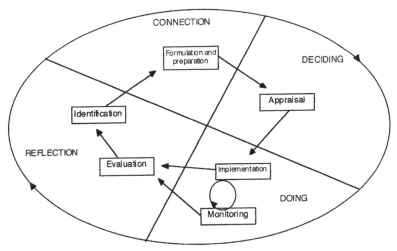

(Building off Kolb 1984; Coleman 1987)

FIGURE 9.6 *Monitoring and evaluation in a learning project context*

tional smoothness of its day-to-day running. Monitoring can take various forms:

- Informal periodic review of users within the context of focus groups.
- Formal analysis of user habits, e.g. a questionnaire dealing with assessment of time spent hands-on, assessment of good and bad habits such as typing skills, **login/logout** procedure, disk care, complaints concerning supervision.

All answers need to be carefully interpreted in the light of the obvious user biases.

Evaluation   This can be annual and can cover such aspects as:

- The general physical condition of equipment compared to previous year.
- Evidence of theft and/or wilful damage.
- User complaints and/or suggestions.
- Staff complaints and suggestions.

9.7.2 Key indicator

M&E should deal with all aspects of the information system – technical, personal and social, soft and hard, formal and informal. This can be seen in broad terms as relating to:

- the human activity system
- the information model
- the socio-technical system
- the human–computer interface
- technical areas.

For example, if all these areas are regularly monitored for problems and the resulting problems evaluated annually and appropriate action taken your system should be fairly successful. For the purposes of the exercise here we will not go into great detail concerning the way in which key indicators are identified and monitored. At this stage it is useful if we have some idea as to the components that are most prone to change. In our own example these are as shown in Table 9.2.

TABLE 9.2   *Selection of areas needing M&E (as related to the Multiview methodology)*

M&E focus	Critical indicators to monitor and evaluate
1 Human activity system	New conflicts of interest
	New departmental linkages
	Widescale changes in senior personnel
	Changes in the economic climate
	Changes in the political arena
2 Information modelling	New functions imposed
	Substantial reworking of old functions
	Changes in decomposition
	New entities
	New attributes
	New events
3 Socio-technical	Changes in the organization's 'vision' of the future
	Changes in personnel responsibilities
	Changes in the economic performance of new IT
	Costs of IT
4 Human–computer interface	Changes in operating systems
	New software
	Changes in the approach to dialogue (e.g. voice-operated systems)
5 Technical areas	Changes in the systems performance with use
	Increasing error levels?
	Retrieval difficulty

The task of the planner is to assess which if not all of the indicators are to be monitored during the run time of the project and what results would constitute the development of a problem. Secondly, the planner will want to identify several of the indicators that can be evaluated at the end of the project cycle.

9.7.3   The logical framework

We will have more to say about this approach in Appendix B. For now, the logical framework has been developed in a number of contexts (e.g. see Coleman, 1970; Cordingley, 1995; Bell, 1996; Thompson, n.d.). It is a four-by-four matrix for developing thinking about a project but it can also be used to model and monitor project progress and project impact.

THINK POINT

In your own organization think about what you would want to monitor to see if:

- the information systems were functioning properly and,
- the users were making the most of them.

Let your thinking take in both social and technical features which are both formal and informal. How much effort would you be willing to put into M&E? How could you 'sell' the cost of this effort to the organization? What would be the benefits arising from good M&E?

9.8   Putting it all together – the technical package

The final package can be seen as a specification that will maintain an information system within what is always assumed to be a hazardous operational environment. The linking together of aspects or areas into one whole should be occurring throughout the design process. Figure 9.7 is one view of the wholeness we are seeking.

Amount of time devoted to analysis so far:
Total for this stage (technical aspects) = 5 days
Cumulative total for path 1 = 30 days
Cumulative total for path 2 = 25 days
Cumulative total for path 3 = 18 days

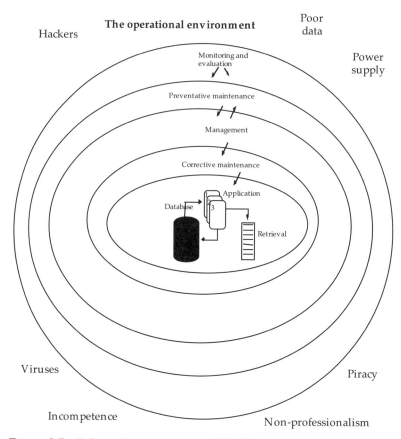

FIGURE 9.7   *Information systems as technical areas*

9.9   Conclusions

This stage of the analysis has provided you with the outline of the completed system. The only requirements that remain are for the outline hardware, software, and training to be followed by an implementation strategy. Make sure that this is the case! Go through your technical areas and make sure that the system that you outline only requires practical details. If your system is deficient at this stage (for example if the system does not provide detail for a software package to be described) rectify the point now.

9.10   Exercise

Using the model from the book set out, in outline, the overall details of the new system in the form of a briefing document for senior company staff. The document has be accessible to a range of different readers and therefore should be quite general. In the document you will need to allude to the total system. This will include items on all the areas outlined above but focusing in particular on:

- the database and the applications aspects
- the management aspect.
- the M&E aspect. This should include some references to: type of M&E procedures, expected problem areas, contingency plans.

Take a look at the model answer in Appendix C.

References and further reading

(Some useful readings on M&E include the following: Rossi and Freeman, 1985; Bell, 1987; Hirschheim and Smithson, 1987; Casley and Kumar, 1988; Mendelssohn, 1989; Lavrijsen, 1994; Theis, 1994; Eyben, 1995; Bell, 1996.)

Avison, D.E. and Wood-Harper, A.T. (1990). *Multiview: An Exploration in Information Systems Development*. Maidenhead: McGraw-Hill.

Bell, S. (1987). A guide to computing systems evaluation and adoption for users in LDCs – some problems encountered in applying standard techniques. *Journal of Information Technology for Development*, **3**(March).

Bell, S. (1996). Approaches to participatory monitoring and evaluation in Dir District, North West Frontier Province, Pakistan. *Systems Practice*, **9**(2), 129–150.

Bicknell, D. (1993). Any takers for a stretcher case? *Computer Weekly*, **14**.

Bicknell, D. (1997). They're on the Road to Nowhere. *Computer Weekly*, **32**.

Casley, D. and Kumar, K. (1988). *The Collection, Analysis and Use of Monitoring and Evaluation Data*. New York: World Bank Publications.

Coleman, G. (1987). Logical framework approach to the monitoring and evaluation of agricultural and rural development projects. *Project Appraisal*, **2**(4).

Collins, T. (1993). Lack of systems backup causes hospital chaos. *Computer Weekly*, **2**.

Collins, T. (1996a). Bank chief learns from computer failure. *Computer Weekly*, **24**.

Collins, T. (1996b). GPís network buckles under huge workload. *Computer Weekly*, **1**.

Collins, T. (1997). IT costs hike up prices of electricity deregulation. *Computer Weekly*, **22**.

Cordingley, D. (1995). Integrating the logical framework into the management of technical co-operation projects. *Project Appraisal*, **10**(2), 103–112.

Davies, T. (1996). GP link suffers network blockage. *Computer Weekly*, **4**.

Dickinson, A. (1996). Virus fever. *Computers in Africa*, 16–18.

Eyben, R. (1995). *Reviewing Impact During Project Implementation*. London: ODA.

Hirschheim, R. and Smithson, S. (1987). Information systems evaluation: myth and reality. In R. Galliers (ed.), *Information Analysis: Selected Readings*. Wokingham: Addison Wesley.

Kaye, J. (1997). Falling at the final hurdle. *Computer Weekly*, **44**.

Kolb, D. (1984). *Experiential Learning: Experience as the Source of Learning and Development*. London: Prentice-Hall.

Lambeth, J. (1996). Managers suffer from information overload. *Computer Weekly*, **3**.

Lavrijsen, J. (1994). *PROMES: an automated system for monitoring and evaluation*. Weijereind: WS Atkins Agriculture.

Lyytinen, K. and Hirschheim, R. (1987). Information systems failures: a survey and classification of the empirical literature. *Oxford Surveys in Information Systems*, **4**, 257–309.

Mendelssohn, G. (1989). The Use of Microcomputers for Project Planning, Monitoring and Evaluation. Inter-Network Papers, No. 1. Overseas Development Institute, London.

Rossi, P. and Freeman, H. (1985). *Evaluation: A Systematic Approach*. San Francisco: Sage.

Sauer, C. (1993). *Why Information Systems Fail: A Case Study Approach*. London: Alfred Waller.

Schein, E. (1996). Can learning cultures evolve? *The Systems Thinker*, **7**(6), 1–5.

Theis, J. (1994). *Review of Monitoring Systems*. London.

Thompson, M. (n.d.). *A TeamUp Case Study: Agriculture Project Design*. Chantilly: Team Technologies Inc.

Chapter 10

THE TOTAL DESIGN, TRAINING, HARDWARE, SOFTWARE AND IMPLEMENTATION

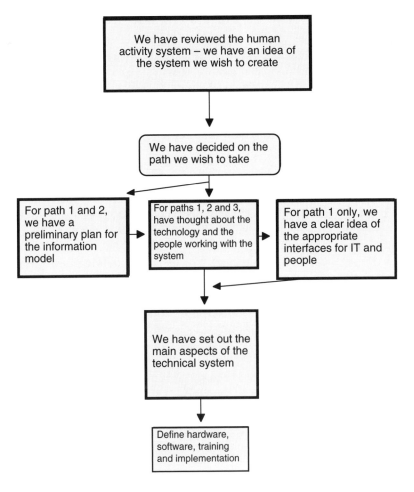

FIGURE 10.1   *Where are we in the process? The sixth stage of the rapid planning methodology*

Keywords:

Training choice, software selection, hardware selection, implementation strategy.

Summary:

The chapter works on the assumption that you have worked through one of the three paths and that you are now ready to embark on the range of training, hardware and software specification and implementation issues. Some brief outlines are given of the types of problem that can arise during this phase.

10.1   Introduction to implementation issues

In the previous chapters we have concluded our review of the stages of the rapid multiperspective approach to planning which we specify as requiring as little as 30 days (six weeks).

It has been our intention to develop in a concise, stage-by-stage manner the means whereby the methodology can be applied to make sense of the information requirements of the organization on the one hand and the best-fit solution to meet those requirements on the other.

The total design has been seen to require considerable labour but we suggest that elements of the methodology can be dropped if time is lacking or certain aspects can be adopted in an abbreviated form. Figure 10.2 demonstrates the unpacking of the total analysis, design and implementation model.

Although planning or analysis and design usually ends with the technical specification of the system, implementation issues will quite often be of concern to us – the learning team who have gone through the analysis and design stages are in a wonderful position to now progress the project through to implementation and beyond. In the next few pages we will look briefly at four areas of interest for implementation of the design:

- training
- software selection
- hardware selection
- implementation

10.2   Training

Before developing the regime, what is good training about?

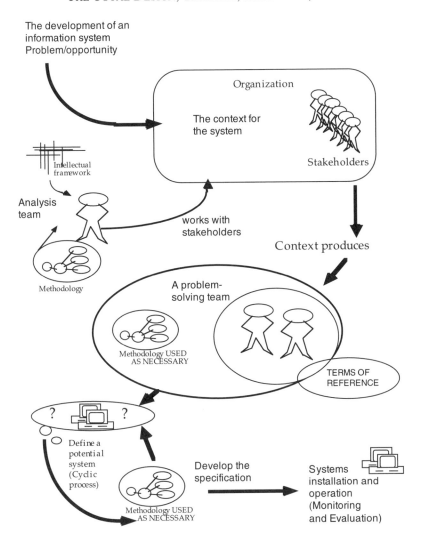

FIGURE 10.2 *Rich Picture of the overall approach*

10.2.1 The communication of skills

Information system and particularly computerized information system use is not intuitive as a rule (despite the development of what are sometimes claimed to be intuitive graphic interfaces). The process of training is usually involved with passing on hands-on skills and confidence in a new system. Other items which may need to be communicated include theory principles, specialist data preparation and fault finding.

Communication requires that the two sides of the informing process are working on the same wavelength. The training programme that you specify might attempt to enhance communication by use of the design factors set out in Table 10.1.

TABLE 10.1   *Design factors for effective communication of skills*

1	User needs clearly determined in cooperation and partnership
2	User capacities evaluated/self-evaluated
3	A training pack is planned with a balance of training items and procedures included. The emphasis is on continuous learning not 'one-stop' training
4	A sequence is set out and agreed for training
5	A schedule is designed and agreed
6	**Milestones** of achievement are mutually identified by potential trainer and trainee
7	Final positions are jointly evaluated

The short-cut to effective communication and therefore training is the primary identification of user need and the secondary evaluation of user capacity. The human activity system and the socio-technical design should have indicated some possible answers to these questions, continuous dialogue between the team and the user groups will aid it.

One means to effective communication lies in the development of the teaching/training package, the precision of its sequence and the organization of its schedule. We need to set out the *content, sequence* and *schedule* of events. We deal with this more fully in section 10.2.3.

10.2.2   Repetition of skills out of the training room context or self-confidence and self-reliance

Training is only effective in so far as the skills developed in the class room can be replicated at the work place. *This of course is obvious!* However, it is essential that training be developed with this object in view. Table 10.2 sets out some means to achieve self-confidence and self-reliance.

The results of not achieving self-sufficiency and self-reliance can be many and varied. The catastrophic outcome would be the folding of the project. Lesser outcomes might be the extreme annoyance to the organization running the new information systems as numerous requests for help come in from worried users, the lowering of morale among newly trained staff and criticism of the training unit that they are not doing their job properly!

TABLE 10.2 *Some means to achieve self-confidence and self-reliance*

1	Including in the training programme plenty of points where the participant has to work on his or her own, e.g. self-assessment exercises and formal examinations of skill
2	Exercises containing trial runs requiring the use of new skills, e.g. demonstrations and simulations
3	Project work, where the participant can develop his or her own themes with the existing training material and reflect on progress and problems

One vital aspect of training is the evaluation of performance. It is all very well performing the training and assessing that the users are up to the job in-hand, however, one should always expect the unexpected. Training is only one aspect of computer installation, for example:

- Hardware and software faults can lead to total system collapse or at least the undermining of staff morale.
- Humidity or dust can lead to system faults.
- Poor data collection, validation or verification all have their problems.
- Trained staff may have a high premium on the local labour market and well-trained staff may leave projects and departments shortly after completing training.

Not to mention the training-related problems such as:

- New software being used which bypasses the existing training.
- The development of new tasks which have not been trained for.
- Large increases in data collection and therefore data processing which alters existing and expected working practices.

All these points indicate the need for a monitoring and evaluation procedure of the situation some time after the completion of training and the return of individuals to their departments. Many analysis and design teams will already have these type of contingencies planned for from the information provided in Chapter 9.

Such an evaluation might make use of the original rich picture concept set out in Chapter 5 and is best carried out by an individual not directly related with the original training but briefed on the training terms of reference and achievements.

10.2.3. Specific training issues to be aware of

There are a number of easy-to-identify issues that can impede your progress with a training schedule. We will, very briefly, run through three of these here.

The first issue is that of senior manager intransigence. Generally speaking, the more senior a member of staff, the greater may be his or her reluctance to adopt the training schedule. This is further complicated if the manager is powerful enough to either daunt the trainer or just tell him to go away! As we have already discussed in Chapter 2, computers threaten many individuals' views of themselves and of their organizational role. Computerized information systems can offend managers' concepts of what constitutes an effective organization. Also, computers can threaten the employment of individuals.

If a training programme is likely to come up against this type of problem certain factors can be usefully applied. The key to winning over reluctant participants is empathy. Understanding the origin of reluctance and sympathizing, while at the same time attempting to dispel needless worry, is half the battle. Remember, participants will respond better to training programmes if they are convinced that the training is 'on their side', empowering them and improving their personal mastery.

The second issue is that relating to the wide range of abilities relating to IT in any organization. It is often the case that computer training sessions tend to have a wider range of abilities among participants than many other forms of training.

Being 'quick' with a computer is not an indication of intelligence. Rapid response to a computer can demonstrate that the participant is good at reading instructions but is not in fact making any mental effort to *understand* the content. It is not possible or desirable to have all students working at the same pace. However, order can be imposed on the potential chaos of a class all moving at different paces by:

- The use of exercises to slow down the faster individuals and make them really take in the content. This provides an additional level of quality to training.
- Self-assessment tests to indicate that milestones have been reached.
- The use of a graduated series of instruction that all can work through at their own pace.

AUTHORS' ASIDE

This is useful but does severely limit the capacity of lectures and presentations, if this type of teaching is used, to come at the 'right' time for everyone.

- Projects that encourage fast and slow participants to work together.

The third issue is jargon. Jargon puts off the newcomer and confuses everyone. It also indicates that the training is not on the same 'side' as the participant. It sets the training apart and reduces comprehension. On the positive side, the occasional use of jargon can be effective in intimidating the aggressive or obstructive individuals ('Have you tied your hexadecimal bootstraps yet?!). But seriously, it is to be avoided at all costs, jargon is generally a negative component. The training programme devised by the team will need to create a common language that provides the trainer and the participant with a format in which both can communicate effectively.

10.3 Software selection

We have already indicated that most applications used in information systems design and development (be they MIS, pay-roll systems, land assessment systems or otherwise) make use of a database. We have also mentioned that in terms of the case study used in these notes a range of standard packages will need to be employed including word-processors, databases and spreadsheets. What we have not yet covered is the area of selection procedure (see Figure 10.3).

There are quite a number of methods for the selection of software. The task is to match the perceived requirements of the users to the capacities of the packages available. The type of information that is needed for the specification to be exact includes the following:

- *Size* How much data is there going to be? How many records per annum (or quarter, or whatever discreet time unit you are going to use) do you expect to add to the base? How large will the database be?
- *Volatility* This refers to the regularity with which you will be deleting old data items and adding the new ones which will keep the base up to date. For example if 50 per cent of the data is to be removed and new entered each year and there are 120,000 data items – this equates to a considerable degree of volatility for a small organization. If you have taken path 1 through the methodology then information modelling will have indicated to you answers to both these questions.
- *Response time* At what rate of speed is the data required by the user? Generally speaking the larger the dataset, the slower will be the response time even if a very powerful computer system is

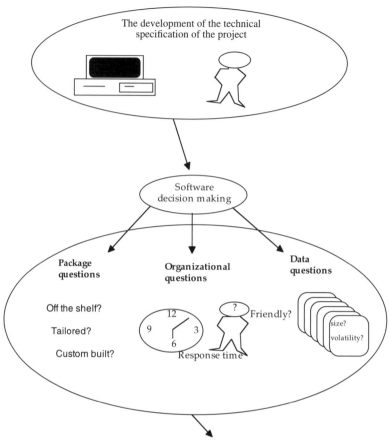

FIGURE 10.3   *Some features of software selection*

used. There is need to select the database system that will meet your requirements in terms of speed not just at the present but, using our future analysis in phase three of the methodology, try to put a figure on the rate of expansion of the system up to the mid-term (five years).

With this basic dataset identification information covered, issues of the range of software options available to you needs to be looked into next. In general terms there are three areas of software that might be explored:

- *Software packages*   These are prewritten and cover a enormous range of applications at the time of writing. What we tend to assume is: 'If I have a software requirement, someone, some-where in the world has already had that requirement and has produced a package to meet it'. Of course, this may not always be the case especially in the developmental/research areas but it is not a bad working assumption. A review of software catalogues and magazines can identify quite a range which can then be reviewed more closely.

- *Tailored packages*   This can be quite expensive and is often required as well as the first option. The tailored package is a development of the standard product. It may involve you (or a hired expert) in adapting elements to your specific requirements. Items to be wary of include poor tailoring leaving considerable **bugs** for you to discover, getting involved in this without thoroughly checking the ready-made market and using spurious experts!
- *Custom-built packages*   This is undoubtedly the most expensive and problem-prone area to deal with. All the items to be wary of that we mentioned above still need to be considered. It is a good practice to get any expert group producing such software to give written guarantees and dates for delivery (as well as cost!). Much modern software is produced with quick build tools which provide developers with the ability to significantly reduce development time.

10.3.1   Case study

For our own example we estimated that any one of a range of software packages would carry out the major database functions which we would be engaged in. The main, specifically *technical* requirements were:

- The database system should be **multi-user**.
- Similarly, spreadsheet and word-processing packages should have multi-user facilities. Specific developmental factors included packages used must be readily available in local markets (remember, our example is set in a developing country), and all selections should be well-established products which had the widest chance of being locally serviceable in terms of training.

Realistically we work on the assumption that most software provided for, and by, developing countries will be prewritten. This will partly be due to the enormous range of software already available and the prohibitive cost of custom-built software. General points to keep in mind (adapted from Kozar (1989)) are the following:

- On reviewing a series of software options, which of the packages actually do the job that you have specified in the logical model of technical specification? Does the package provide you with the levels of control that are essential for successful running?

- Does the software fit the outline hardware configuration that we are forming? Will the software interact smoothly with the operating system?
- How well do the performance times of the software rate? Can a trial dataset be run on each system for comparison with standard workloads?
- Can the system be made as user friendly as was set out in the human–computer interface of the methodology?
- How adaptable to change is the software?
- Is the vendor for the packages reputable?

10.4   Hardware selection

Having made a choice of software that meets the needs that your analysis has arrived at you are now ready to specify hardware for the system. Again there are a number of key factors that have to be considered (see Figure 10.4).

The process involved with hardware selection can be delineated as follows:

- System evaluation which includes information gathering on potentially appropriate systems (e.g. trade magazines and visits). Following this the team needs to identify vendors, request details of total cost (which includes all hardware components, hardware training, hardware support/maintenance). Another important question: is hardware flexible enough to adapt to the user environment? The end of this stage is to produce a short-list of potential systems.
- Installation evaluation which includes such issues as what precise local factors will affect installation? For example humidity, temperature, dust, seasonal fluctuation in atmospheric conditions, the budget for spares, the availability of spares locally and the availability of finance. More specifically, how easy is the system to use?
- A useful approach to adopt is to request details of existing users. In discussing the system with existing users particular attention can be paid to runtime problems in similar environments but beware defensive attitudes following 'bad' decisions (individuals are rarely likely to tell you if the system they have bought has been no good).
- Finally, test drive (benchmark test) the proposed new system.

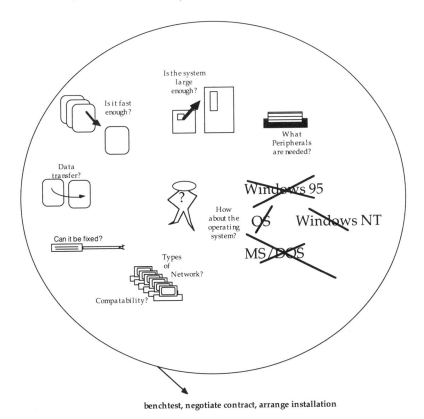

benchtest, negotiate contract, arrange installation

FIGURE 10.4 *Hardware specification*

10.4.1 Case study

For our example we decided upon a microcomputer network. Our final hardware selection was for a standard PC-based Novell network on compatibles with uninterruptible power supplies. The market standard PC was selected because it was the fastest, reliable and well-tested chip at the time. Novell was selected because it had well-established, international support.

In making the decision the major contenders to the choice were existing IBM compatibles or IBM PCs. We decided that on the grounds of local support and international compatibility with similar activities that the selection was IBM compatible. We decided against the IBM PC on the grounds of its lack of international availability at the time of the work and also because there was no local support, spares would be costly and there was a question mark over capability in humid, tropical conditions.

Trial MIS operations had already been run on IBM compatible

hardware in similar conditions. The benchmark test was therefore dispensed with.

10.5   Implementation

Following the nuts and bolts of hardware and software purchase, implementation is the next stage. Several factors need to be kept in mind:

- In new environments rigorous management techniques will need to be applied (see Chapter 9, the management aspect).
- Staffing will need sufficient initial and recurrent training in the use of the technology (see the training structure given in this chapter).
- The monitoring and evaluation procedure will have to be continued on an annual basis. Initial (within three years) success should not create undue complacency.

Actual systems installation can take a number of forms (see Figure 10.5). The precise form will depend upon the circumstances in which you are working, the perceived benefits of each approach as perceived by yourself and the major stakeholders. Kozar (1989) lists four consideration to keep in mind when selecting the installation structure:

- *Stress considerations*   The least stressful of the four approaches is probably the parallel system. In this case there is a fall-back and the various agencies within the host institution should not feel too 'exposed' with the new system.
- *Cost considerations*   Although the parallel approach appears the most costly, purely in terms of keeping two systems running at the same time, it may reduce some runtime costs because of the reduced stress on operators and managers. This is yet another example of the local environment being the major force in the adoption of a system.
- *Duration considerations*   This refers to the speed for systems uptake and the length of time which it is envisaged that the system will be partially implemented. Again the parallel approach would appear to be the most costly in terms of duration. Users of the old system are more likely to hang onto functions that they know and are happy with.
- *Human resource management considerations*   Resistance is one major factor in terms of staff consideration. The rich picture at the beginning of the analysis should have provided us with some idea of likely centres of resistance. All implementation procedures should be based around a strategy for ensuring minimum

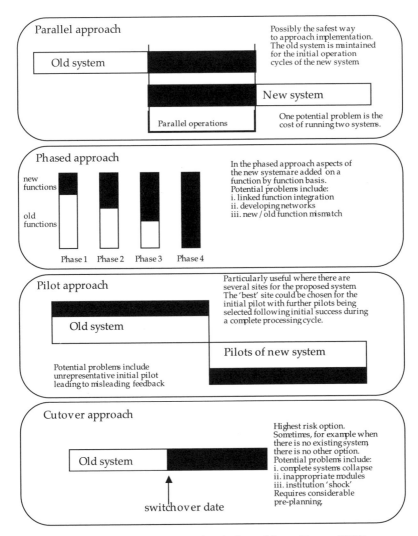

FIGURE 10.5 *Installation approaches (adapted from Kozar, 1989)*

disruption to key personnel. The parallel approach should provide the major problems in terms of staff selection for two systems. The cutover approach will produce the most stress in terms of sudden workload and untried procedures.

10.6 Conclusions

With implementation the information system moves from the planning and design phase through to operation. You are the proud owner of an information system 'solution' as the technology salespeople like to put it. However, it is dangerous to think of the development process as now being over. Your problems are probably just about to begin! The new information system *will* have teething problems, hopefully your monitoring procedure will pick these up before they become too acute and your maintenance shell and guard should keep the worst of the environmental hazards at bay. As we have hinted throughout, the greatest concern in the field of information science is undue complacency concerning the power and efficiency of information systems. A healthy attitude to cultivate is that your learning curve is just beginning, the first year or two after installation are often the most valuable in terms of gaining experience, this period can also be quite painful!

10.6.1   The Multiview methodology

The five stages of the foregoing analysis should provide you with tools that will allow you to plan and develop information systems for most organizational requirements. Any information system you design will have to be as dynamic as the organization it is going into. If the system cannot adapt to the changing needs of the organization then you will have problems. Our intention has been to demonstrate not only good practice in information systems planning but to emphasize the need for caution and the capacity to adapt to changing situations. Ultimately the information system is part of the wider social system and this in turn is part of, and dependent upon, the global system. The sources of potential interference and disruption are almost endless but this realization should encourage rather than disincline us to plan as effectively as we can.

10.6.2   The learning organization methodology

We have attempted to demonstrate throughout this book that the process of information systems analysis and design throws up a range of powerful opportunities for organizations to learn about their internal processes. There is also a terrific opportunity for teams to develop and generate real knowledge about the organization. This team-based knowledge base can be seen as being a compatible and linked outcome from the analysis procedure. Analysis and design teaches the organization about its data and information processes, the learning organization provides unique insights into the knowledge within the organization.

   As a total picture of the learning that can be gained from using our approach see Table 10.3.

TABLE 10.3   *RISD and the learning organization*

Discipline	Value in RISD	Outcome?
Systems thinking	Information systems can be seen as being remote objects and problems to users or they can be seen as being part of the organization as a whole. Systems thinking encourages us to see information systems as part of the complex whole which is the organization	Arising from our focus on wholeness and not dealing with information systems in a piecemeal fashion generates systems which are better geared to deal with real needs, provide more relevant information and grow and change with the organization
Personal mastery	Each stage of RISD provides opportunities for the team involved to develop their confidence and understanding of their own organization as well as its information flows	From the empowerment of being involved, if not architect of an information system come a range of potential personal mastery outcomes: • over the informing function • over the function of the organization as a network • over group processes within the organization
Mental models	Within RISD you are encouraged to model your context from many (multi) views. Each mental model, from the rich picture to flow diagrams provides a different and yet valuable insight into the organizations processes	Many outcomes are possible: • the capacity to stand back from the context and consider it according to one variable • the recognition that different perspectives are possible and all can have value • the liberation of mind to show that no single way of thinking is absolute
Shared vision	In RISD we have emphasized the value of shared thinking and working. The result is an information system which is more than a single view. Being the outcome of group processes it reflects that group and the various needs which it represents	Outcomes include: • an information system that is for the organization not one individual • informing processes that support the organization's vision of what it should be • information systems that can evolve with the vision of the organization
Team learning	Above all RISD is a team learning opportunity. The team should be selected carefully to represent the richness of the organization but once selected the team can learn cooperatively through the process of finding out how the organization actually functions	Numerous potential outcomes: • team cohesion in the organization • technology supporting team working • the establishment of networks within the information • more effective use of, and valuing of, the organization's knowledge

References and further reading

(Some general reading on learning with information systems includes
    Argyris, 1982; Checkland, 1984; Boud, 1985; Checkland, 1985;
    Episkopou and Wood-Harper, 1986; Honey and Mumford, 1986;
    Bawden and Macadam, 1988; Hulme, 1989; Mason and Kaye, 1989;
    Weil, 1989; Pedler *et al.*, 1991; Boud, 1993; Boud and Walker, 1993;
    Ison, 1994; Mason, 1994; Ackoff, 1995; Andreu and Ciborra, 1996;
    Bell, 1996a; Bell, 1996b; Fals Borda, 1996; Heron, 1996; Reason
    and Heron, 1996; Schein, 1996; Chambers, 1997.)

Ackoff, R. (1995). Whole-ing the parts and righting the wrongs.
    Systems Research, **12**(1), 43–46.
Andreu, R. and Ciborra, C. (1996). Organizational learning and core
    capabilities development: the role of IT. *Strategic Information
    Systems*, **5**, 111–127.
Argyris, C. (1982). *Reasoning, Learning and Action*. San Francisco:
    Jossey Bass.
Bawden, R. and Macadam, R. (1988). *Towards a University for
    People – Centred Development: A Case Study of Reform*. New
    York: Winrock International.
Bell, S. (1996a). *Learning with Information Systems: Learning Cycles
    in Information Systems Development*. London: Routledge.
Bell, S. (1996b). Reflections on learning in information systems prac-
    tice. *The Systemist*, **17**(2), 54–63.
Boud, D. (1985). *Reflection: Turning Experience into Learning*.
    London: Kogan Page.
Boud, D., Cohen, R. and Walker, D. (1993). *Using Experience for
    Learning*. Milton Keynes: Open University Press.
Boud, D. and Walker, D. (1993). Barriers to reflecting on experience.
    In D. Boud, R. Cohen and D. Walker (eds), *Using Experience for
    Learning*. Milton Keynes: Open University Press.
Byrne, B.K. and Wood-Harper, A.T. (1997). The effect of analytical
    thought on ethical issues in the information systems discipline.
    Association for Information Systems. 2nd American Conference,
    Indianapolis, 15–17 Aug.
Chambers, R. (1997). *Whose Reality Counts? Putting the First Last*.
    London: Intermediate Technology Publications.
Checkland, P.B. (1984). Systems thinking in management: the devel-
    opment of soft systems methodology and its implications for social
    science. In H. Ulrich and G. J. Probst (eds), *Self Organisation and
    Management of Social Systems*. Berlin: Springer-Verlag.
Checkland, P.B. (1985). From optimisation to learning: a develop-
    ment of systems thinking for the 1990s. *Journal of the Operational
    Research Society*, **36**(9), 757–767.
Episkopou, D.M. and Wood-Harper, A.T. (1986). Towards a frame-

work to choose appropriate IS approaches. *The Computer Journal*, **29**(3), 222–228.

Fals Borda, O. (1996). Power knowledge and emancipation. *Systems Practice*, **9**(2), 177–181.

Heron, J. (1996). *Co-operative Inquiry: Research into the Human Condition*. London: Sage.

Honey, P. and Mumford, A. (1986). *The Manual of Learning Styles*. Maidenhead: Peter Honey.

Hulme, D. (1989). Learning and not learning from experience in rural project planning. *Public Administration and Development*, **9**, 1–16.

Ison, R. (1994). Designing Learning Systems: How can systems approaches be applied in the training of research workers and development actors? International Symposium – Systems Orientated Research in Agriculture and Rural Development, Montpellier.

Kamsah, M. and Wood-Harper, A.T. (1997). *Intergrating into the Existing Systems – a Malaysian Case Study*. 8th Austrialian conference on information systems, Adelaide, 29 Sept. – 2nd Oct.

Kozar, K.A. (1989). *Humanized Information Systems Analysis and Design: People Building Systems for People*. New York: McGraw-Hill.

Mason, R. (1994). *Using Communications Media in Open and Flexible Learning*. London: Kogan Page.

Mason, R. and Kaye, A. (eds) (1989). *Mindweave: Communication, Computers and Distance Education*. Oxford: Pergamon.

Pedler, M. *et al.* (1991). *The Learning Company: A Strategy for Sustainable Development*. London: McGraw-Hill.

Reason, P. and Heron, J. (1996). Co-operative inquiry. In R. Harre, J. Smith and L. Van Langenhove (eds), *Rethinking Methods in Psychology* (in press).

Schein, E. (1996). Can learning cultures evolve? *The Systems Thinker*, **7**(6), 1–5.

Weil, A.W. (1989). *Making Sense of Experiential Learning: Diversity in Theory and Practice*. Milton Keynes: The Open University.

Wood-Harper, A.T., Wood, J.R.G. and Goh, P. (1993). Assumptions in information systems. *The Systemist*, **15**(4), 218–220.

GLOSSARY

4GL (Fourth Generation Language) A computer program which is semi-intelligent, allowing the computer to be more interactive with the user.

Action research The person undertaking research is part of the research context. The researcher tries to understand the context by linking theory with practice.

Application The term used to define the main activity of a computer-based information system (for example an MIS is an application).

Attributes The basic features evident in an entity, for example the first name, second name, address, telephone number, etc. in an entity called 'address book'.

Backup files/disks The process of making security copies or backups of files and disks of files.

Bugs Faults in computer software. These usually arise because tailored or purpose-built software has not been adequately tested prior to installation.

Case studies Examination of phenomena with no clear boundaries at the outset.

CASE (Computer Assisted Software Engineering) tools These are software packages that assist analysts in the process of developing software packages. They were particularly designed to work with structured analysis and design approaches (an early and widely used CASE tool was 'Excelerator').

Computer-based information system The computer is the processing basis and storage facility of the system that provides on demand a number of key information products requested by an identified user community.

Conceptual model Usually describes an activity model to achieve a transformation of some kind.

Conceptual study A form of research also known as 'armchair' research.

Consolidated computing The second period of the computer age. Mainframe based and programmer orientated.

Context A word always being used by information system planners. The context of the system is vital to the workability of what is being proposed. For example a complex mainframe system dependant upon a sophisticated support system would be contextually inappropriate in a remote location with few trained staff. This is an extreme case but the principle is; IS requirements and feasibility varies with context.

Data Unstructured, unverified, unvalidated material which is the basic foundation for information products. Some form of process must be undertaken to transform the data into information (for example sales data can be compiled as information on company turnover).

Database This is the store for data.

Debugging The procedure whereby a new item of software is analysed to make sure that it has no built-in faults or 'bugs'.

Decision support system A computer-based system which provides users with the capacity to carry out 'what if' analysis (for example: 'If I increase inflation by 4 per cent and decrease output by 7 per cent what does this do to my balance of trade?). Decision support systems or DSS are usually based on spreadsheets.

Decomposition The process of working out functions to subfunctions and if necessary sub-subfunctions. Decomposing a task down to subtasks.

Desktop microcomputers The most common computers. Generally these are on the individual user's desktop, run common software packages and are versatile enough to go into quite harsh environments. The most common microcomputers are PCs (Personal computers with Intel processors running to a common standard originally set by IBM – thus named 'IBM compatibles') and Macs (computers manufactured by Apple Co.).

Dialogue systems The screen formats and protocols which a computer uses to inform users and explain procedures.

DOS (Disk Operating System) The software that controls the user interface to the computer and the working of the computer. Used in Chapter 7 to indicate the wide range of microcomputers that use the industry standard operating system MS DOS which controls graphic interfaces such as Windows 95/98.

Drive alignment Refers to the ability of the disk drive to read the removable disks. If the drive is out of alignment then there will be problems with both reading and writing data.

Eclectic An approach to problem solving with systems analysis and systems design methodologies where a number of different approaches are brought together, linking the best or most appropriate parts of each, in order to arrive at a newly evolved approach. Multiview might be said to be an eclectic methodological framework.

Eductive We tend to be familiar with deduction and induction but eduction is less common. It means to 'draw forth' and shares the same root with education. Ideally to educate is not to pump full of data but to draw forth the genius which each of us contains in potential.

Entities The description of anything about which we wish to store data.

Error messages Often incomprehensible message (for example a really great message that users used to be afflicted with was BDOS ERR ON B:) sent to the computer screen to inform the user that something is amiss!

Events These are the triggers which will spark of functions in an information model (for example the end of a financial year may be the trigger that sparks the function 'do the annual accounts').

Expert imposition An attitude which is summed up in the anonymous quote: 'I am the computer expert, please let me get on with sorting out your problem without interruptions!'.

Field experiments Data is collected on the behaviour of the independent variable. The dependent variable is measured.

Focus group These are usually small groups of stakeholders in an enterprise who are brought together with a facilitator to gain quality information about specific problems and issues.

Fragmented files Files which have been separated into many small pieces by the software process.

Functions In information modelling these are the activities that are associated with entities and which prompt information processing to occur (for example the function 'sort into alphabetic order' may occur upon the entity 'store of data on library books').

Geographic Information System (GIS) Numerous packages which handle spatial data (for example maps and satellite images) and produce composite maps, overlays, planning guides, etc.

Hackers Any individual using a computer-based information system without authorization. In recent years this term has been most specifically related to users of the Internet breaking into supposedly secure systems such as that belonging to NATO.

Hard Term used to denote a technocratic approach to problem solving.

Hard copy   Usually refers to the printed output from a computer system.

Hard disk   A fixed disk drive which is usually located in the computer and is not designed to be removed. Hard disks are usually large ranging from hundreds of megabytes to gigabytes of storage.

Hardware   The computer unit itself and its related components. This usually works out as the visual display unit or monitor, the main processor box, a keyboard, printers, modems, fax machines and optical scanners.

Human Activity System (HAS)   A concept used and extended by Professor Peter Checkland in the soft systems approach to systems thinking and practice. The human activity concept includes initially understanding the problem context (often by use of a rich picture), discovering central themes with the root definition and setting out proposed activities.

Human–computer interface   The label given to work which attempts to make the connection between the human side of an information system and the technology as easy as is feasible.

Information   A product which has gone through a process which derived it from data. It is assumed that information provides the basis for knowledge which can in turn facilitate decision making, for example company turnover information, derived from sales data, provides the basis for making knowledgeable decisions on production, marketing, etc.

Information modelling   A hard analysis and design technique. The technique is concerned with setting out what are the major entities of a system, what are their functions and attributes and what events will trigger the functions into activity.

Information systems   Any system which provides the user with the necessary information to engage in action.

Install software   All software needs to be set up or 'installed' on a computer before it can be used. Installing usually is the method for making sure that the software makes best use of the computer processor, screen type and printer.

Internet   The word used to describe the global connectivity between computers of all types.

Intranet   Computer-based connectivity within an organization, usually based upon Internet technologies.

Isolated computing   The first period of the computer age. Firmly related to mainframe computers and mainframe systems.

Knowledge   A condition of being informed which is the result of good information. Knowledge is the basis of good decision making, for example knowledgeable decisions arising from company turnover information can affect the overall strategy of an organization.

Laboratory experiments   The researcher manipulates the independent variables. All 'noise' is controlled.

LAN (Local Area Network)   A network of computers linked together on a particular site (such as in one organization).

Learning organization   An organization which is developing a 'blame-free' culture of understanding both in terms of its own internal processes and those which relate to its environment. The outcome of such a culture is heightened awareness, improved efficiency, professional satisfaction and enhanced capability to deal with change.

Login/logout   The term for getting into and out of a computer system.

Lost clusters   A cluster is a group of sectors allocated to a file. Lost clusters are just as they sound!

Mainframe   A large computer, usually occupying an entire room. This type of computer requires a very highly controlled environment and several trained operators under the authority of a computer manager.

Maintenance   An aspect of the fifth stage of the methodology. Maintenance includes both corrective and preventative aspects.

Management   This is the technical aspect of the fifth stage of the methodology and its focus is to control but also to learn and encourage participation from users.

Management controls and constraints   The third period of the computer age, referring to the stage where computer functions began to be harnessed by the business managers within organization.

Management Information Systems (MIS)   Such systems are usually based on computers but do not have to be. Usually they are designed around the idea of supplying management at set times or on demand with key information products called performance indicators.

Mathematical modelling   In this form of exploration all variables are known. Therefore, analysis is reduced to a set of equations.

Menu-driven system   The term used to describe a computer-based system which works according to users selecting a series of menu options in predesigned sequence in order to arrive at the information products required.

Methodology   A term used in this book to refer to any approach for planning information systems although more properly it means the science of considering methods. Methodologies usually provide the user with guidelines and procedures for accomplishing tasks.

Mice or mouse A small, oblong box with a ball in it used to move the cursor on the screen by making contact between the ball and a surface.

Milestones Significant points for the evaluation of achievement. For example a milestone for the implementation of a new infor-mation system might be 'review progress on data incorporation into the computer system at the end of the financial year'.

Mindset Sorry about using this term but it is quite useful. A mindset indicates all the aspects of your state of mind on a given issue at a given time. If we are working on a rich picture in a participatory fashion, the picture should represent the mindsets of the analyst and the major stakeholders involved in producing the overall diagram.

Minicomputer Not at the scale of a mainframe, or that of the microcomputer or PC, the minicomputer is a large piece of furniture and requires support in the form of environmental control and skilled operators.

Microcomputer or personal computer (PC) or desktop computer The range of machines which sit on the user's desk and act as standalone or networked facilities operating a range of office software packages.

Multi-user A computer system with a network that allows a number of users to use the same software at the same time.

Multiview An eclectic methodology initially designed by D.E. Avison and A.T. Wood-Harper and developed with other authors.

Network The name for linking together computers so that they can share information. Popular networks include Ethernet-based systems linked Internet and running an Intranet.

Outsourcing The practice of letting third parties handle organizational functions. In terms of this book it relates to allowing a third party to control and develop the information processing function. Outsourcing avoids the organization covering the cost of information systems development. The risk is that a third party may not look after the organization's interests as well as internal staff.

Partition The term used to describe separating a hard disk into several different logical disks. For example the hard disk might be called drive C:. By partition we can make several logical drives (C:, D:, E:) on that single actual drive.

Performance indicators An MIS will often be measuring a number of key factors to ascertain the relative success of failure of elements of an organization or of its functioning. The factors selected for this monitoring are often called performance indicators.

Phenomenological research This type of research focuses on understanding the essence of experience.

Pirated/piracy The illegal copying of software products.

Presenting problem The superficial problem, often this is not the real problem at all but a deeper problem lies beneath it as its cause.

Problem context This refers to the situation in which an analyst and designer is working. The assumption is that an information system is required because something is not working as well as it might. Therefore, the system and the planner of the system inhabit a problem context.

Prototyping This usually requires a programmer with access to sophisticated software tools to iteratively develop the MIS application in consensus with users and user teams.

Rapid Application Development (RAD) This is not related to the rapid information systems analysis and design approach used in this book. RAD is a form of prototyping which makes use of CASE tools to iteratively produce systems quickly.

Recipient community That group of stakeholders and users who will be the eventual information system managers, operators and clients.

Reductionist The traditional, scientific approach to problem solving which claims to be objective. In a reductionist approach the whole is broken down to the parts which are then studied in isolation. Reductionism is usually contrasted to systemism.

Retrieval The production of information from a database via an application.

Rich picture The overall structure and content of the problem context visually set out as a cartoon including hard and soft structures and processes.

Role of the user The fourth period of the computer age. At last the term 'user' is adopted and is seen as being important. IT begins to be orientated towards user requirements.

Root definition A technique to set out the main transformation resulting from systems analysis. The definition usually includes identification of the customer, actors, problem owners, environmental constraints and major assumptions of stakeholders.

Screen burn If a computer is left on and not used for a considerable time the screen will eventually have a burnt on image left. Thus, you will be able to see what has been on the screen even when the computer is off. This is easily avoided by use of screen savers.

Social and technical systems analysis The linking together of human and technological resources to make the 'best' combination for the specific problem context.

Soft The term used to denote a non-reductionist, empathetic approach to problem solving

Software This refers to the application (for example word-processors, databases, etc.) that run on the hardware.

Software-hardware mismatch The wrong software on the wrong hardware.

Stakeholders Any individual with an interest in the existing or proposed information system.

Standalone A computer that works independently from other computers. That is a computer which is *not* networked.

Structured analysis This is a specific form of analysis which makes use of some of the tools set out in this book. The main concepts are dataflow diagrams, data dictionary, store structuring and process logic representations.

Survey Also known as 'opinion research'. Sampling is dependent upon judgement and convenience.

Sustainable A very important word. An information systems that is sustainable is one that can be maintained and will be the basis for evolution into the future. It is the obverse of a 'one-hit-wonder' system which does splendidly for a month or so but then collapses or, an information system that operates well but cannot be developed for future needs.

System The splendid definition has been provided by Peter Senge (1994): 'A system is a *perceived* whole whose elements 'hang together' because they continually affect each other over time and operate toward a common purpose. The word descends from the Greek verb sunistánai, which originally meant: ' to cause to stand together'. As this origin suggests, *the structure of a system includes the quality of perception with which you, the observer, cause it to stand together'* (Emphasis added. p. 90).

Systemic An approach to problem solving which is based upon an holistic approach. Pragmatic and sometimes subjective, systemism is interested in understanding the complexity of processes and relationships in wholes. Systemism is usually contrasted with reductionism.

Systems analysis and systems design The process of discovering what an information system should do and setting out a plan for a feasible development.

Systems model A diagram which sets out the main components of the context as systems and subsystems.

Technical aspects The range of component aspects which combine to produce the total information system.

UNIX A computer operating system originally designed by Bell Laboratories. Long thought of as the natural system for minicomputers it is also being adopted for microcomputers.

User/machine interface The latest and fifth period of the computer age. The focus is the communication between the user and the machine.

Viruses Software, sometimes designed for fun sometimes with malign intent, which will make a computer break down in a minor or major way. Viruses are usually brought into computers on pirated software. They can lead to total system collapse.

WAN (Wide Area Network) A system which links local computers with national and sometimes international computer systems and databanks.

Web An approach in systems analysis and systems design which attempts to see all aspects of an organization (management systems, financial systems, information systems) as an integrated whole. Web is generally seen as being opposite to discrete entity analysis which sees all systems within an organization as separate.

Web site A unique address on the World Wide Web where organizations and/or individuals can produce multimedia information about themselves.

Wordprocessing The most commonly used packages in modern computing. Much more than clever typing, these software applications provide users with the ability to input ideas, develop themes, write, work and rework text and usually produce top quality printed output as well as draft.

Workspace The amount of store or memory or time or all three which is allotted to a user.

Worldview The overall conception of the world for any one individual or organization (also known as *Weltanschauung*).

World Wide Web A growing element of functionality available on the Internet providing users with multimedia images and information in a graphic format.

SYSTEMS ANALYSIS AND SYSTEMS DESIGN – METHODOLGIES IN RELATION TO EACH OTHER

In our opening chapters we discussed the problems which organizations have with developing information systems. Problems seem to arise no mater what methodology is applied. In Chapter 2 we looked at the thinking behind methodologies to information systems analysis and design and in particular we looked at the reductionist and systemic tendencies in information systems thinking. Reductionist thinking is traditional 'scientific' thinking. It treats the world as an object to be studied. Figure A1 is a representation of this type of approach.

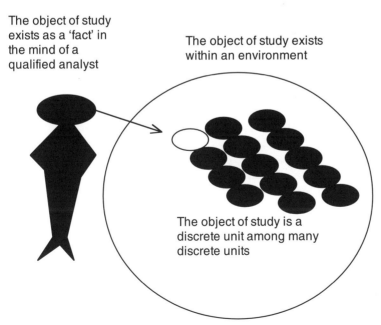

FIGURE A1   *Reductionist approaches*

The reductionist measures elements of wholes to understand them. By taking things apart and putting them back together again the reductionist gains understanding. The weakness of the approach can be that the whole is not given due importance being seen as too complicated to understand in its entirety. By contrast we discussed systemic or holistic thinking which considers the whole and the processes which it includes. This is demonstrated in Figure A2.

Figure 2. Systemic approaches

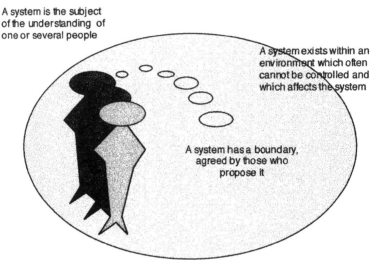

A system is the subject of the understanding of one or several people

A system exists within an environment which often cannot be controlled and which affects the system

A system has a boundary, agreed by those who propose it

FIGURE A2   *Systemic approaches*

If we were to describe these two approaches we might draw out their main differences as shown in Table A1.

In this book we have proposed that the 'hard' approaches have tendencies towards the reductionist model and the softer approaches

TABLE A1   *A comparison of systemic and reductionist approaches*

Systems approach	Reductionist approach
The problem is shared by legitimate stakeholders in the problem context	The problem is in the mind of the expert
The system as a whole is reviewed	A part of a complex whole is analysed
The environment affects the system	The environment is controlled
The boundary of the system is flexible and dependent upon the perception of the stakeholder	The boundary of the part is defined by the expert

tend to the systemic. This is not an infallible fact but an observation derived from experience (and assented to by many practitioners). For a thorough analysis and comparison of the range of approaches available the authors recommend that the reader see Avison and Fitzgerald's (1995) book. For the purposes of this book we would like to indicate where we feel the various approaches 'fit' in terms of the tending to reductionist and tending to systemic. Those which tend to people issues and those which tend to the technology. We set out the methodologies in Figure A3.

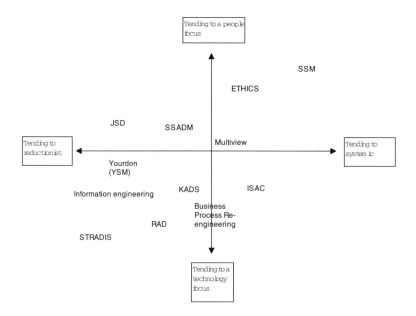

FIGURE A3   *Methodologies – systemic and reductionist, people and technology*

None of these methodologies is 'right' or 'wrong', they are different and emphasize different types of tools and techniques. They are derived from different mindsets and do different things differently. In our estimation the Multiview approach is appropriate for the development which we have given it in this book because it is closest to the central point, offering the best chance to cover the widest range of issues across the breadth of the organization. Each of the five stages of Multiview looks at the organization and the information which it contains in a slightly different way. This provides the analysis team with a good chance of covering issues of concern and including in analysis the majority of problem items.

Further reading

(In the areas we cover there is a great deal of information and we do recommend the Avison and Fitzgerald book for those who want to gain a view of the big picture regarding methodologies. Other references regarding the methodologies are as follows: Gory and Scott-Morton, 1974; De Marco, 1979; Gane and Sarson, 1979; Mumford and Weir, 1979; Checkland, 1981; De Marco, 1982; Land, 1982; Lundeberg, Goldkuhl, 1982; Parker and Benson, 1987; CCTA, 1988; Cameron, 1989; Martin, 1989; Tagg and Brown, 1989; Avison and Wood-Harper, 1990; Checkland and Scholes, 1990; Galliers, 1990; Stowell, Holland, 1990; Martin, 1991; Galliers, 1992; CCTA, 1993; Davenport, 1993; Yourdon, 1993; Eva, 1994; Avison and Fitzgerald, 1995; Mumford, 1995; Bell, 1996a; Bell, 1996b; Land, 1996; Yeoman *et al.*, 1996).

Avison, D.E. and Fitzgerald, G. (1995). *Information Systems Development: Methodologies Techniques and Tools* (second edition). London: McGraw-Hill.

Avison, D.E. and Wood-Harper, A.T. (1990). *Multiview: An Exploration in Information Systems Development*. London: McGraw-Hill.

Bell, S. (1996a). *Learning with Information Systems: Learning Cycles in Information Systems Development*. London: Routledge.

Bell, S. (1996b). Reflections on learning in information systems practice. *Systemist*, **17**(2), 54–63.

Cameron, J. (1989). *JSP and JSD: The Jackson Approach to Software Development*. Los Angeles: IEEE Computer Society Press.

CCTA (1988). *SSADM – The Open Standard for Information Management*. Norwich: CCTA, Information Systems Engineering Division.

CCTA (1993). *Applying Soft Systems Methodology to an SSADM Feasibility Study*. London: HMSO.

Checkland, P.B. (1981). *Systems Thinking, Systems Practise*. Chichester: Wiley.

Checkland, P.B. and Scholes, J. (1990). *Soft Systems Methodology in Action*. Chichester: Wiley.

Davenport, T. (1993). *Process Innovation: Reengineering Work through Information Technology*. Boston: Harvard Business School.

De Marco, T. (1979). *Structured Analysis: System Specifications*. Englewood Cliffs: Prentice Hall.

De Marco, T. (1982). *Controlling Software Projects: Measurement, Management and Estimation*. New York: Yordon Press.

Eva, M. (1994). *SSADM Version 4: A User's Guide* (second edition). London: McGraw-Hill.

Galliers, R. (ed.) (1992). *Information Systems Research: Issues, Methods and Practical Guidelines*. London: McGraw-Hill.

Galliers, R.D. (1990). *Choosing Appropriate Information Systems Research Approaches: A Revised Taxonomy*. Amsterdam: North Holland.

Gane, C. and Sarson, T. (1979). *Structured Systems Analysis: Tools and Techniques*. Englewood Cliffs: Prentice Hall.

Gory, G.A. and Scott-Morton, M.S. (1974). A framework for management information systems. In R. Nolan (ed.), *Managing the Data Resource Function*. St. Paul: West Publishing Company.

Land, F. (1982). Adapting to changing user requirements. *Information and Management*, **5**, 59–75.

Land, F. (1996). The new alchemist: or how to transmute base organization into coporations of gleaming gold. *Journal of Strategic Information Systems*, **5**, 7–17.

Lundeberg, M., Goldkuhl, G. and Nilsson, A. (1982). *Information Systems Development – A Systematic Approach*. Englewood Ciffs: Prentice Hall.

Martin, J. (1989). *Information Engineering*. Englewood Cliffs: Prentice Hall.

Martin, J. (1991). *Rapid Application Development*. New York: Macmillan.

Mumford, E. (1995). *Effective Requirements Analysis and Systems Design: The ETHICS Method*. Basingstoke: Macmillan.

Mumford, E. and Weir, M. (1979). *Computer Systems in Work Design – The ETHICS Method*. Associated Business Press.

Parker, M. and Benson, R. (1987). Information economics: an introduction. *Datamation*, 86–96.

Stowell, F.A., Holland, P., Muller, P. and Pnar, R. (1990). Applications of SSM in information system sesign: some reflections. *Journal of Applied Systems Analysis*, **17**, 63–69.

Tagg, C. and Brown, J. (1989). TBSD: Notes on an evolving methodology. Hatfield: Hatfield Polytechnic.

Wood-Harper, A.T. and Fitzgerald, G. (1982). A taxonomy of current approaches to systems analysis. *Computer Journal*, vol. 25, no. 2.

Yeoman, I. *et al.* (1996). Effective group knowledge elicitation through problem structuring methodologies. *Systemist*, **17**(2), 79–91.

Yourdon, I. (1993). *Yourdon Systems Method: Model-driven Systems Development*. Englewood Cliffs: Yourdon Press.

Appendix B

A PROJECT CYCLE: SEEING THE TASK IN PERSPECTIVE

The nature of the cycle

The object of this appendix is to set the systems analysis and systems design stage in the perspective of a total project. It is quite easy not to see the fuller picture when you are working on the detail of specific design.

Analysis and design can be said to fall into the stages of the project cycle known as *formulation* and *preparation*, and *appraisal*. This is not the place to go into great detail on these matters but it is useful to introduce the fuller picture, to set analysis and design in context and indicate key texts that can be pursued for a fuller appreciation. Figure B1 indicates the major components of most projects and shows five distinct phases in the project cycle with the monitoring function as being continuous.

- *Identification.* This is usually very general and non-specific. The identification is usually of some general need or general issue such as: 'the need to improve the delivery of sales and purchase

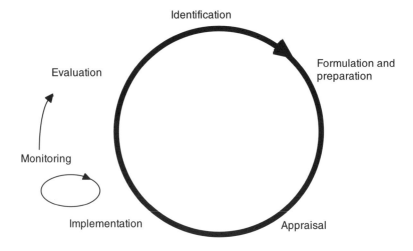

FIGURE B1   *Simplified project cycle (adapted from Coleman, 1987)*

data from regional offices to head office in order to give the company competitive edge', or 'the need to increase the efficiency of core government operations by means of management information system functions'. The identification stage usually occurs without any reference to systems analysis and systems design.

- *Formulation and preparation.* This stage is also known as feasibility. It is at this stage that the workability and outline terms of reference for the project is decided. If those involved in the formulation and preparation stage think that the project will deliver the required end within the scheduled time then the real work of planning can begin. Sometimes analysis and design is involved at this time. Quite often an IT-orientated project will make use of a systems analyst expert witness to provide details of the feasibility and cost of given project plans. The tools discussed in Chapter 5 relating to the human activity system may be applied at this stage.
- *Appraisal.* This is the major planning stage of the project. Appraisal requires systems analysis and systems design because it will be the appraisal document which will form the basis of the implementation plan. It will be during the appraisal period that we would expect the five stages of analysis and design (as we have described them here) to be undertaken.
- *Implementation.* In our book we have set implementation outside the analysis and design stage but still within the analyst/planner's mandate of activity. This is often not the case for an entire project. There will often be many non-computer functions related to the project. For example in our case study used throughout this book there was a communications improvement function which was running with the analysis and design of the MIS and yet had no direct linkage to the analysis/planning team. Implementation will mean that all the threads of the project are now brought together.
- *Evaluation.* Most projects should end with some form of evaluation, setting out the original themes for the project work and measuring the level of success in achieving these goals.

In Chapter 4 we set out a project cycle drawn from the Kolb learning cycle (Kolb, 1984) of reflecting, connecting, deciding and acting. We feel that all cyclic project activity should be reflective and thus a learning experience.

In Chapter 9 we briefly described another tool for considering projects, the logical framework (Logframe). The framework is shown in Figure B2.

While not providing a cyclic activity, it can be a profound way of considering the vertical and logical structures of an IT project. Popular project management tools such as PRINCE (e.g. see

GOAL	VERIFIABLE INDICATORS	MEANS OF VERIFICATION	ASSUMPTIONS
The higher-level objectives towards which the project is expected to contribute (Mention target groups)	Meassures (direct or indirect) to verify to what extent the Goal is fulfilled	The sources of data necessary to verify status of Goal level indicators	Important events, conditions or decisions necessary for sustaining objectives in the long run
PURPOSE The effect which is expected to be achieved as the result of the project	**VERIFIABLE INDICATOR** Measures (direct or indirect) to verify to what extent the purpose is fullfilled	**MEANS OF VERIFICATION** The sources of data necessary to verify status of Purpose level indicators	**ASSUMPTIONS** Important events, conditions or decisions outside the control of the project which must prevail for the Goal to be obtained
OUTPUTS The results that the project management should be able to guarantee (Mention target groups)	**VERIFIABLE INDICATOR** Measures (direct or indirect) to verify to what extent the outputs are produced	**MEANS OF VERIFICATION** The sources of data necessary to verify status of Activity level indicators	**ASSUMPTIONS** Important events, conditions or decisions outside the control of the project necessary for the achievement of the Purpose
ACTIVITIES The Activities which have to be undertaken by the project in order to produce the outputs	**VERIFIABLE INDICATOR** Goods and services necessary to undertake Activities	**MEANS OF VERIFICATION** The sources of data necessary to verify status of Activity level indicators	**ASSUMPTIONS** Important events, conditions or decisions outside the control of the project necessary for the production of the Outputs

Figure B2   *The logical framework*

HMSO (1990)) go into great depth in terms of the control and procedure in IT projects. As we have shown throughout this book, this type of control is often not possible for IT projects. Often staff, time and resources are not available or maybe, the project is just too small for the effort involved in PRINCE. The logical framework on the other hand is now widely used across a range of projects (e.g. see Coleman (1987a, b), Thompson and Chudoba (1994), Cordingley (1995), Team Technologies (1995), Thompson (1995), Bell (1996), and Thompson (n.d.)) and can be used at a number of levels:

- As a 'thinkpad'. As a means to just consider the levels of the project.

- As a detailed analysis tool for thinking about the times and dates for various interventions.
- As a preliminary tool for developing a project which will require further tools (e.g. Gantt charts, work breakdown structures, etc.).

Perhaps the greatest value of the Logframe is that it can be done collaboratively or alone, in depth or superficially, in a quantifiable or quality-orientated way, focusing on soft and/or hard issues and events, problems or opportunities. It is flexible. Figure B3 shows the way in which the Logframe can be integrated into the learning cycle.

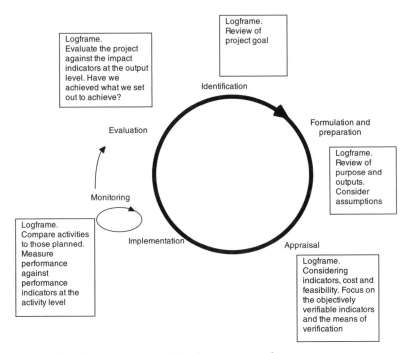

FIGURE B3   *The Logframe within the project cycle*

In perspective

Systems analysis and systems design is usually a component part of any ongoing project. Throughout this book we have tried to indicate the importance of the analyst/planner being humble in terms of his or her relationship with those who will inherit the system that is being devised. Humility is also required with regard to these wider project considerations.

Any work undertaken will need to fit into a greater whole. To some extent all analyst/planners have to be multidisciplinary in their approach if they are to survive in the project environment.

Further reading

Bell, S. (1996a). Approaches to participatory monitoring and evaluation in Dir District, North West Frontier Province, Pakistan. *Systems Practice*, **9**(2), 129–150.

Bell, S. (1996b). *Learning with Information Systems: Learning Cycles in Information Systems Development.* London: Routledge.

Coleman, G. (1987a). Logical framework approach to the monitoring and evaluation of agricultural and rural development projects. *Project Appraisal*, **2**(4).

Coleman, G. (1987b). M&E and the Project Cycle. Norwich: Overseas Development Group, University of East Anglia.

Cordingley, D. (1995). Integrating the logical framework into the management of technical co-operation projects. *Project Appraisal*, **10**(2), 103–112.

HMSO. (1990). *PRINCE: Projects in Controlled Environments.* Norwich: HMSO.

Kolb, D. (1984). *Experiential Learning: Experience as the Source of Learning and Development.* London: Prentice Hall.

Team Technologies (1995). *TeamUp 2.0.* Chantilly: Team Technologies Inc.

Thompson, J. (1995). User involvement in mental health services: the limits of consumerism, the risks of marginalisation and the need for a critical approach. Hull: Centre for Systems Studies, University of Hull.

Thompson, M. (n.d.). *A TeamUp Case Study: Agriculture Project Design.* Chantilly: Team Technologies Inc.

Thompson, M. and Chudoba, R. (1994). Case Study Municipal and Regional Planning in Northern Bohemia, Czech Republic: a participatory approach. World Bank Report. Washington DC.

SOME THOUGHTS ON ANSWERS TO THE EXERCISES

Exercise in Chapter 1

In the first chapter we asked you to read the article 'GPs' network buckles under huge workload', and asked you to consider if any of the 'Problems with IS' identified in that chapter were relevant. Thoughts you might have included:

- Task-machine development mismatch. The system as first conceived could not deal with its own success. As the load increased so the system came apart.
- Maybe in the same line we have an example of over-ambition on the part of managers of the system.
- The system may have been conceived with a poor analysis perspective. It seems to have outperformed its capacity and maybe this might have been foreseen if managers and clients were included in the original planning.

Other possibilities for comparison may occur to you. The point we would like you to carry forward is that the five examples of problems we have given can be used as models to compare real situations in order to see if there are some fairly common basic problems with the IS with which you are familiar.

Exercise in Chapter 2

There is not a right answer to this but the case seems quite clear on the evidence we have here. This case has quite large reductionist content. Reductionism should deal with technical and quantitative issues within a tight technical boundary. Such items abound, the 'bug', the number of courts, the size of the data and the need for reports to schedule. However, the problems and 'soft' features seem to predominate. Soft would cover the political and social problems for the IS and draw a large boundary around the potential context. The original bid was 50 per cent lower than rival bids – how was this achieved? Would we not expect problems with such cost-cutting? How will the delay rebound on the confidence of the agencies providing the funding? Might there be a case now for a renegotiation of the contract or at least of the technical roll out? Given the context, the need is to properly understand the nature of the problems and their real causality rather than applying a technical fix which might lead to the whole thing happening again.

Exercise in Chapter 3

This is a tricky scenario. The analyst will have to deal with a complex meshing of powerful interests (being paid by a publisher while working under a charismatic director and for a harassed senior administrator). On the other hand the need for technical ability is also evident. The information might be global, and be in a wide number of formats and for a diverse range of reporting and delivery needs. In our estimation the core need is for technical ability here. The NGO is in the UK and the budget for the project is given. In this sense the publisher is the major client and can push through the system. Although the ability to work in the context and to understand and draw out the needs of the NGO staff is vital, to get the basic system designed in a technically feasible manner might be thought to be the main consideration.

Exercise in Chapter 4

- *Strength.* Software is preselected and the staff are well trained also, the project is a pilot and can therefore be allowed to learn from mistakes without expecting catastrophe.
- *Weakness.* The hostility of the head of schools so far.
- *Opportunity.* The potential to 'sell' the idea to the schools in terms of showing from the pilot how they can gain control of their organization and access to additional funding by cooperation.
- *Threat.* The potential for non-inclusion of the schools and therefore the further development of hostility into open anger at what is seen as being useless additional bureaucracy.

In terms of the approach, path 2 might be best at the outset. There will probably not be a need to focus on the HCI if the software is prewritten and is known to work – the proviso being that the systems interface is sufficiently acceptable to British users. There may need to be participation on the structure of the application (and therefore information modelling) – it depends how much the US and British systems are alike.

Exercises in Chapter 5

5.1   The rich picture

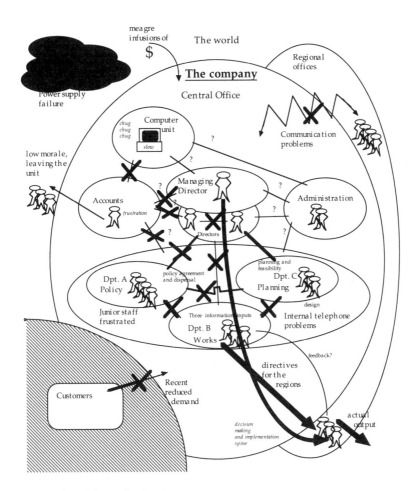

FIGURE C1   *The rich picture*

Figure C1 illustrates the rich picture. This is a picture for the analysts use only. It indicates a decision-making spine based on the strong family interests running through senior management. The overriding message from the picture is ignorance. We simply do not know enough about the core management and administration functions of the organization. The worst mistake we could make at this point is to disguise or ignore this ignorance. We need to know more about core functions. We have read between the lines and indicated a fair degree of frustration and anger in the management section.

Initial indications would suggest that more details are required concerning:

- present use of computing
- role and attitude of administration
- the working relationship between the three departments
- attitude of the regional offices to head office practices. This is the result of a sideways look at the project. The project terms of reference are stressing MIS at headquarters level. The business of the company takes place in the regions. Are the terms of reference right?

These items could be further developed in a second rich picture.

5.2   The root definitions

The analyst
Customer – Primarily the donor (the bank), secondly the company
Actor – Self, senior and MIS company staff
Transformation – MIS for key functions aimed at assisting key management with a unified purpose
Worldview – Improved efficiency of operations and the reduction in internal wrangling. A sneaking feeling that the main problem is not so much the management function of the company but its line function, that is the dirty work in the regions
Owner – The company in the long term, the bank in the short term
Environment – Company head office initially, then the regional offices. All work would need to take the regional offices into account

The donor
Customer – Primarily the donor
Actor – Primarily the analyst working within the donor's terms of reference
Transformation – Improving the efficiency and profitability of the company through improving the management function
Worldview – Increased profitability
Owner – The company
Environment – The company head office

Head of department
Customer – Primarily the company
Actor – Company employees working with the analyst. Responsibility for work undertaken is seen as being on the shoulders of the analyst
Transformation – Efficiency, MIS functions, status of the company improved

Worldview – Improved competitiveness and status
Owner – Company and analyst
Environment – The company

Consensus
Customer – Donor and company
Actor – Company employee and analyst working to agreed terms of reference
Transformation – Action to develop efficiency and profitability
Worldview – Cost effectiveness
Owner – The company and in the short term the analyst
Environment – The company

This consensus is not completely agreed. The view of the analyst is not quite that of the bank or the managing director. Putting the view in a cone format it would look like Figure C2.

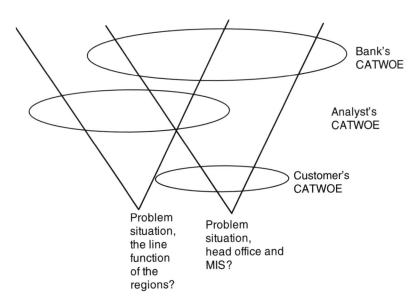

FIGURE C2   *Overlapping root definitions of the problem*

It is not possible for the analyst to alter the terms of reference for the entire project, but it is worth noting down at this stage that there is a divergence of views.

5.3   The top level systems model.

Figure C3 illustrates the top level systems model.

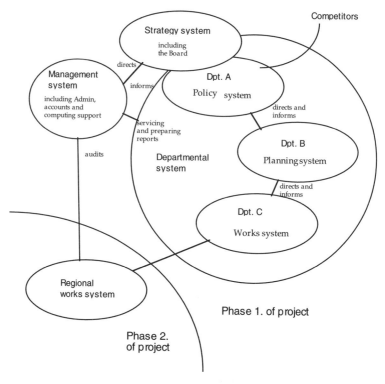

FIGURE C3   *Top level systems model*

The top level systems model does take some liberties with the rich picture. We assume here that there is a clear line of command between the three departments working its way out to the regional offices. We have taken a further liberty by salving our consciences concerning the need of the regional offices by setting out their needs as a second project. The other point of note is the strategy system lying outside and above the management system. The reason for this is the impact of the bank on strategy.

Exercise in Chapter 6

6.1   The entity model

The entity model in Figure C4 shows that we have simplified the new MIS down to two primary areas – daily administration on the one hand and core planning on the other. Administration has to do mainly with equipment, staff and pay-roll details, Core planning is concerned with project progress. This model could be further simplified – see Figure C5.

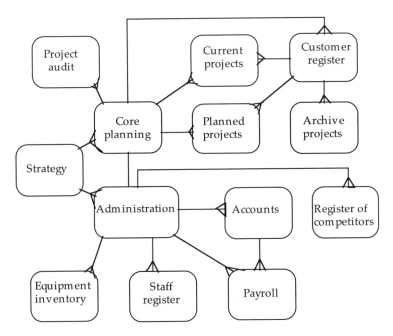

FIGURE C4   *The first entity model*

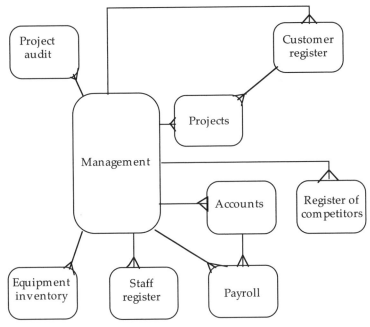

FIGURE C5   *Focusing the entity model*

But we thought that this line of approach was too lacking in detail so we opted for Figure C4.

6.2 Primary attributes

The main attributes are illustrated in Figure C6. These details could be developed.

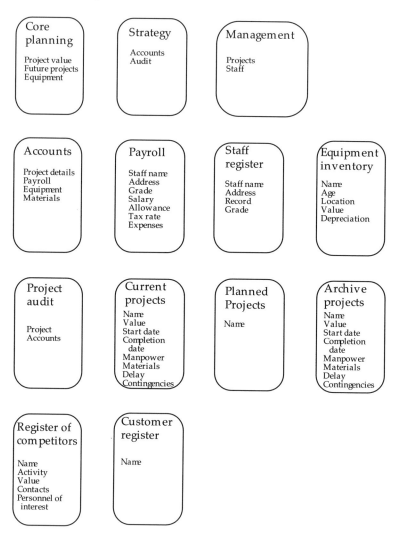

FIGURE C6   *The main attributes*

6.3 Major functions

The functional decomposition is illustrated in Figure C7. The basis of all functions in the MIS is to support the strategy formulation function. This is therefore our logical first level.

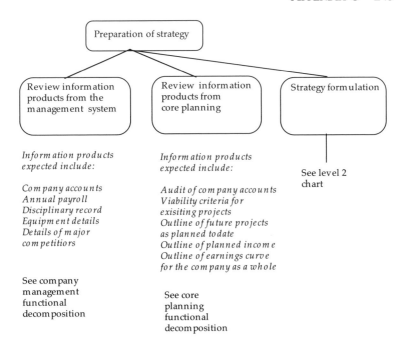

FIGURE C7   *First level functional decomposition*

Figure C8 develops the second level theme of strategy formulation.

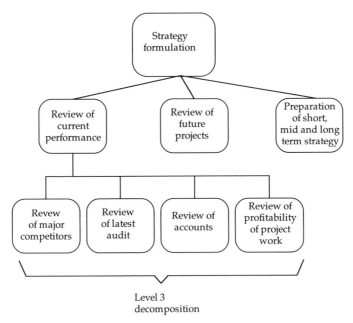

FIGURE C8   *Second level functional decomposition*

To carry the analysis one level further, we look at the details of the review of major competitors shown in Figure C9.

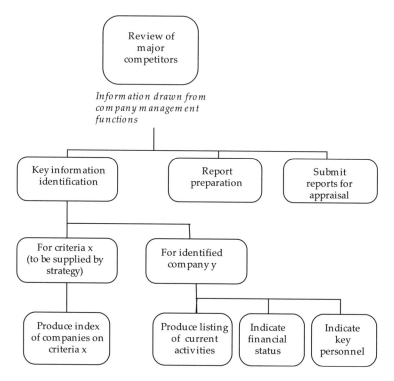

FIGURE C9   *Third level functional decomposition*

6.4   Key events

The flow diagram in Figure C10 shows the action of events upon the functions related to the review of major competitors.

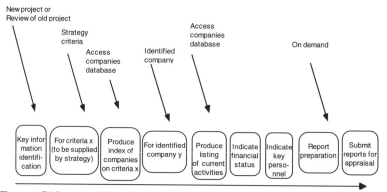

FIGURE C10   *Level 3 related events*

Exercise in Chapter 7

The approach taken to socio-technical modelling builds off that discussed at the end of Chapter 7. Here social objectives are seen to drive technical objectives i.e. each social objective works its way out in one or more technical objectives.

Social objectives	Technical objectives
Appear credible	Improve communication
	Timely decision making
Improve professionalism	Improve technical skills
Improve budget	Improve timeliness in budget planning
	Demonstrate effective budgeting
	Demonstrate efficient subcontracting
Improve planning	Technical skills
	Automated features
	Networking decision making
Improve office management	Networking
	Standards
	Rapid processing
	Learning processes initiated

The alternatives arising from the objectives given are as follows:

Social alternatives	Technical alternatives
S1. Retrain key staff	T1. Computerizable manual system
S2. Retrain all staff	T2. PC standalone + T1
S3. New staff + S1	T3. PC network + T1
S4. New staff + S2	T4. Network

The main point of note here is that we are linking social and technical alternatives in combination (e.g. T3 = T1 – computerizable manual – + PC network).

The two best options shown in Table C1 indicate a desire to base any new system on new staff bringing in skills at present unobtainable in the organization. The point difference between S3T2 and S4T2 is the level of retraining within the organization – all or just key staff. In terms of making a proposal based on this analysis it would be quite simple to indicate an expansion path for the incoming system, from a small, highly trained group dealing with the initial micro/manual system, gradually spreading out training to the wider community as appropriate. This would also link to the analysts indicated preferred direction of the project as a whole – outward to the regions.

TABLE C1

Alternatives	Social costs	Technical costs	Social constraints	Technical constraints	Social resources	Technical resources	Total	Rank
S1T1	2	2	2	7	4	4	**21**	**2**
S1T2	2	4	3	6	4	5	24	
S1T3	3	6	4	6	5	5	29	
S1T4	4	7	5	6	6	6	34	
S2T1	3	2	3	7	4	4	23	
S2T2	3	4	3	6	4	5	25	
S2T3	3	6	4	6	5	5	29	
S2T4	4	7	5	6	6	6	34	
S3T1	4	2	3	7	3	3	**22**	**3**
S3T2	**4**	**2**	**3**	**5**	**3**	**3**	**20**	**1**
S3T3	4	3	4	3	4	4	**22**	**3**
S3T4	4	4	4	4	4	4	24	
S4T1	4	2	3	7	3	3	**22**	**3**
S4T2	**4**	**2**	**3**	**5**	**3**	**3**	**20**	**1**
S4T3	4	3	4	3	4	4	**22**	**3**
S4T4	4	4	4	4	4	4	24	

Exercise in Chapter 8

8.1   Impact of the new information system on the company

Because we have opted for a development path working off established manual practices and because there is an existing computer unit we might expect impacts of the system to be fairly minimal. This would certainly not be the case if a new and very powerful computer-based information system were being installed from scratch. The main problem will probably lie with the existing computer staff having to introduce and work equitably with the new, highly trained staff being brought in. Also, as a wide ranging change in practice will eventually follow the new system we might expect senior management to need a considerable degree of awareness training and general encouragement. There may be some displacement of clerical workers but hopefully most can be moved into the new areas of data entry and data edit.

8.2   Suggested measures

1. General organization-wide awareness raising
2. Training on all new equipment for existing computer staff
3. General keyboard and computer package use training for clerical staff
4. Senior management awareness training

8.3   Avoiding risks

We have avoided the worst risks for a new system by avoiding a networked computer option, although this may occur at some time in the future. A manual/standalone microsystem can be made fairly secure by ensuring:

1. That all machines are in safe zones (lockable offices with access only to authorized staff).
2. A procedure for authorizing staff to access the system.
3. Levels of access to any computer information. Access would work broadly on the lines of:
   - level 1. basic data input
   - level 2. basic data edit
   - level 3. data edit
   - level 4. department wide information retrieval
   - level 5. organization-wide information retrieval
   - level 6. basic system fault finding
   - level 7. access to the total system

4. Usual software and data backup procedures as set out in this book.

8.4   Screen interfaces

The priority with a mixed manual/micro system is for the two components to work well together. Standard paper forms will still be in evidence, particularly in the early stages of the operation. We would therefore expect that screen interfaces (in terms of data entry) would imitate these standard forms being based on a form filling practice as shown in Figure C11.

On the other hand, the managers who are going to be using the final information products will require a system that is menu based (see Figure C12). It is assumed, in line with the information given in Chapter 8, that computer staff will not require specialized screen interfaces.

```
        Construction Project Form 1A        Screen  1 of 6
Name of project:            [_____]
                            [_____]
                            [_____]

Location                    [_____]
                            [_____]

Start date                  [_____]

Proposed completion date    [_____]

Type of project (new or     [_____]
maintenance)

Initial budget              [_____]

Officer in charge           [_____]

Team size                   [_____]

Team details (numbers)

Senior managers             [_____]

Senior engineers            [_____]

Engineers                   [_____]

Labourers                   [_____]

  Details for machinery on screen 2. Hit PgDn for 2.
```

FIGURE C11   *Form filling screen interface*

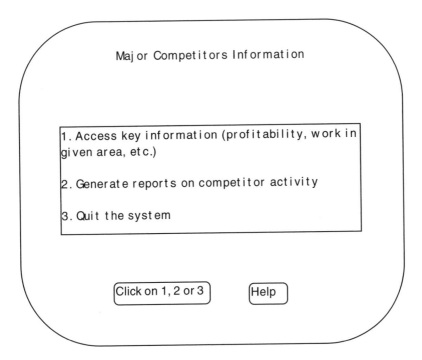

Major Competitors Information

1. Access key information (profitability, work in given area, etc.)

2. Generate reports on competitor activity

3. Quit the system

Click on 1, 2 or 3   Help

FIGURE C12   *Information products screen interface*

8.5   Measures to reduce staff resistance

The key to reducing staff resistance is the demonstration of:

- The value of the system to the individual user.
- The fact that the system does not threaten.

The awareness training sessions are the ideal vehicle for this type of assurance. Awareness raising sessions involving computers too often tend to focus on the use of computers rather than the use of information systems. Ideally a replica of the incoming system should be provided for the users and a range of normal tasks should be set out which will demonstrate to the user that:

- The system will make life easier.
- The system is open to change if there are problems – the user has ownership of the system.
- The system should result in a notable increase in the efficiency and work satisfaction of the user.

Where there are problems (widescale changes in work practice, changing job terms of reference) these can be introduced in the context of other positive elements (more pay, better conditions).

Exercise in Chapter 9

Technical briefing to all senior company staff

The outline of the new information system   The system arising from the review to date can be seen as having at least six distinct component parts:

1. an application
2. a database
3. retrieval in the form of reports
4. maintenance of the system
5. management of the system
6. monitoring the working of the system and evaluating annual success.

Without going into too much detailed, technical information now we will set out the general details of the system. From our analysis and design the overall need for the application is quite clear. Strategy formulation has to be supported by information in the headquarters section of the company being made available in a packaged format. The information required for strategy is derived both from the general IT system and also from core planning. Therefore the overall application is designed as a management information system but more clearly – a strategy support system. The application is designed for interaction at three levels:

1. The production of strategic information products for senior managers
2. The input of basic data by clerical staff
3. The control, of the system by computer staff

The primary implications of such a system can be seen in the information to be stored, that is the databases.

Initially we would expect that all project details would be required on a computerized database. This information would be cross-referenced with company information such as pay-roll, staff details and equipment inventory. These information areas would be related to, and further supported by, information on current and past customers and a register of competitors.

The activity of the system would be centred on the production of reports. These can be broken down into two key areas:

1. Reports for the support of strategy.
2. Reports for the increased efficiency of the company.

Reports in support of strategy   These would relate to the major areas of competitive advantage over other organizations, the review of current performance in specified areas such as cost control and project profitability, the results of company audit and analysis of future project trends – key areas to become involved in, old areas to drop.

Reports for increased efficiency   These would need to focus on the effectiveness and value of staff, staff costs as set against returns, the effective use of capital plant, internal accounting, staff records and staff turnover. The applications, database and reporting areas would come under the overall control of management.

The management of the information system   In our case management would initially be undertaken by existing computer staff but would eventually probably become the responsibility of new staff to be employed. The central need for management is to ensure that the system is maintained secure irrespective of changes in the organization. Effective management requires that the following areas be effectively controlled:

1. The operating system of the incoming system. This includes that all user interfaces are in place and that levels of control are established through the use of the operating system.
2. Job priority control. Computers cannot provide all information to all users at all times. The central objective of the system is the support of strategy. Access to the system for this priority job would need to be ensured. Strategic decision making is often quite unstructured and requires that the system have the capacity to respond flexibly to need. This may mean that one computer unit is constantly available for strategy enquiries. The information for the management and administration of the company can normally be scheduled in terms of the production of daily, weekly, monthly and annual reports. Clerical input has to function effectively if the information products are to be provided. Clerical use needs to be carefully controlled and information products need to be passworded off from casual or accidental access.
3. Security. Building on the items raised in 2; security for hardware (power supply, theft and accidents) can be improved if effective control is exerted over the working environment. Because the system will initially be used by only a small number of staff the threats to hardware should be reduced through control over physical access to the machines.
4. User support. We have already mentioned a wide range of training support for the various user groups. Related to this should be

effective day-by-day supervision of users (a function which can
be provided by the computer unit staff) and a clearly defined line
of communication, feedback and learning to, and from, the user
body and those who control the technical system. This is important in allowing users to feel that they have some say in the
future development of the information system and that their
learning is important in the evolution of the system. A user
support committee with attendance by computer unit staff should
fulfil this need.

One aspect of effective management of the system is to ensure
that regular maintenance is carried out. The initiation of a preventative maintenance shell linked to corrective maintenance guard is
dependent upon the organization getting appropriate staff trained in
this area or employing new staff who already have these skills.
Given the hazardous nature of the environment in which the
company operates (as depicted in the rich picture) the maintenance
area will require development prior to system implementation.

Finally we come to the monitoring of the process of the system
installation and the evaluation of preliminary information products.
Table C2 indicates key items to monitor and the critical indicators
to watch.

The final evaluation of the system should occur following a

TABLE C2   *Selection of areas requiring M&E*

M&E focus	Critical indicators to monitor and evaluate
1 Human activity system	New conflicts of interest between family members Changes in the local economic climate Changes in the relationships between headquarters and regions
2 Information modelling	New functions arising from strategy Changes in decomposition New entities required New attributes for existing entities New events requiring new reports
3 Socio-technical	Changes in personnel responsibilities Settling in of new staff Performance of technology Integration of manual and IT systems
4 Human–computer interface	New dialogue systems required relating to new information
5 Technical areas	Effective user support? Regular monitoring at the level of the systems impact

three-year run cycle to give the new system time to adjust to the environment. The evaluation should focus on the relative performance of the new system as set against the details of the systems analysis and systems design contained here. Of critical importance will be the reporting procedures – are the strategic reports being produced on demand and are these reports of relevance in developing better planning policies?

INDEX